MANCHESTER MERCHANTS

AND FOREIGN TRADE

Volume I

1794-1858

MANCHESTER MERCHANTS

AND FOREIGN TRADE

1794-1858

BY

STUDENTS IN THE HONORS SCHOOL OF HISTORY IN
THE UNIVERSITY OF MANCHESTER

AND

ARTHUR REDFORD

[1934]

AUGUSTUS M. KELLEY PUBLISHERS
MANCHESTER UNIVERSITY PRESS

© 1934 Manchester University Press.

First Published 1934 by
Manchester University Press

Reprinted 1973 by
Manchester University Press
316-324 Oxford Road
Manchester M13 9NR England
ISBN 0 7190 0546 9

Augustus M. Kelley Publishers
305 Allwood Road
Clifton New Jersey 07012 U. S. A.

Library of Congress Cataloging in Publication Data

Redford, Arthur.
    Manchester merchants and foreign trade, 1794-1858.

    Original ed. issued as no. 233 of Publications of
the University of Manchester and as no. 11 of
Economic history series.
    Includes bibliographical references.
    1. Manchester, Eng.--Commerce. 2. Merchants,
British. 3. Great Britain--Commerce--History.
I. Title. II. Series: Victoria University of
Manchester. Publications, no. 233. III. Series:
Victoria University of Manchester. Publications.
Economic history series, no. 11.
HF3510.M2R42   380'.09427'2   73-1675
ISBN 0-678-00750-0

PRINTED IN THE UNITED STATES OF AMERICA
by SENTRY PRESS, NEW YORK, N. Y. 10013

PREFACE.

THIS book is based primarily on the manuscript records of the Manchester Commercial Society (1794-1801), the Manchester Commercial Association (1845-58), and the Manchester Chamber of Commerce, which was founded in 1820. The main part of the volume is concerned with the activities of the Chamber of Commerce, but no attempt has been made to write an official history of the Chamber, complete with lists of Presidents and Directors. The stubborn struggle of the Manchester merchants to surmount the barriers which obstructed the expansion of their export trade stands out as the central theme ; yet many aspects of Manchester's foreign trade are described only incidentally, or altogether neglected. Our purpose has been to analyse the chief problems which confronted Manchester merchants during a most formative period of the city's history, and to trace the development of local commercial policy, so far as that policy reflected itself in the proceedings of the merchants' organisations.

Many of the questions to which the Manchester merchants claimed to have found satisfactory answers were national in scope, and were the subject of widespread agitation in all the main commercial centres and industrial districts. The petitions and memorials sent up from Manchester were often the result of carefully organised co-operation with Liverpool, Glasgow, Leeds and other great provincial towns ; if public policy was swayed by such means, the victory was not to be claimed by Manchester alone. Nevertheless, the traditional cocksureness of the Lancashire men, and their boast that they said to-day what England would say to-morrow, were often justified ; on many questions of public policy the Manchester merchants gave a lead which the country followed, for good or ill. If some passages of our book seem to exaggerate this influence of the Manchester merchants upon national policy, it is hoped that the defect will be charitably excused as arising partly from the limitations of our documentary material. In further extenuation of the offence, it may be pleaded that we have been more concerned to reflect the special point of view of the Manchester merchants than to attempt a general survey of the forces moulding British commercial policy during the early nineteenth century. The latter task would have involved prolonged research on a scale much larger than lay within our compass ; it may be doubted, indeed, whether all the materials for this larger study have yet been made accessible to research students.

Some other imperfections of our book may fairly be attributed to the circumstances and method of its compilation. The initial stimulus came from Mr. Raymond Streat, the Secretary of the Manchester Chamber of Commerce, who suggested to me that the records of the Chamber might repay close study. At that time (1928) I was engaged upon another book, for which the publishers were already pressing me, and I was reluctant to undertake work which I had no reasonable prospect of finishing within the next few years. I was equally reluctant, however, to let slip such a favourable opportunity for research into local economic history, especially after I had inspected the long row of fat folio volumes which Mr. Streat displayed to me in the Board Room of the Chamber. In this dilemma, I suggested that it might be possible to organise a team of senior undergraduates, who would each work through a few years of the Chamber's *Proceedings*, and would use these records as raw material in preparing academic theses. To this experiment the Directors of the Chamber readily consented, and further agreed to deposit their records in the University Library for as long a period as might be necessary.

Six undergraduate members of the History School (Cyril Ward, Annie Niven, Agnes Kerrigan, Dorothy Goodreid, Mary Provost, and Donald Johnston) agreed to take part

in the work, and to study the records covering the period
1794 to 1858; the choice of 1858 as a terminal date was
more or less arbitrary, but some reasons for considering it
as not altogether inappropriate are given in the concluding
chapter of the book. Mr. Ward undertook the difficult task
of analysing the operations of the Manchester Commercial
Society between 1794 and 1801; to Mr. Johnston fell the
very laborious work of collating the records of the Manchester
Commercial Association with those of the Manchester
Chamber of Commerce in the 'fifties. The other members of
the team each took one massive volume of the Chamber's *Proceedings*, and by co-operation among themselves attempted to
trace some continuity of policy running through the activities
of the Manchester merchants during the generation which
followed the end of the Napoleonic Wars.

The theses submitted were of varying quality, and it was
clear from the outset that my task of co-ordinating them
and moulding them into the shape of a book would not be
easy. At first I tried to confine myself to the work of editing
and re-arranging what the students had written; but in
the end I found it necessary to re-write rather than merely
to revise. The students' theses were invaluable as a guide
to my re-reading of the records, and as giving me the raw
material for a rough draft of the book; but for all defects
in the constructional framework, for all lapses in literary
style, and for all errors in quotation I must bear the sole
responsibility.

A brief outline of several chapters of this book was
included in a paper on " Some Problems of the Manchester
Merchant after the Napoleonic Wars," which I read before
the Manchester Statistical Society in December, 1930;
several passages quoted in the book will be found also in
this paper, and it is possible that other instances of auto-
plagiarism may be detected. Where discrepancies occur between the paper of 1930 and the book of 1934, it may be
assumed that the later version is more reliable. In particular, it may be noted that the records referred to as
Minutes in the paper of 1930 (and in the works of earlier
historians of the Manchester merchants) are identical with

the records more correctly described as *Proceedings* in the footnotes of the present volume.

Earlier use of these records has been made by Elijah Helm (*Some Chapters in the History of the Manchester Chamber of Commerce*), and by Messrs. E. Raymond Streat and A. C. Walters in the *Monthly Record of the Manchester Chamber of Commerce* for 1921. In each case the difficulty and tedium of the work led to its abandonment before the original project was completed. Mr. Helm gave a reasonably full account of the activities of the Manchester Commercial Society, but his courage failed after he had written two scanty chapters on the early work of the Chamber of Commerce. Mr. G. H. Wright found equal difficulty in compiling his *Chronicles of the Birmingham Chamber of Commerce*; after planning " to construct a history of the Chamber," he was finally content " to offer, in place of a history, properly so-called, a series of chapters illustrative of the life and work of the Chamber." These earlier writers were officials of the institutions about which they wrote ; they were experts in framing (and interpreting) resolutions, petitions and memorials. The academic student cannot hope to have attained complete success in a task which the expert officials found too difficult ; but he can at least hope that the magnitude of the task may be properly appreciated by those who know the complexity of modern business life, as reflected in the proceedings of our great commercial organisations.

I owe especial thanks to Mr. E. Raymond Streat for encouragement in the planning of this book, and for friendly help at several points in the lengthy process of compilation. The Directors of the Manchester Chamber of Commerce showed great generosity and public spirit in making their records accessible to young students under conditions most favourable to research ; they have added to our debt of gratitude by offering to bear part of the expense of publication. I have received generous help from my academic colleagues at every stage in the final preparation of the book. Professor G. W. Daniels read through the typescript, and mingled sage advice with kindly encouragement. Mr.

T. S. Ashton, while busily engaged in writing his history
of the Manchester Statistical Society (*Economic and Social
Investigations in Manchester, 1833-1933*), found time to read
my galley proofs and gave me the benefit of his special knowledge on many points.   Mr. A. P. Wadsworth read the page
proofs with meticulous care, and convinced me once more
that proof-reading is a skilled occupation.   Finally I have
to thank Mr. H. M. McKechnie, the Secretary of the Manchester University Press, for much patient help in smoothing
out the technical difficulties of publication.

Tentative explorations, by a fresh team of students,
have already been made into the later history of the Manchester Chamber of Commerce, and a further volume,
covering the second half of the nineteenth century, may
appear in the course of the next few years.   It is hoped
that this announcement will be regarded as a promise rather
than as a threat.

ARTHUR REDFORD.

MANCHESTER, *July*, 1934.

CONTENTS.

PAGE

PREFACE V

CHAPTER

I. ORGANISATIONS OF MERCHANTS BEFORE 1794 . . . 1

II. THE FOUNDATION OF THE MANCHESTER COMMERCIAL SOCIETY, 1794. 15

III. EUROPEAN TRADE IN WARTIME: CONVOYS AND EMBARGOES 25

IV. THE DECLINE OF THE ASSOCIATED COMMERCIAL SOCIETIES, 1798-1801 45

V. THE BEGINNINGS OF THE MANCHESTER CHAMBER OF COMMERCE 63

VI. THE VICISSITUDES OF MANCHESTER TRADE, 1820-58 . 74

VII. FOREIGN TRADE AND TARIFF PROBLEMS: (i) EUROPEAN COUNTRIES 85

VIII. FOREIGN TRADE AND TARIFF PROBLEMS: (ii) AMERICAN STATES 97

IX. TRADE WITH THE FAR EAST 108

X. THE STRUGGLE FOR FREE TRADE: (i) ORIGINS AND EARLY STAGES, 1785-1828 126

XI. THE STRUGGLE FOR FREE TRADE: (ii) SPECIAL QUESTIONS AND THE CORN LAWS, 1820-46. 139

XII. CURRENCY AND BANKING QUESTIONS 158

XIII. INLAND TRANSPORT AND COMMUNICATIONS . . . 169

CONTENTS

CHAPTER   PAGE
    XIV. Postal Services and Steam Navigation   .   .   . 188

    XV. Legal Questions and Joint-Stock Legislation .   . 205

    XVI. The Supply of Raw Cotton   217

    XVII. Conclusion 229

Appendices   237

Index   247

CHAPTER I

ORGANISATIONS OF MERCHANTS BEFORE 1794.

THROUGHOUT the last quarter of the eighteenth century the Lancashire cotton industry was expanding at an unprecedented rate, and was being radically reorganised. The introduction of power-driven spinning machinery necessitated the rapid development of a factory system ; the imports of raw cotton increased enormously, and there was a corresponding expansion of the export trade in manufactured goods. The established merchant employers found themselves overshadowed by the rise of a new class of industrial mill-owners or factory masters, many of whom attained great wealth with meteoric rapidity. Naturally, the changes in industrial organisation called for corresponding changes in commercial relations. The new industrial capitalists were manufacturing on a scale which demanded free access to world-wide markets ; they early realised the necessity for organisation in defence of their common interests. Large-scale industry was, of course, already honeycombed with marketing agreements and other informal combinations among industrial employers for the regulation of prices, output and wages. Even Adam Smith, who seems to have had little detailed knowledge of the profound industrial changes which were taking place during his lifetime, was well aware that " Masters are always and everywhere in a sort of tacit, but constant and uniform combination " ; [1] and the combination was not always merely tacit.

Whenever important questions arose, concerning the common interests of a whole industry or industrial district, it was usual for the employers to form special committees, and to raise funds for the execution of measures agreed upon in general meetings of the subscribers. In the textile districts, under the old " putting-out " system, such committees had

[1] *Wealth of Nations*, Bk. I, Chap. VIII.

I

been frequently formed to deal with questions such as the embezzlement of raw materials by the domestic workers, or their neglect of work undertaken for a merchant employer. Thus the employers in the Lancashire worsted industry had in 1764 formed a prosecuting committee, which appointed inspectors to secure information and bring offenders to justice at the joint expense of the manufacturers. In 1772 a strong committee of manufacturers, formed for " the Detection and Prosecution of Felons and Receivers of stolen or embezzled Goods," was advertising its existence in the *Manchester Mercury*, and was offering rewards to informers.[1] Similar committees were being formed throughout that generation, not only in Lancashire and Yorkshire, but also in many other industrial districts. In most cases these committees were formed for a particular defined purpose, and had a very short term of life ; but occasionally the transient grouping of interests led to the formation of quasi-permanent organisations, with regular constitutions and a wide range of functions. Thus, the succession of special committees among the Manchester manufacturers and merchants, during the third quarter of the eighteenth century, may be said to have foreshadowed the establishment of the Manchester Committee for the Protection and Encouragement of Trade in 1774. This latter committee may be regarded as a forerunner of the Manchester Commercial Society (founded in 1794), which in its turn foreshadowed the foundation of the present Manchester Chamber of Commerce.

On Tuesday, the 1st February, 1774, a general meeting of merchants and manufacturers was held at Crompton's Coffee House, in Manchester, " to consider of proper measures for the security and encouragement of the cotton, linen and other manufactures of this Town and Neighbourhood." [2] From this meeting a committee of nineteen was appointed, with a Chairman, Treasurer and Secretary. During the next few months this body met regularly, and took various measures for the improvement of local trade. Evidently there was no lack of public business to be transacted, for by the beginning of March the committee was planning to reorganise itself upon a more permanent basis. In its

---

[1] Wadsworth and Mann, *The Cotton Trade and Industrial Lancashire, 1600-1780*, 1931, pp. 397-8.
[2] *Manchester Mercury*, 8th March, 1774.

opinion, " the great extent and variety of the manufactures and commercial interests of Manchester and the
neighbourhood render the appointment of a committee not
only proper, but necessary ; for there are scarcely any
regulations of trade that can be proposed in Parliament
by which they may not be affected." An appeal for subscriptions was therefore made to " gentlemen in trade."
" Leaving the whole expense and trouble of promoting these
public interests to a few generous individuals in Manchester
has on former occasions been a matter of very just complaint ;
it is now reasonable to expect the generous aid of all persons
in trade, not only in Manchester, but in the several towns
and villages in the circuit of its manufactures. . . . Whatever sums are subscribed will be applied under the direction
of the committee with the utmost care and frugality, and
a just and regular account kept, which will be open to the
inspection of the public." This announcement is not very
explicit as to the functions of the committee ; but from other
evidence it appears that one of the main aims of the movement was to facilitate the importation of raw cotton. The
" free-port law " of 1766 had relaxed the Navigation Laws by
opening certain ports in the British West Indies to foreign
vessels, and is said to have enabled British merchants to buy
French colonial cotton 30 per cent. cheaper through the
" free ports " than through France.[1] This law was due to
expire in 1774, but was renewed by the Government at the
request of the organised merchants and manufacturers.

A more direct attempt to secure a satisfactory supply of
raw material was made by Manchester business men in the
same year, through the establishment of a Cotton Manufacturers' Company for the purpose of buying large quantities
of cotton in bulk for re-sale to individual firms. This
company was evidently formed as the result of a general
meeting of cotton manufacturers held in September, 1774,
at which " a Resolution was agreed upon, which, if once
generally adopted, it is believed, will be of great Service to
the Trade in general, by keeping the Price of Cotton upon a
more regular Footing." [2] In an attempt to forestall criticism
and opposition, the promoters of the company threw the

---

[1] W. Bowden, *Industrial Society in England towards the End of the
Eighteenth Century*, 1925, p. 202. See also Wadsworth and Mann, *op. cit.*,
pp. 190-1.
[2] *Manchester Mercury*, 27th September, 1774.

membership open to the public : " Not meaning to proceed upon any narrow confined Principles, or to give Offence to any Person of Property and Integrity, such as chuse to become Members of the said Company are desired to give in their Names . . . to Mr. *Josiah Birch*, or to Mr. *George Walker*, at their Warehouse (late Mr. Hague's) and they will be balloted for, agreeable to Rules already approved of." [1] The formation of the company was part of a scheme by which the manufacturers hoped to escape from the control of the specialised cotton dealers or jobbers, who were accused of manipulating the market and of refusing to grant the usual six months' credit to manufacturers.   This attempt to eliminate the speculative middleman by co-operative action foreshadowed many modern experiments in marketing organisation ; but the commercial and financial difficulties which arose during the American War of Independence were too great a strain upon the new company, and in 1778 its accounts were closed. [2]

Meanwhile, the Committee for the Protection of Trade continued to issue frequent notices in the local newspapers, and was especially active in warning the citizens of Manchester against nefarious schemes of foreigners in their midst, who were suspected of stealing trade secrets.   Questions concerning the supply of raw cotton remained important, however, and evidently became more serious as the American War dislocated oceanic transport.   In 1780 (the year of the Armed Neutrality) the committee petitioned the House of Commons to permit the importation of cotton in neutral ships, on the plea that the cotton manufacture was being injured through the monopolistic organisation of British shipping. In spite of strong opposition from the ship-owning and West Indian interests, the Government gave the manufacturers some relief by permitting imports contrary to the Navigation Acts until the end of the war. [3]

Among the more domestic problems with which the Commercial Committee was concerned during these years, prominence must be given to the movement against exclusive patent rights over textile machinery.   As early as 1776, the committee had begun to challenge the exercise

---

[1] *Manchester Mercury*, 4th October, 1774.
[2] G. W. Daniels, *The Early English Cotton Industry*, 1920, p. 101, n. 1 ; see also Wadsworth and Mann, *op. cit.*, pp. 234-5.
[3] Bowden, *loc. cit.*

of patent rights over machines which were asserted to be already known to the trade. This question became more serious after 1780, since the use of new and improved machinery was being restricted through fear of infringing Arkwright's patents, the original specifications for which had been deliberately left obscure. Early in 1781 Arkwright served writs on several Manchester manufacturers, and his claims (if they had been successful) would have given him an almost monopolistic hold over the development of the cotton industry. Under the leadership of Robert Peel (later the first baronet) meetings of the local merchants and manufacturers were held, and legal opposition to Arkwright's patents was organised; subscriptions towards the legal expenses were invited, and twenty-two firms subscribed at the rate of one shilling per spindle.[1]

To strengthen the movement against Arkwright's claims, the Manchester Commercial Committee was reorganised on a wider basis. On the 26th June, 1781, notice was given that " a general meeting of the merchants, manufacturers, and all others interested in the cotton, linen, silk, and small-ware trades " would be held at the Bull's Head Inn, " in order to elect by ballot a new Committee for the Protection and Encouragement of the Trade and Manufactures of this Town and Neighbourhood, under such regulations as will then be produced." As eventually constituted, the new committee consisted of sixteen members (ten for cotton and linen, three each for silk and smallwares); and during the early months of its existence the committee appears to have met, on the average, about twice each month. In a report issued on the 10th December, 1782, the committee summarised its activities, which included attempts to oppose the patent system, particularly in the case of Arkwright's patents, and to devise other methods of encouraging and rewarding inventors; to secure the repeal of restrictions on the use of cotton goods; to obtain larger and cheaper supplies of raw materials by modifications of restrictions on imports; to facilitate the punishment of buyers and receivers of stolen goods; to aid employers in their dealings with employees, checking the emigration of artisans, and fighting combinations of workers; and to bring the manufacturers into more effective relations with other industrialists and with public officials.[2]

[1] Wheeler's *Manchester*, 1836, pp. 521-2.   [2] Bowden, *op. cit.*, p. 167.

From this ambitious programme it appears that the committee regarded itself as representing the general interests of the Lancashire textile industries ; but it is not easy to discover the relationship between this general body and the organisations which existed among employers in special branches of industry, such as the fustian manufacturers, the dyers and crofters, the calico manufacturers and printers. When the important question of the fustian tax and the " Irish Propositions " came into prominence in 1784-85, it seems to have been the committee of the fustian manufacturers which took the lead, and the committees of the various branches of the textile trades held separate meetings.   In September, 1784, in the midst of the agitation against the fustian tax, a meeting was called of the " Committee for the Protection of the Calico Manufacture and Print Trade," and complaints were there made of the large quantities of calicoes and linens being smuggled into the kingdom.[1]   Frequent notices also appeared of meetings called by the " Dyers and Bleachers," and by the " Callenderers, Dressers, and Makers up of goods."   From some of the notices issued it almost looks as if the Committee of the Fustian Trade claimed priority over such organisations as those of the dyers and bleachers ; and it may be significant that among the signatories of the trade notices at this time appear men who were prominent as officials of the Manchester Commercial Society organised during the early stages of the French wars.[2]

The movement towards the formation of commercial organisations in the main industrial towns received a great stimulus during the years of expanding trade and unsettled economic policy which followed the American War of Independence.   In 1783 there was formed at Birmingham a General Commercial Committee, to watch over the public interests of the town and neighbourhood, and " to correspond with other Commercial Committees that may have been established." [3]   Among the other Commercial Committees of the period were those at Leeds, Halifax and Exeter ; and the attempt to secure unanimity among the provincial merchants and manufacturers was an interesting anticipation

---

[1] *Manchester Mercury*, 5th October, 1784.

[2] *Cf. ibid.*, 5th and 12th October, 1784 (Notices of the Committee of the Fustian Trade, signed by J. Silvester).

[3] G. H. Wright, *Chronicles of the Birmingham Chamber of Commerce*, 1913, pp. 11-12 ; J. A. Langford, *Century of Birmingham Life*, 1868, Vol. I, pp. 315-30.

of future developments. The initial stimulus to the formation of the Birmingham Commercial Committee was a proposal to repeal the laws against the exportation of brass ;
but the committee's functions were soon widened to include
the discussion of such questions as the excise laws, the export
of tools, impediments to trade, and the seduction of British
artisans by foreign manufacturers. As at Manchester, so
also at Birmingham, the Commercial Committee aimed at
representing the general economic interests of the district ;
but the various branches of the midland metal industries
had also their special organisations, some of which were
intimately associated in aims and policy with the Commercial
Committee.[1]   Some degree of unanimity was already possible
by means of correspondence between the different districts ;
and the trend of public policy now seemed to call for still
closer co-ordination, in order that the merchants and manufacturers of the whole country might present a united front
in negotiating with the Government.

In 1784 the younger Pitt adopted a programme of drastic
fiscal reforms, to assist the country in recovering from
the financial instability of the war period. Among other
measures, he introduced a new excise which increased the
duties to be paid upon dyed stuffs of cotton or of a mixture
of cotton and linen.   To facilitate the assessment and collection of the excise duties, various vexatious regulations were
framed, concerning such matters as the excise officials' right
of inspection, and severe penalties were imposed for any in-
fringement of the regulations or any obstruction of the excise-
men.   The new excise, which became commonly known as
the fustian tax, aroused great opposition in Lancashire,
especially among the fustian manufacturers, whose interests
were most seriously threatened.   Even before the Excise Bill
passed, the dyers and bleachers declared at a public meeting
that they would abandon their occupation if the Bill became
law, and that such a stoppage would ruin the whole cotton
industry, throwing out of employment several hundred
thousands of the King's industrious and loyal subjects.[2]

Soon the Lancashire agitation was reinforced, not only by
the merchants and cotton manufacturers of Glasgow, but

[1] See T. S. Ashton, *Iron and Steel in the Industrial Revolution*, 1924,
pp. 164-5.
[2] *Manchester Mercury*, 31st August, 1784 ; *cf. ibid.*, 7th September,
1784.

also by the midland iron masters and the Birmingham merchants. The movement in favour of united action received an additional stimulus from Pitt's " Irish Proposi- tions," which came up for consideration early in 1785. Pitt's scheme was for a measure of commercial reciprocity between England and Ireland. Ireland was to share in England's colonial and foreign trade, with certain restrictions in favour of English merchants, and the customs duties on manufactured goods passing between England and Ireland, in either direction, were to be reduced to the rate of the country in which the existing duties were the lower. To a later generation of Lancashire manufacturers such proposals would have been warmly welcome ; in 1785, however, freer trade between England and Ireland was thought to jeopardise the prosperity of English industry. Many of the cotton manufacturers, including Robert Peel, threatened to transfer their enterprises to Ireland, where manufacturers were encouraged by the payment of bounties, where water-power was plentiful, where labour was cheaper and taxes were lower than in England. No doubt the attitude of the Lancashire manufacturers to the Government's Irish policy was partly determined by the political friction which had already been created by the imposition of the fustian tax. " The Manchester people," wrote Lord Lansdowne, " have contrived artfully enough to confound the taxes lately imposed on manufacturers with the Irish Propositions." [1] In the agitation which was thus aroused, the main com- mercial and industrial interests throughout the country gained, for the time being, a new solidarity in opposition to the Government.

So early as February, 1785, the Birmingham Commercial Committee had resolved that " it is become necessary to correspond with the Commercial Committees and eminent Merchants and Manufacturers in different parts of the kingdom. . . . And it is essential for persons, who are most intimately acquainted with all the connections relative thereto, and most immediately interested in the prosperity of Mines, Manufactures and Commerce, to form some mode of corre- sponding, in order to remonstrate against injudicious taxes upon any article of export." [2] These resolutions of the

---

[1] *Hist. MSS. Commission*, Rutland MSS., III, 201-2 ; quoted by Bowden, p. 176.
[2] *Manchester Mercury*, 15th February, 1785.

Birmingham merchants were reported in the Manchester papers, and the response was prompt. The Committee of the Fustian Trade declared " that it is highly necessary to correspond with every manufacturing body in the kingdom, to prevent, as far as possible, the fatal and ruinous system of taxing manufactures " ; and letters in the local press called on the Lancashire industrialists not to confine their loyalty to " associations of *single* and *detached* bodies of Merchants and Manufacturers," but to support the movement, which was already on foot in London, for organising " *the whole manufacturing Interest of the Island*." [1]

In this new movement the initial stimulus came from Josiah Wedgwood, representing the Staffordshire pottery industry. Wedgwood wrote to Matthew Boulton in February, 1785, suggesting the formation of " a Committee of Delegates from all the manufacturing places in England and Scotland to meet and sit in London " ; his primary purpose was to organise resistance to the Irish Propositions, but he hoped that such concerted action on the part of the provincial manufacturers might lead to the establishment of a permanent association. On the 7th March, 1785, a meeting of industrialists from various parts of the country was held at the London Tavern, and framed resolutions hostile to the Government's Irish policy. A further meeting was held later in the same week, and a standing committee was appointed, which called a general meeting of the delegates for the 14th March. It was at this general meeting on the 14th March, 1785, that the decision was taken to form a permanent national organisation, which was to be called the General Chamber of Manufacturers of Great Britain. The cotton manufacturers had been numerically predominant on the committee, and the plan for the new Chamber was presented to the general meeting by a Manchester delegate.[2] The Chamber was to consist of " Manufacturers and such Delegates (being commercial men of the same description) as may be appointed by Provincial Chambers." A General Meeting was to be held every year soon after the opening of Parliament. A committee was to be appointed, to consist of twenty-one manufacturers, residing in London, who were to meet on the first Thursday in every month, and of this

---

[1] *Manchester Mercury*, 8th and 15th March, 1785.
[2] Bowden, *op. cit.*, pp. 177-9.

committee all the delegates from provincial Chambers were to be members.[1]

Credit for the formation of the General Chamber may be divided among the pottery, cotton and iron interests ; but in supporting the Chamber, Manchester seems to have been particularly active, for the Birmingham Commercial Committee later exhorted its members to emulate the Manchester men in their liberality. In November, 1785, an important meeting was held at the Exchange Coffee House, Manchester, under Peter Drinkwater's chairmanship, " to consider the best means of giving a proper and effectual support to that useful and highly necessary institution, the General Chamber of Manufacturers of Great Britain." Mr. Thomas Walker, who had been a delegate in London, made a long speech in favour of the General Chamber, and especially commended its work in securing the rejection of the Irish Propositions. This initial success, he maintained, showed the desirability of continued support to the Chamber as a permanent institution. " How many other important matters may yearly arise, and call for the like promptness both in decision and execution, the wisest amongst us could not now foresee ; and if this institution, even in its infant and unsupported state, had rendered us such essential services, what might we not expect from its riper years when Government should be convinced of its integrity and place confidence in its informations." Moved by Mr. Walker's eloquence, the meeting resolved to support the General Chamber by an annual subscription ; and a committee of twenty (which included Samuel Oldknow) was appointed to collect contributions from manufacturers not present at the meeting.[2]

Birmingham was not tardy in following Manchester's lead. On the last day of January, 1786, the Birmingham Commercial Committee passed a resolution " that the present conjuncture of affairs peculiarly demands the firm union, the serious attention, and the vigorous and judicious exertions of the whole body of British manufacturers. . . . The voice of the whole will be heard, while the complaint of individuals, or the clamours of the manufacturers in a single branch would be disregarded." The committee therefore

---

[1] *Plan of the General Chamber of Manufacturers of Great Britain*, quoted Ashton, *op. cit.*, p. 169 ; *cf. Manchester Mercury*, 16th August, 1785.
[2] *Manchester Mercury*, 29th November, 1785.

hoped that the General Chamber of Manufacturers would be adequately supported by the citizens of Birmingham. Indeed, the Birmingham Committee, as having been partly responsible for the institution of the General Chamber, considered itself pledged to contribute a due proportion of the expenses incurred; subscriptions were therefore invited, and a sub-committee was appointed to collect further contributions.[1]

The unanimity existing amongst the members of the General Chamber was not destined to last very long. They held together firmly on such matters as the excise laws and the Irish Propositions; but there was no such general agreement concerning freer trade with France under the Eden Treaty of 1786. The leading employers in the large-scale industries were all in favour of such a treaty, for their productive powers were expanding so rapidly as to demand an extension of the overseas markets. The cotton, iron and pottery manufacturers had much to gain by freer access to the French market, and little to fear from French industrial competition. On the other hand, the industrialists of an older type, manufacturing such articles as silks, ribbons, paper, clocks, leather and glass, were not in such a strong competitive position, and were still in favour of high import duties for the protection of their home market. This conflict of industrial interests within the General Chamber was at first dormant, since it was the large-scale industries which had taken the initiative in the formation of the Chamber. During the negotiations which led up to the treaty, the activities of the Chamber were dominated by the northern and midland delegates; and after the signing of the treaty, the Committee of the Chamber (of which all the provincial delegates were members) passed a resolution of enthusiastic approval.

Thereupon, the employers in the older type of industries, and especially the London manufacturers, rallied in opposition. At general meetings of the Chamber, held in London early in February, 1787, the malcontent party found themselves in a majority, and passed resolutions deprecating the terms of the treaty; they petitioned Parliament to withhold its ratification, and asked for a reconsideration of the question. This repudiation of the committee's policy by the general meeting shook the public credit of the Chamber, and

[1] G. H. Wright, *op. cit.*, pp. 24-5.

caused the secession of the northern and midland manufacturers, who had been the backbone of the movement.   Less
than a fortnight after the obnoxious resolutions were passed
in London, the Committee of Fustian Manufacturers met in
Manchester and resolved : " That, as several resolutions have
been published in the London papers, by the General Chamber
of Manufacturers of Great Britain, expressing doubts relative
to the expediency of the Treaty of Commerce lately concluded between this Kingdom and France, . . . We, the
Committee appointed at a general meeting of the Fustian
Manufacturers, for the purpose of corresponding with the
Lords of the Committee of Council, respecting the commercial arrangements between this Country and France,
think it incumbent on us to declare, that no person has been
appointed by us as a delegate to the General Chamber of
Manufacturers. . . . We are unanimously of opinion that
the Commercial Treaty . . . will be highly beneficial to the
cotton manufacturers of this town and neighbourhood." [1]

In the iron industries there was some conflict of opinion
between the producers of pig and bar iron, who were in
favour of the treaty, and the hardware manufacturers, who
remained protectionist ; but the main industrial leaders of
the Birmingham district were predominantly in favour of
freer trade.   In March, 1787, James Watt recommended that
the Birmingham manufacturers should withdraw from the
General Chamber and form a new organisation, to which
only delegates from associations should be admitted ; the
individual manufacturers, whose votes had turned the scale
at the general meetings of the General Chamber in London,
were to be excluded.   This proposal was quickly taken up in
Birmingham.   On the 27th March, 1787, the Birmingham
Commercial Committee met under the chairmanship of
Matthew Boulton (Watt's business partner), and resolved
unanimously that the recent proceedings of the General
Chamber of Manufacturers had been highly injudicious ;
that these proceedings were in no way authorised by the
committee, or by any delegate of the Birmingham manufacturers ; that the dissension which had arisen in the
General Chamber had tended to lessen its " respectability " ;
that the constitution of the General Chamber should be
" new modelled and such regulations made as may tend to
prevent such conduct in the future, and also to prevent

[1] *Manchester Mercury*, 6th March, 1787.

improper persons from being admitted members of that Chamber ; and that until such regulations were adopted the Committee would decline to send any delegate to the General Chamber, and would not consider that it represented in any way the manufacturers of this town and neighbourhood." [1]

Four months later, in a letter to Josiah Wedgwood, James Watt gave further details of his plan for the establishment of a new Chamber of Manufacturers, which was still being favourably considered by the Birmingham Committee. " The Idea now started but not any ways fixt is the union of the Chambers of Manchester, the Iron masters, Sheffield, the Pottery, Nottingham, and such others as are in the neighbourhood to meet at Manchester, Birmingham, the pottery, etc., either in rotation or as may be convenient and to maintain a regular correspondence and to have nothing to do with Londoners except on particular occasions." [2] The scheme does not appear to have materialised, and later meetings of delegates from the various provincial committees were organised in a much looser fashion ; but it is evident that the northern and midland industrial interests were unwilling to take any further part in the proceedings of the original Chamber. With their secession, the influence of the General Chamber over public policy became negligible. Pitt continued to consult the great industrial capitalists on important economic questions ; but with the " Chamber of Commerce " (as he called it) he would have no further dealings.

From this time, until after the outbreak of war against revolutionary France in 1793, attempts at the national organisation of the commercial and industrial interests appear to have been suspended. In some cases even the local Commercial Committees became dormant. At Manchester, during this period, committees seem to have been appointed at public meetings called from time to time, for specific purposes, and to have been dissolved when such purposes were accomplished. Organisations continued to exist in almost all the separate branches of the cotton industry, but it is not certain which (if any) of these were bodies meeting at regular intervals to conduct general business. In the agitations of the years preceding 1787 the Committee of the Fustian Trade had been particularly prominent ; but even this committee had a precarious and intermittent existence. Thus, in the spring of 1786, when the obnoxious

---

[1] Wright, *op. cit.*, pp. 25-6.   [2] Ashton, *op. cit.*, p. 173.

fustian tax had been repealed, the Committee of the Fustian Trade presented its accounts to a public meeting, disposed of its surplus funds, and dissolved itself.[1]   The commercial negotiations with France soon caused the appointment of a new Committee of the Fustian Manufacturers ; but in this case, also, the organisation dissolved itself (after a triumphal dinner at " the Hotel ") as soon as its specific object was achieved.[2]

The inactivity of the Manchester Commercial Committee during these years was doubtless due largely to the friction and ill-feeling which existed between different branches of the Lancashire textile industries, especially between the fustian manufacturers and the finishing trades.   As early as 1784, at the time of the agitation against the fustian tax, the fustian manufacturers were at loggerheads with the dyers and bleachers ; and similar friction between the fustian manufacturers and the manufacturers of calico and muslin gave rise to curious proceedings in 1788, when the latter group combined with the printers in asking for Government assistance against the competition of the East India Company.   At a meeting of the opposing groups, " Mr. Thomas Walker (fond of popularity) took the lead and speeched away for the fustian makers ; Mr. Robert Peel and others for the printers ; at last they were so warm that Mr. Lawrence Peel and Mr. Walker collared each other, and all was violence." [3]   In such an atmosphere, the establishment and maintenance of a central organisation, representative of the whole cotton industry and trade, was evidently a very remote possibility.   The shock of warfare against France, and the consequent dislocation of commerce, transport and credit, were necessary before the various branches of the cotton trade could be induced to present a united front to the common danger.

[1] *Manchester Mercury*, 9th May, 1786.   [2] *Ibid.*, 8th May, 1787.
[3] Bowden, *op. cit.*, p. 168, quoting *Board of Trade Papers*, 6/140, Doc. 45 (" A letter from Manchester ").

CHAPTER II.

THE FOUNDATION OF THE MANCHESTER COMMERCIAL SOCIETY, 1794.

WAR broke out between England and France in February, 1793, and at once led to measures which threatened to strangle the overseas trade of the two countries. The economic warfare had, indeed, already begun before the end of 1792 ; Great Britain had detained cargoes bound for French ports, and France retorted by repudiating the Eden commercial treaty of 1786. At the beginning of March, 1793, only a month after the actual outbreak of war, the French Government began to pass a series of prohibitory measures which seemed to be especially aimed against British trade. The import of various classes of textile, metal and earthenware articles was specifically prohibited, and all goods not expressly exempted were to be excluded from France if they came from an enemy country. Before the end of the year all goods made or manufactured in countries subject to the British Government had been excluded from France.[1] The reaction of this economic warfare upon the activities of the Manchester merchants was immediate. In April, 1793, a meeting of " the Gentlemen, Merchants, and Tradesmen of the town and neighbourhood of Manchester " resolved " that the present state of the Trade and Commerce of this country calling for the local superintendence and attention of the merchants and manufacturers of this town and neighbourhood, a committee be appointed for this purpose under the collective name of a ' Committee for Commercial Affairs '." [2] Later in the year this committee was active in appointing a deputation to confer with delegates from other commercial towns concerning the times to be fixed for the departure of convoys.

[1] See Heckscher, *The Continental System*, 1922, pp. 24-6.
[2] *Manchester Mercury*, 30th April, 1793.

As the economic dislocation caused by the war became more serious, a more permanent form of organisation became necessary. Early in February, 1794, a general public meeting was convened by advertisement in the main Manchester papers, to take into consideration the report of a committee appointed by the merchants and manufacturers of Manchester for the purpose of looking into the " abuses which have of late years crept into the export trade on the Continent of Europe, the Chicaneries, and the want of regularity." As a result of the general public meeting, it was decided to form a Society, to carry the propositions of the committee into effect. The committee whose report was laid before the public meeting was evidently the Committee for Commercial Affairs appointed in 1793 ; and the society which resulted from the meeting was the Manchester Commercial Society. Many of the merchants who had been appointed members of the Committee for Commercial Affairs became active in the new Commercial Society ; especially prominent were the names of Brandt, Richardson, Entwistle, Hardman, and Barton. Messrs. Brandt and Richardson were the two Manchester delegates to the conference on convoys in October, 1793, and were among the first twelve elected as members of the new Commercial Society. Charles Frederick Brandt, a German " merchant and manufacturer " who had come to Manchester about 1781, became the first President of the Society. At an adjourned meeting held on the 13th February, 1794, the Chairman and five others, out of the twenty-eight already elected as members of the projected Commercial Society, were requested to wait upon twenty-eight other merchants and manufacturers, to invite their approval of the general principles upon which the committee's propositions were based. As a result of this missionary work, twenty-three new members were elected at the next meeting ; it was then resolved to proceed upon the principle of the Chamber of Commerce at Leeds, and the rules of the latter society were circulated for the consideration of the Manchester merchants. Finally, at a further meeting held on the 27th February, the new organisation was formally constituted as " The Commercial Society of Merchants trading on the Continent of Europe."

The Society's name was not without significance as indicating the scope and main direction of the work to be undertaken. Needless to say, it must not be assumed that membership was confined to merchants, to the exclusion of manufacturers ; even at the end of the eighteenth century, the distinction between merchant and manufacturer was not very clearly drawn in Manchester. Most of the members of the new Society were described in the directories of the time as " merchants and manufacturers." Some of them had originally been manufacturers, and had only gradually assumed commercial functions ; on the other hand, some of the members had originally been merchants, and had subsequently engaged in manufactures. " The Firm at the commencement of business would style themselves Merchants, . . . and afterwards their attention was drawn to something more lucrative ; some turned Dyers, others Calico Printers, while some became Drysalters and even Medly Manufacturers." [1] Nevertheless, although most of its original members were both merchants and manufacturers, the objects and activities of the new Society were mainly commercial. The Society did not concern itself with such problems as the relations between industrial employers and their workmen ; nor did it express any opinion upon political, military, or naval affairs, except as these affected the interests of commerce. There is only one brief reference to the problem of raising troops ; yet great prominence was given to this question in the local newspapers, and many loyal associations were formed, in which members of the Society played a very active part.

Still more curiously, the Society's *Proceedings* do not contain a single reference to the serious financial crisis of 1797, which resulted in the suspension of cash payments by the Bank of England. This was apparently considered a matter of too general importance to come within the scope of the Commercial Society ; in such cases the ordinary procedure was for the boroughreeve to call a town's meeting. On the 3rd March, 1797, a public meeting was called to consider the financial situation, and the following resolution was passed : " We, the undersigned Bankers, Merchants, Manufacturers, Shopkeepers, and others . . . do approve of the measure adopted by the Bank of England, in issuing notes from one Pound and upwards, and we do engage to receive as cash, Bank of England notes of every description." Over

---

[1] John Scholes, *Manchester Foreign Merchants, 1784-1870* (Manuscript in Manchester Reference Library), p. 14.

two hundred signatures were appended to this resolution, including the names of many citizens who had not joined the Commercial Society ; but five out of the first six signatures were those of prominent members of the Society.[1]

The silence of the Commercial Society's records upon many other questions of national importance will appear less curious when it is remembered that the northern manufacturers and merchants of the period " experienced a species of pride in their aloofness from politics, other than for the promotion of economic policies directly involving their interests."[2]   The Manchester merchants seem, indeed, to have had a definite prejudice against political action.   It was with indignant contempt that Mr. Brandt, the President of the Commercial Society, described the Exeter representatives, at a conference held in 1796, as " more politicians than merchants " ; and the Exeter men evidently felt the sting of the imputation, for they protested that they had " no intention of interfering or appearing in a political light, but merely as commercial men in stating the situation of their trade."[3]

Even in the commercial sphere, the name of the Manchester society suggests a fairly narrow limitation of activities. The " Merchants trading on the Continent of Europe " controlled only one section (though an important section) of Manchester's foreign trade, and in that respect the Commercial Society of 1794 was far from being a Chamber of Commerce in the modern sense.   There had evidently been other and earlier organisations of the merchants trading to particular European countries, for in the summer of 1794 five members of the Manchester " Spanish Committee " attended a meeting of the Commercial Society, and decided that the books and papers of their committee should be handed over to the Secretary of the new Society.[4]   On the other hand, it is clear from a later reference that the merchants " trading to the West Indies and America " remained outside the Commercial Society,[5] so that for the discussion of questions affecting the general interests of the Manchester export trade

<hr/>

[1] *Manchester Mercury*, 7th March, 1797.

[2] Bowden, *op. cit.*, pp. 162-4.

[3] *Proceedings of the Manchester Commercial Society*, 1st December, 1796.

[4] *Ibid.*, 18th June, 1794.

[5] *Ibid.*, 28th February, 1798.

it was still necessary to call special public meetings. This transitional stage in the evolution of a modern Chamber of Commerce will be easier to understand when the history of the Liverpool commercial organisations comes to be written. At Liverpool, overseas trade was necessarily more specialised, and various commercial organisations (such as the Liverpool Brazil Association, the Liverpool East India and China Association, and the Liverpool West India Committee) exerted an influence over the different sections of Liverpool trade all through the earlier nineteenth century. The strength of these separate organisations may partly account for the fact that no general Chamber of Commerce was formed at Liverpool until 1849.

The constitution of the Manchester Commercial Society was decidedly democratic ; there were no directors, and all members had equal voting powers. Each firm could be represented by one member only, and the rights of members were safeguarded by the rule that no proposition brought forward at one meeting was to be decided upon until the next meeting. Prospective new members were to be proposed at one meeting and balloted for at the next, a three-quarters majority being necessary. A president (who was also to act as treasurer) and a secretary were to be elected annually. The secretary was to conduct the correspondence and other business of the Society, under the direction of the president, and was to receive £20 as an annual allowance. The Society was to meet on the first Thursday of each month at Spencer's Tavern, but the president was empowered to call extraordinary meetings at the request of two or more members. The annual fee of each firm was fixed at two guineas, which went to the general fund from which the expenses of the Society were defrayed ; any deficiency of funds was to be met by an equal levy on all members. Copies of these rules (which were evidently based on the rules of the Chamber of Commerce already established at Leeds) were to be circulated to the Commercial Societies of other towns, or to the principal business houses in towns where such societies had not yet been formed.

The Society never had many more than sixty members, and there were important branches of Manchester trade which remained outside its scope. Moreover, since the Society was primarily a commercial organisation, the industrial and manufacturing interests of the district were not likely to be fully represented. The owners of cotton-spinning factories, who were becoming an increasingly important class in the community, were not numerous among the members of the Society : though several of the members, who were primarily merchants and fustian makers, were also master cotton-spinners. Mr. Drinkwater, in whose cotton-spinning mill Robert Owen received some of his training as a mill manager, was one of the earliest members of the Commercial Society ; and many other well-known families of cotton factory owners, like the Gregs and the Peels, were represented in the early debates of the Society, especially on such semi-industrial questions as the exportation of cotton yarn. It cannot be denied, however, that serious friction sometimes arose between the Commercial Society and the organised manufacturers of the district ; this conflict of interest necessarily weakened the Society's position in its negotiations with the Government or with other bodies.

There can be no doubt that the foundation of the Commercial Society in 1794 was a result of the economic warfare which had arisen between England and France. Needless to say, there were other circumstances which made the formation of such a body desirable. It has already been noticed that the Committee of 1793 had inquired into " abuses that have of late years crept into the export trade on the Continent of Europe, the Chicaneries, and the want of regularity." The phrase " of late years " suggests that such abuses had existed for some time before the outbreak of war with France ; in the first instance the war merely aggravated existing evils, though it was later to create new problems of a very pressing character. The fact that commercial credit may be injured by various causes, independently of war, was forcibly argued by Mr. George Rose in 1793 : " The rapid increase of our Commerce, Navigation, and Manufactures [he wrote] has exceeded the most sanguine expectations on the subject. . . . The advantages resulting from thence have, however, suffered an interruption from a concurrence of temporary circumstances, very little connected with the war with France ; it would be extremely difficult to ascertain to what extent the demand for our Manufactures is lessened by the disturbances prevailing on the continent of Europe, but the only immediate consequence in that respect of the hostilities in which we are engaged, is the excluding us from Exports to the French dominions, to the value of £717,000

per Annum, on an average, since the Commercial Treaty." [1]
Evidently there were circumstances which for a time shel-
tered England from the worst effects of continental warfare.
England had remained at peace whilst the rest of Europe
was arming. Therefore "our funds became a favourite
object of purchase for those monied men on the Continent
who wished to secure their property." The war had also
given a stimulus to some of the English manufacturing
industries, through the increased demands from the belligerent countries for munitions and army clothing.

Even before England's entry into the war, however, her
trading position had been rendered less favourable by the
partial collapse of continental credit. Continental bankruptcies had become ominously frequent, and the security of
bills of exchange had become impaired. The partition of
Poland had led to the failure of the Bank of Warsaw, which
had brought down with it many other European financial
houses, especially in Petersburg, Hamburg and Amsterdam.
" The general wreck of credit among our allies on the Continent deprived us in a great measure of the markets there.
Orders did not arrive, or, if they did arrive, could not be
executed ; the security of the correspondent was doubted, or
the channel of payment shut up. . . . The general result of
these particulars is, that whereas, before the war, bills were
discountable, and of course entered into circulation from every
part of the world, at perhaps eighteen months' date, and
sometimes at even longer, distrust and bankruptcy have, for
the present, rendered three-fourths of the whole waste paper ;
and those of the very first credit are in general negotiable at
two months' date only. . . . Bankruptcies have spread, and
are spreading everywhere over the continent of Europe,
through France, Holland, Germany, Poland, Russia, Italy,
and Spain ; and everywhere private as well as public credit
is impaired or destroyed. . . . The governments of Russia,
Austria, Poland, France, and Spain are either bankrupt, or
on the verge of bankruptcy, and have had recourse to
practices that differ little from open rapine. . . . Of the
[European] houses that remain solvent, it is known that
the greater part are struggling with difficulties ; that these

[1] George Rose : *A Brief Examination into the Increase of the Revenue,
Commerce, and Navigation of Great Britain, since the Conclusion of the Peace
in 1783* (1792.   4th edition, 1793), pp. 9-10.

are hourly increasing ; and that distrust and dismay prevail universally." [1]

The general impression of commercial insecurity is amply confirmed in the early records of the Manchester Commercial Society.   The Society's declared objects were :

> " (1) To resist and prevent as much as possible depreda-
> tions committed on mercantile property in foreign
> parts, detect swindlers, expose chicaners and
> persons void of principle and honour in their
> dealings.
>
> " (2) To adopt such regulations as may tend to the
> benefit of their trade, add to its safety and
> promote more regular payments.
>
> " (3) To watch over the interests of their trade at large
> and co-operate jointly in all applications to
> Government, or in any measure which may from
> time to time be thought necessary for the good
> of the whole." [2]

It was resolved that individual members should disclose the names of any of their foreign customers who were " guilty of unjustifiable abatements, chicanery, prolongation of pay-ments, or any unmercantile proceeding " ; and that, if the Society found such complaints to be well grounded, the names of the defaulters and the grounds of complaint should be entered in the Society's books.   At a later meeting it was decided that no member of the Society, not already in actual correspondence with the accused person, should execute any orders received from such a person after the time when the name was entered in the book, until reparation had been made.

Actually, the Society's Black Book seems to have been very seldom used, though it may have served its purpose by exercising a deterrent effect.   Only one case of the " collective boycott " is recorded in the Society's minutes, and in that instance the system produced satisfactory results.   In October, 1794, Messrs. Rawlinson and Alberti (a Manchester firm which was a member of the Commercial Society) com-

---

[1] Jasper Wilson (Dr. James Currie), *A letter, commercial and political . . . in which the real interests of Britain in the present crisis are considered,* 1793 (4th edition reprinted in W. W. Currie's *Memoir of James Currie,* 1831, Vol. II, pp. 391 ff.).

[2] *Proceedings of the Manchester Commercial Society,* 27th February, 1794.

plained to the Society concerning the ill-treatment they had
suffered from one of their correspondents, Luca Buonocore of
Naples ; and it was resolved " that the name of the latter
deserved to be entered upon the Black Book of the Society,
to guard others from experiencing similar treatment." [1]   The
form of entry, as prepared for confirmation at the next
monthly meeting, ran as follows :

" November 6th, 1794

Buonocore, Luca, of Naples by Messrs. Rawlinson and Alberti
As being unworthy of confidence from his
arbitrary and unfair practices."

The grounds of complaint were then stated : that the
Italian had dishonoured the drafts of the English firm, and
had also caused them to suffer " by losses in the Exchange,
and by abatements they were obliged to make." [2]   Twelve
months later the Secretary reported that Luca Buonocore
had paid Messrs. Rawlinson and Alberti the balance of his
account, and his credit was accordingly restored.   " Losses
in the Exchange " evidently constituted a serious wartime
grievance, for one of the early actions of the Commercial
Society was to frame a definite ruling, which was to be
applied uniformly in all such cases.   The Society declared by
resolution that " the goods are sold here in English measure,
weights, and money, and the exporter cannot be responsible
for any fluctuation in the exchange : the goods, once shipped,
becoming the absolute property of those who ordered them." [3]
This declaration was to be printed in the main foreign
languages, and copies were to be distributed to the members
of the Society for circulation among their correspondents
abroad.

The third main object of the Commercial Society was
(as already stated) to " co-operate jointly on all applications to Government."   This method of exerting a collective
influence over public policy was no novelty ; it had been
quite commonly used by the various industrial and commercial committees of the preceding generation, and the
advantages of co-operation with the commercial organisations
of other provincial towns were already well understood.
The economic dislocation caused by naval warfare forced the
Commercial Society to correspond with several departments
of the Government on a host of problems concerning the

[1] *Proceedings of the Manchester Commercial Society*, 2nd October, 1794.
[2] *Ibid.*, 6th November, 1794.   [3] *Ibid.*, 6th March, 1794.

provision of convoys, the seizure of British property abroad, and the desirability of concluding commercial treaties with various European states. The necessity for fixing regular periods and dates for the sailing of convoys, to protect merchant ships taking part in the Mediterranean trade, had already become urgent before the Manchester Commercial Society was formed ; the organisation of collective applications to Government, on this subject, was one of the main reasons for the foundation of the Society, and became one of its main functions.

CHAPTER III.

EUROPEAN TRADE IN WARTIME : CONVOYS AND EMBARGOES.

DURING the later eighteenth century the export of Manchester goods to countries on the Continent of Europe had been expanding rapidly, and the older markets, such as Africa, North America and the West Indies, had become relatively less important.   This change in the direction of the Manchester export trade arose partly from the failure of Manchester checkmakers to compete successfully with Indian goods in the African trade, and partly from the constitutional struggle with the North American colonies, which cut off a great part of the plantation trade as well as reacting adversely upon both the West Indian and African markets.   Fortunately, while their western overseas outlets for checks and printed cottons were shrinking, Lancashire manufacturers were evolving new lines of goods in the fustian branch. These new materials, of which cotton velvets, velverets and velveteens were the most important, proved unusually attractive to continental customers, especially after 1763, when three Manchester firms obtained a direct connection with the German market.   During the following generation, and down to the outbreak of war between England and France, the expansion of Manchester's export trade to the Continent was amazingly rapid.[1]

The best European outlets for Manchester goods, especially after the clogging of the French and Dutch markets by naval hostilities, were to be found in Italy and Germany. In both these countries the chief centres for the distribution of imported goods were the great fairs held periodically in some of the larger cities.   The fair of Salerno, which began on the 15th September, was said to be " by much the most considerable of any in Italy for the sale of the manufactures and

---

[1] See Wadsworth and Mann, *op. cit.*, pp. 164-9, 174-5.

produce of this Kingdom." [1]   Another great Italian fair was
that held at Aversa in April ; at this fair Manchester cotton
goods intended for summer wear found a ready sale.   For
the German and eastern European markets the most important fairs were those of Leipzig, Frankfort, Brunswick
and Nuremberg.   The Easter fair at Leipzig was " justly
celebrated for the immense quantities of British manufactures
sold there." [2]

The increasing demand for British textiles in the continental markets, and the concentration of this demand in
the great periodical fairs, may help to explain the urgency
with which the Manchester Commercial Society, and the
other commercial organisations of the war period, impressed
upon the Government the necessity for regular convoys of
merchant ships.   The demand for particular lines of Manchester cotton goods was seasonal ; if the goods intended for
summer wear arrived too late for the Easter fairs at Leipzig
or Frankfort, or the fair at Aversa in April, they might miss
their market altogether and become a dead loss.   In the
early phases of the war, when nearly all Europe was allied
against the French, the chief preoccupation of the Commercial
Society was to ensure that the convoys sailed at the proper
times, so that the goods would not be too late for the fairs.
Later on, however, when the success of the French armies
caused the secession from the allied cause of such states as
Prussia, Spain and Tuscany, the greatest anxiety of the
Commercial Society arose from the Government's action in
placing an embargo on all ships in English ports destined for
continental markets.   The situation became still worse when
Napoleon had conquered Italy, for the Commercial Society
had subsequently to face serious problems arising from the
confiscation of British property in enemy territory.   The
main objects of the Society then became to secure redress
for the property confiscated, and to see that the English
manufacturers received payment for the goods exported.
Underlying and closely connected with these difficulties were
various complicated questions of marine insurance and payment by bills of exchange.

The necessity for organising regular naval convoys to
protect English merchant shipping had become urgent

---

[1] *Proceedings of the Manchester Commercial Society,* 11th June, 1795.
[2] Charles Reinhard, *The Present State of the Commerce of Great Britain,*
1805, p. 7, note.

before the end of 1793. In October of that year a deputation, consisting of Mr. Turnbull and four other London
merchants, two delegates from Birmingham, two from
Manchester, and one from Halifax, had " waited on the Right
Honourable the Lords Commissioners of the Admiralty . . .
to represent to their Lordships the necessity that regular
convoys should be appointed for the protection of trade. . . .
The gentlemen of the said deputation received every satisfaction, . . . and such arrangements were made, for the
future departure of the convoys to the different ports of
Spain and Italy, as they were unanimously of opinion would
be perfectly sufficient for the convenience and protection of
the trade of England, to those countries, during the continuance of war." [1] In the actual working of the convoy
system, however, this unanimity of opinion soon faded, for it
frequently happened that the convoys failed to sail on the
dates fixed, with consequent prejudice to the sale of the
cargoes at the continental fairs.

The unpunctuality of the convoys was often, of course,
caused by bad weather or the vicissitudes of naval operations ; but the smooth working of the system was also
endangered by the frequency with which the merchants
of various towns attempted to delay the sailing of the
convoys when their own goods were not ready for shipment
by the official date. Apparently the Leeds merchants
were at first the chief offenders in this respect. In April,
1794, the Manchester Commercial Society resolved [2] that
the Admiralty should be requested to give instructions
for the convoys to sail at the times fixed, notwithstanding
any application to the contrary. Letters stressing the need
for punctuality were also sent to the Commercial Societies of
Exeter and Birmingham ; and in a letter to Messrs. Lees,
who represented the Halifax merchants, the Manchester
Society complained " that the convoy fixed for the 15th March
had been delayed at the request of the Leeds merchants."
The same difficulty arose again later in the year. Early in
June, 1794, the Manchester Commercial Society wrote to
Mr. Turnbull of London (who was sometimes referred to as
the " Chairman of the General Committee of Merchants ")[3]
to protest against the action of the Leeds merchants in

---

[1] *Manchester Mercury*, 29th October, 1793.
[2] *Proceedings of the Manchester Commercial Society*, 14th April, 1794.
[3] *Ibid.*, 1st October, 1794.

requesting the postponement of the convoy which had been arranged for the 15th June. The Manchester merchants were particularly anxious that this convoy should not be delayed, because the goods sent under its protection were intended for the September fair at Salerno. The Commercial Society even went so far as to instruct Messrs. Earle of Liverpool that the two ships intended for the Mediterranean trade (one for Naples and Salerno, the other for Genoa and Leghorn) should meet the convoy appointed for the 15th June at Falmouth, but should not wait for the appearance of the convoy beyond the 10th July. Eventually the Admiralty ordered the convoy to sail on the 1st July.[1]

From the proceedings of a special meeting of the Manchester Commercial Society, held on the 21st October, 1794, the general framework of the convoy system can be perceived. The meeting resolved that the times for the sailing of convoys in the coming year should be the same as those fixed twelve months previously, except that the convoy then appointed for the 10th October should sail instead at the end of the month. There were to be four convoys to the Mediterranean ports during the year ; the first was to sail from Spithead between the 15th and 20th January, the second between the 15th and 20th March, the third between the 15th and 20th June, and the fourth between the 20th and 30th October. It was further suggested that, if possible, there might be an additional convoy about the 20th December, and also one between the June and October convoys. These times were suggested because " they suit the times of the different fairs where manufactured goods are chiefly disposed of." The Manchester resolutions were submitted (through the agency of Mr. Turnbull) for the approval of the London merchants, who proposed by way of amendment that there should be five convoys during the year, to sail from Spithead on the 30th January, the 30th March, the 30th June, the 30th August, and the 15th November ; to these amendments the Manchester merchants eventually assented.

If the convoys were unpunctual, there was not only a danger that the goods would miss their market, but also a chance that they would deteriorate through waiting too long on board ship at Falmouth. On one occasion when an application had been made for the postponement of the convoy, the Manchester Commercial Society instructed

[1] *Proceedings of the Manchester Commercial Society*, 18th June, 1794.

Messrs. Earle that the goods should be loaded later at Liverpool rather than have to wait at Falmouth. Normally the Manchester merchants had to send off their goods to Liverpool about a fortnight before the convoy was due to sail from Spithead. The last day for sending goods from Manchester for the January convoy was fixed at the 17th ; and the ships had to sail from Liverpool not later than the 21st, to be sure of joining the convoy at Falmouth by the 30th of the month.[1] When the convoy was due, the merchant ships would have to put out of harbour in order to join the convoy without delaying it ; when the convoy did not appear punctually, the merchant shipping had to wait for it outside the harbour. To evade this difficulty the Manchester society (at the suggestion of Messrs. Earle) made application to the Admiralty for a frigate or cutter to be appointed, which should be sent ahead of the convoy, and should give sailing orders to the captains of the merchant ships waiting at Falmouth. The application was successful, but the system did not always work satisfactorily. On one occasion early in 1796 the Admiralty cutter split her sails before arriving at Falmouth, and was unable to enter the harbour. Consequently, when the Mediterranean convoy arrived off the town, and put out a signal, the captains of the two merchant ships waiting at Falmouth thought it was the West India convoy, and did not go out to meet it ; the convoy therefore went on without them.[2] To remedy this mistake the Lancashire merchants asked that an additional convoy might be provided, since the cargoes were specially intended for the spring market ; if they missed the Easter fairs they could not be sold until the following year, and would then probably be out of fashion.

As the war went on it became clear that most of the applications for the postponement of the convoys were from the London merchants. A large part of the export trade of the London merchants consisted in the re-export of goods brought in by the East India Company ; as the arrival of the East India goods was not always at fixed and certain dates, the London merchants wished to secure more elasticity in the times for the sailing of the Mediterranean convoys. The Manchester merchants, whose goods had in many cases

---

[1] *Proceedings of the Manchester Commercial Society*, 18th December, 1794.
[2] *Ibid.*, 4th March, 1796 : letter from Messrs. Earle of Liverpool.

to compete with the Indian textile goods, naturally opposed any such relaxation of the system.   In June, 1795, the Manchester Commercial Society formally protested against Mr. Turnbull's having applied for a postponement of the convoy without having consulted the manufacturing towns ; and the President of the Society complained to Mr. Turnbull that such applications would give the Admiralty an excuse for further delays in the future, since " their Lordships must infer that we do not all agree in the periods . . . agreed upon, and finally concluded upon, on the most deliberate and mature consideration . . . for the general interest of all the trade of the Kingdom." [1]   In his reply, and in justification of his action in delaying the convoy for eight days, Mr. Turnbull pleaded that he had made the application " at the urgent request of the London merchants," and with due regard to the date of the opening of the fair at Salerno. "As time was pressing " (he wrote), " I trusted to the candour of the manufacturing towns and the confidence which I flattered myself they reposed in me that they would approve without the delay of consulting them of a measure which I felt to be so clearly and essentially expedient. . . . In the northern parts of England, at Leeds and Halifax &c., they have been thankful for the application I made." [2]

Disagreement concerning the Mediterranean convoys threatened to become a chronic source of friction between the London and Manchester merchants.   In August, 1795, the Manchester Commercial Society had once more to consider an application from the London merchants for the postponement of the next convoy from the end of August to the end of September, on the ground that one convoy had only just departed.[3]   To this postponement the Manchester merchants consented, on condition that no alteration was proposed in the sailing of the more important convoy fixed for the 15th November.   Even the postponement of the August convoy by a month, however, proved insufficient to satisfy the London merchants ; for a further letter was received from Mr. Turnbull to the effect that on the 7th October the East India Company would hold a sale of various commodities, especially pepper, a great part of which would be bought for re-export to Spain and Italy.   It would therefore be more convenient to the London merchants if

[1] *Proceedings of the Manchester Commercial Society*, 11th June, 1795.
[2] *Ibid.*, 2nd July, 1795.   [3] *Ibid.*, 13th August, 1795.

the convoy agreed on for the 30th September could be further postponed to the 15th October.[1] Once more the Manchester merchants, " although desiring general adherence to the times fixed for the sailing of convoys," acquiesced in the proposed delay, though they again stressed their objection to any postponement of the convoy appointed for the 15th November. Ironically enough, when the Admiralty announced that this convoy would definitely sail on the 15th November, it was the Manchester merchants who requested that its departure should be postponed until the end of the month. Actually it did not sail even then, for Mr. Turnbull wrote later to explain that the delay which had occurred in the sailing of the convoy fixed for the 30th November was chiefly due " to the captains of the transport vessels, who, having no inducement for dispatch, are generally very dilatory." [2] Seven months later the Manchester society learned that the London merchants had once more asked that the convoy fixed for the 30th June should be delayed until the 15th July, in order that they might complete their cargoes, the shipping of which had been suspended owing to the critical state of affairs in Italy. The June convoy was, however, the most important of the year to the Manchester merchants, because on its punctuality depended the market for Lancashire cotton goods at the fair of Salerno. The Manchester Commercial Society therefore protested strongly against any postponement, and in this instance the London merchants seem to have given way.

The convoy problem caused anxiety to Manchester merchants not only in the Mediterranean trade but also in the trade with northern and central Europe by way of Hull and Hamburg. Hull was a most convenient port for Manchester goods going by water either to London or to the Baltic countries ; the export of Manchester goods through Hull was already important before the French wars, and tended to increase after the beginning of hostilities. Naval operations in the Channel and the Atlantic, the closing of many southern ports to English manufactures, and the increased risks of navigation in the Mediterranean, caused much trade to be diverted to the northern route, even though the goods exported might be destined ultimately for Switzerland or northern Italy. In 1795, however, the French

---

[1] *Proceedings of the Manchester Commercial Society*, 3rd September, 1795.   [2] *Ibid.*, 7th January, 1796.

invasion of Holland jeopardised the northern route also, and led the provincial merchants to ask for the organisation of a convoy service from the Humber to the Elbe. In February the Hull merchants sent a memorial to the Lords of the Admiralty, requesting that regular convoys should sail at intervals of about three weeks from Hull to Hamburg and Bremen. This application was supported by the Manchester Commercial Society, which declared :

" That the Manchester manufacturers and merchants constantly export considerable amounts of manufactured goods to Germany and to the Southern Ports of Europe through the ports of Hull and Hamburg. That the late irruption of the French into Holland has endangered this route, and that such danger has caused an exorbitant advance of premium on insurance, which, unless protection is given, will become so extravagant as to amount eventually to a prohibition. That several ships with valuable cargoes are now waiting at the port of Hull for convoys to take them to Hamburg and other ports of the Hanse Towns." In an accompanying letter, the Manchester merchants explained to the Secretary of the Admiralty that the trade between Hull, Hamburg and Bremen was " the key through which our manufactures can alone find a passage for the markets of Germany, Switzerland, and the borders of Italy." [1]

The Government acceded to the requests of the northern merchants, and organised a service of convoys from Hull ; but by this time the European war was assuming a more formidable aspect, and made necessary a more drastic regulation of merchant shipping. For the greater part of 1793 and 1794 Holland, Prussia and Spain were among the allies of England, but towards the end of 1794 the coalition began to disintegrate. In October, 1794, Prussia withdrew her forces from the conflict ; before the end of the year Holland had been overrun, and in the following summer peace was concluded between France and Spain. By the end of 1795 Saxony, the two Hesses, Portugal, Naples, the Duke of Parma and the Pope had all made their peace with France. These withdrawals from the allied cause made the naval position of England less secure, by reducing the number of ports open to English shipping. Moreover, the naval strength of revolutionary France was by no means negligible ;

---

[1] *Proceedings of the Manchester Commercial Society,* 3rd February, 1795, *et seq.*

though it was not able to cope with the British navy, it was capable of inflicting much damage upon English merchant shipping. The numbers of English merchantmen captured by French warships and privateers showed a tendency to increase down to 1797, in spite of a steady rise in the number of British frigates and corvettes detailed to patrol such danger zones as the Bay of Biscay.[1]

So early as 1794 it was evident that the convoy system, though useful, did not give adequate protection, partly because the captains of many merchant ships had orders to proceed without convoy rather than run the risk of being too late for the Italian fairs. The loss of ships and cargoes, which too frequently resulted from such evasions of convoy, was one of the factors which led the Government, early in 1795, to place an embargo on all English ships sailing for the Continent of Europe. Exemption from the embargo was given to ships sailing under the protection of the Mediterranean or Baltic convoys, and from this point of view the embargo might be regarded as a method of enforcing the convoy system; but the provincial merchants, though they were all in favour of an effective convoy system, found the embargo much less to their interest. In March, 1795, the Manchester Commercial Society decided to present a memorial to the Privy Council, to protest against the embargo on vessels loading at Hull for Hamburg and Bremen; particular anxiety was felt lest the *Frankfort*, which was already much delayed because frost had prevented goods from reaching Hull, should be too late for the Easter fair at Frankfort-on-Main.[2] Mr. Burstall of Hull, who had gone up to London to negotiate concerning the embargo, reported that orders had been given to allow certain vessels to sail for Hamburg which were laden on or before the 16th March, but not those which took on goods after that date; this relaxation would not cover the case of the *Frankfort*. Subsequently, however, special permission was given for the *Frankfort* to sail, provided that no more goods were taken on board. The Manchester merchants were grateful for the partial lifting of the embargo, but greatly disappointed that the *Frankfort* should have to sail without her full cargo. Hoping that the ship would be in time, if not for the fair at Frankfort, at any rate for that at Leipzig, the shippers

[1] See *Cambridge Modern History*, Vol. VIII, p. 485.
[2] *Proceedings of the Manchester Commercial Society*, 5th March, 1795.

" had their chests and bales in lighters moored all round the vessel, covered with sail cloth and watched both day and night in expectation of the hourly arrival of the order liberating the ship." When the order came, allowing the ship to sail but prohibiting the loading of any more goods, all the goods in the lighters had to be returned to the warehouses, and the ship had to sail half empty.[1] The procedure seemed gratuitously vexatious to the provincial merchants, especially as there was at Hull a lack of neutral vessels suitable for the transport of the surplus goods. In a letter to Colonel Stanley, who was one of the two Members of Parliament for the County of Lancaster, the President of the Manchester Commercial Society explained that " The trading ships between Hull and Hamburg not only serve for the conveyance of the goods of our manufactures, but for those of all Yorkshire, Nottingham, and Birmingham, for all Germany, Switzerland, and the borders of Italy : as such you will easily conceive how important it is that this communication should not be interrupted, but that it should, on the contrary, be effectually protected by frequent and periodical convoys."[2]

The embargo had even more vexatious effects upon shipping for the Mediterranean. Vessels which were to join the Mediterranean convoy were held up in a half-empty condition at Liverpool ; their cargoes could not be completed until the lifting of the embargo was announced, and they would then require about a month before they could join the convoy at Falmouth. The uncertainty as to when the embargo would be lifted naturally unsettled trading conditions ; and commercial instability threatened to react seriously upon industrial employment. The Manchester merchants emphasised the embarrassing difficulty of the situation by asking the Government whether goods for the fair of Salerno would be allowed to sail with the June convoy, " for without such assurance we cannot go on finishing our goods, nor will the Shippers lay on any Vessels."[3]

To make matters worse, Messrs. Earle reported that there was not a single neutral vessel unemployed in the port of Liverpool, and that such as arrived were immediately engaged to load for Hamburg and other ports of the North, because such short voyages were more profitable than those

---

[1] *Proceedings of the Manchester Commercial Society*, 23rd March, 1795.
[2] *Ibid.*, 2nd April, 1795.
[3] *Ibid.*, 11th April, 1795 ; *cf. ibid.*, 7th May, 1795.

to the Mediterranean. As a means of safeguarding English shipping and commerce, the embargo was evidently worse than useless. Actually, however, the conservation of merchant shipping and cargoes was not the Government's main motive in putting on the embargo ; the British navy was badly in need of seamen, and the embargo was intended to facilitate the work of the naval pressgangs. Between 1792 and 1799 over 90,000 extra seamen were taken into the Navy, and the vast majority of them had previously been serving in the crews of merchant ships. Many of the naval recruits were secured by voluntary enlistment, generally with a bounty ; but many others were forcibly enlisted by the pressgangs, from whom no British seaport or merchant-man was safe. When all other expedients had failed to produce a sufficient number of sailors, an Act [1] was passed in 1795 requiring from the various counties quotas of men, the numbers ranging from twenty-three in the case of Rutland to a thousand and eighty-one in the case of Yorkshire. A few weeks later this was supplemented by another Act [2] requiring quotas of men from the various ports.

The connection between the embargo and the problem of naval man-power is clear from Orders in Council of March, 1795, which lifted the embargo from ships employed in the coasting trade, on condition that the ships " shall not take any seamen on board who are under the age of fifty years and above the age of sixteen years," and also from ships laden with goods for the German fairs, under similar conditions.[3] Mr. Burstall (the Hull merchant who was negotiating in London for the removal of the embargo) advised the Manchester merchants to include in their applications to Government an assurance that vessels carrying their goods would comply with the Order in Council. The Manchester society, in reply, asked Mr. Burstall for the names of the " constant traders " then in Hull, so that these vessels might be specifically named in the application for the removal of the embargo ; it was also suggested that the owners of these ships might be requested to give a guarantee to the Government that they would employ only such hands as were not liable to serve in the Royal Navy. A satisfactory answer was soon received, giving the names of three " constant traders " in the port of Hull whose owners were willing to give the

[1] 35 Geo. III, c. 5. [2] 35 Geo. III, c. 9.
[3] *Proceedings of the Manchester Commercial Society*, 23rd March, 1795.

necessary guarantee.   On this basis the matter was satisfactorily arranged ;   the Secretary to the Privy Council
announced that the general embargo could not be taken off,
but that it would be relaxed in favour of vessels specifically
named and fully loaded, under the usual restrictions.

The restrictions were even more severe in the case of
ships sailing to the Mediterranean.   In April, 1795, Mr.
Turnbull informed the Manchester society that, at a meeting
of the Privy Council attended by a deputation from the
Levant Company, a Mediterranean convoy had been appointed to sail on the last day of that month, and that the
embargo would be lifted from all vessels wishing to join this
convoy.   The names of such vessels were to be stated, and
they were to sail " on the same or rather more favourable
conditions than have been granted to the West India convoy."
Each vessel should have no more than five English seamen
(the master, two mates, boatswain, and carpenter) ;   the rest
of the crew must be made up of foreigners, English seamen
under fifteen or over sixty years of age, or seamen invalided
from the King's service.[1]   The Manchester merchants pointed
out that it was much harder to obtain foreigners as seamen
in the outports than in London ;   but their protest was in
vain.   When the question of the important June convoy
came up for discussion, the Manchester Commercial Society
was naturally very anxious to know whether the convoy
would sail at the appointed time, and whether merchant ships
would be allowed to join the convoy, if the general embargo
had not been lifted.   Once again the Manchester merchants
emphasised the special and seasonal nature of the goods
exported for the Italian fairs ;   these goods (they wrote)
" consist of a great variety of fancy articles prepared purposely for those markets . . . should we get them ready
and they could not be sent away in time, the loss would be
serious as the patterns are not suitable for other markets."
They were anxious for a speedy reply from the Admiralty,
" since our articles are tedious in their operations of finishing
for the market, and the time required for that purpose is
already too short." [2]   It is satisfactory to be able to add that
the reply from the Admiralty came without delay, and was
reassuring.

[1] *Proceedings of the Manchester Commercial Society*, 13th April, 1795 :
letter dated 8th April.
[2] *Ibid.*, 7th May, 1795.

Napoleon's invasion of Italy in the spring of 1796 made English commerce with the Mediterranean even more precarious. Before the end of June English property had to be removed from Leghorn to Corsica, owing to the dangerous proximity of the French armies, and it was already anticipated that a special embargo would be laid on merchant ships bound for the Tuscan port.[1] Much English property which remained in northern Italy was confiscated, the trade with southern Italy was in danger, and a serious check was given to the circulation of Anglo-Italian bills of exchange.

The Corsican situation now became a subject of deep anxiety to the English merchants, especially those of London. The Corsicans, under the leadership of Paoli, had declared their independence of France in 1793, and the island had been under English control since 1794. It was therefore reasonable to ask that the English merchants who had fled from Leghorn to Corsica should receive adequate protection, especially as "from Corsica, the markets in Italy, the Levant, and the African coast may be supplied; and that island may be rendered a safe and useful depot for the manufactures of this country."[2] The London merchants considered that free ports should be established in Corsica, or (better still) that trade with the island should be completely free. Import duties, which could not possibly be of much advantage to the revenue because of the miserable poverty of the Corsicans, should be abolished; such action would make the islanders more loyal to the British Government. For these views the London merchants found strong support in Manchester; but Corsica was not destined to become a pivot of English trade, for in the later months of 1796 the English navy lost control of the Mediterranean, and the island had to be evacuated.

Meanwhile, the London and Manchester merchants had been wasting their energies in trying to get compensation for the property confiscated by the French at Leghorn and other neutral ports. They based their claims on a proclamation issued by the Governor of Leghorn on the 25th June, 1796 (just before the entry of the French armies), exhorting everybody to "remain tranquil," since the

[1] *Proceedings of the Manchester Commercial Society*, 27th July, 1796: letter from Mr. Turnbull, dated 20th July.

[2] *Ibid.*, 30th July, 1796.

neutrality of Tuscany would be respected.   This proclamation was disregarded, of course, by the victorious French. They seized all goods left behind in the town by British subjects, and (with the acquiescence of the Tuscan Government) discovered the debts due to English merchants ; even neutral property deposited at the British factory did not remain inviolate.[1]

This was a distressing situation for the English merchants concerned, but it should have been clear that they were not likely to obtain redress while Tuscany remained in the hands of the French.   Nevertheless, the English merchants held a solemn conference on the subject in November, 1796.   Delegates from the commercial organisations of London, Manchester, Liverpool, Leeds, Halifax and Birmingham met in London and passed several resolutions, one of which asserted that the French, by damaging British property at Leghorn and by collecting for their own use the debts due to British merchants, had " violated all rules of political justice, which constantly tends to lessen the miseries of war by making the enemy suffer as little as possible individually, although from necessity as much as possible collectively."   The French Government was to be requested to pay compensation, not only for the confiscations at Leghorn, but also for similar outrages elsewhere, especially at Milan and Bologna.   The British Government was requested to claim compensation from the Tuscan Government for the losses sustained in trusting to its official and public proclamation ;   the associated merchants were especially anxious that " the Tuscan subjects may not be permitted for a moment to imagine that by paying extorted sums to French Generals and Commissaries they can be exonerated from their legal debts to British merchants."   An application for compensation was actually made to the Tuscan Government in 1797 by the British factory at Leghorn ;   but, as might have been foreseen, the application produced no tangible results.

Not only did the English merchants fail to get compensation for their property which had been seized at Leghorn, but further trade with that port became progressively more difficult as Napoleon strengthened his hold on Italy and the Mediterranean.   In August, 1796, the Manchester Commercial

---

[1] *Proceedings of the Manchester Commercial Society*, 3rd November, 1796 : letter dated 31st October, from John Drake of Chester, a member of the British Factory at Leghorn.

Society learned that the Privy Council had placed a special embargo on all ships loaded in England for Leghorn, but that every facility would be given for the cargoes to be deposited in the King's warehouses, either to be re-shipped to neutral ports or returned to the owners.   There was as yet no embargo upon the vessels loaded in England for Naples, but if necessary the ships would be stopped at Gibraltar or Corsica. Even this latter arrangement, however, had been upset before the end of the year by the English navy's failure to maintain its control of the Mediterranean.   Since November, 1795, Sir John Jervis had been in command of the English fleet in the Mediterranean, and had taken a personal interest in the organisation of the Mediterranean convoys.   The usual arrangement was that a strong convoy should protect the merchant ships across the Bay of Biscay, and then a weaker convoy should take them on to Gibraltar.   As soon as the convoy left Spithead a messenger was to be dispatched overland to Leghorn, and a cutter, kept always in readiness, was to set sail to report to Sir John Jervis.   The Admiral was then to act according to the reports he received from the cruisers stationed off the French and Spanish coasts. If enemy ships were reported to be hovering in force, a strong convoy would accompany the merchant ships from Gibraltar to the Italian ports ; if not, an ordinary convoy, consisting of a seventy-four-gun ship, a frigate, and a sloop of war, would be considered sufficient.[1]   During the summer of 1796, however, French successes in Italy and the growing hostility of Spain made it increasingly difficult for the English fleet to give adequate protection to merchant shipping in the Mediterranean.   Jervis had been obtaining his supplies from the Italian coast, and when that came under French control he found it difficult to keep his seamen in good health. Moreover, his lines of communication were imperilled when, in August, 1796, Spain concluded a treaty of amity with France.   The Spanish navy with twenty-six sail moved to Toulon, and was there joined by twelve French sail of the line ; in face of such a formidable enemy force, Jervis had to retreat.   He evacuated Corsica, and in December, 1796, reached Gibraltar in safety with his whole fleet and a large convoy of merchantmen.

---

[1] *Proceedings of the Manchester Commercial Society,* 4th February, 1796.

The dislocation of English trade with the Mediterranean had already become acute through the declaration of open warfare between England and Spain; this gave rise to various commercial problems similar to those occasioned by the French occupation of Leghorn. Early in September, 1796, the Spanish Government had secured information on oath of all British property in Spain and of all debts due to British merchants. Soon afterwards, orders were issued forbidding the payment of debts to English creditors, and British property was confiscated. The payment of bills of exchange was prohibited, though this was afterwards modified by leave to discharge bills drawn and accepted before the declaration of war. War was declared on the 6th October, and at the beginning of the following month all sums due to English merchants were ordered to be paid into the Spanish Treasury. In consequence, several Spanish business houses gave notice that English creditors must consider the Spanish Government their debtor at the end of the war. This procedure violated a specific treaty undertaking that six months should be mutually allowed by the English and Spanish Governments, in case of war, for the removal of persons and property and the recovery of debts. It was therefore urged that the British Government should apply to Spain for the recovery of outstanding commercial debts according to the treaty obligation, and that this application should be strengthened by a proposal to permit the importation of Spanish produce into England in neutral bottoms during the war.[1]

The English merchants were strongly against any retaliation upon Spanish property in England; on this point they received an assurance that the British Government, " actuated by superior motives of honour," would not imitate the Spanish example, and that the Spanish merchants would be informed of this decision, " to prove to Europe the justice of the British Government." [2] In later diplomatic exchanges between Lord Grenville and the Prince de la Paz, the Spanish Government denied the charges made against it. It declared that the English naturalised in Spain were ordered to move twenty leagues into the interior, and that those not naturalised were given the stipulated six months in which to settle their

---

[1] *Proceedings of the Manchester Commercial Society*, 2nd February, 1797.   [2] *Ibid.*, 23rd December, 1796.

affairs.[1] The Irish " domiciliated " Catholics were not in the least molested. No property was confiscated, but only detained or embargoed in order to prevent embezzlement and to facilitate its return with all possible speed when the proper time should arrive.[2] Whatever may have been the truth on this point, it is certain that some London firms received considerable remittances from Spanish houses after the beginning of the war ; these payments were made quite openly, and without any suggestion that the operation was illegal.

The naval abandonment of the Mediterranean dealt a serious blow at the trade between England and Italy ; regular convoys could no longer be granted beyond Lisbon. Even before the evacuation of Corsica, Captain Curzon of the *Pallas* had declined to take his convoy on from Gibraltar to Naples ; and the Mediterranean convoy had later been ordered into Lisbon by Admiral Parker. At the very time that Jervis was preparing to withdraw to Gibraltar, delegates from the English manufacturing towns were passing resolutions urging that a strong naval force should be maintained in the Mediterranean to protect the trade with Italy and the Levant, which kept in employment over 200,000 manufacturers.[3] A strong naval force (it was pointed out) would also enable English merchants to import the essential raw materials, such as cotton, silk, mohair, and goats' wool, without which the manufactures of England could not be carried on, and its presence would increase the possibility of securing redress for damage done to British property. To such resolutions the Admiralty could only reply that it would do its best to maintain a strong fleet in the Mediterranean, but that the measures adopted " must depend upon further intelligence and on the comparative pressure of other services."

Conversations later between Mr. Turnbull (representing the associated commercial societies of England) and Lord Spencer (First Lord of the Admiralty) emphasised the difficulty of giving adequate naval protection to Mediterranean trade. Lord Spencer " appeared to be perfectly sensible that the great object of the French was to shut us out from commercial intercourse as far as was in their power

[1] " And even several exceptions have been made to this general rule, in favour of persons whose circumstances have recommended them, by their being permitted to reside in the ports, and remain in Spain."
[2] *Proceedings of the Manchester Commercial Society*, 18th March, 1797.
[3] *Ibid.*, 3rd November and 6th December, 1796.

with every port in Europe," and he justly observed that the
trade with Italy and the Levant could only be maintained
" so long as the Italian states bordering on the Mediterranean
were enabled to support their neutrality." In the existing
unsettled condition of Mediterranean affairs, it was decided
that the port of rendezvous for convoys should be Lisbon
rather than Gibraltar, since the former was less exposed to
the enemy's fire. Sir John Jervis could then take charge of
the convoy onwards from Lisbon with a strong force ; and
it was hoped that the Court of Portugal might be prevailed
upon to exempt the convoy ships from port charges.[1] Later
in 1797 the naval victories of Jervis at Cape St. Vincent and
Duncan at Camperdown raised hopes that a more adequate
convoy system might once more become possible ; but to
the inquiries of the associated merchants Lord Spencer had
to reply that the re-establishment of regular trade in the
Mediterranean was as yet impossible, owing to the variety of
services which were required from the Royal Navy.[2]

The impracticability of ensuring the safety of cargoes in
the Mediterranean at this time gave rise to a somewhat
fantastic scheme, propounded to the Manchester Commercial Society by a certain Mr. Season of Naples, for sending
goods to Italy by an overland route. Mr. Season suggested that an armed English frigate might be detailed to
cruise between Trieste and Manfredonia. Goods could then
be sent from Hamburg by land to Trieste, and the freight
charges across Europe would be lower than the wartime
insurance charges on goods going across the Mediterranean.
The merchants of Naples were willing to bear the expense of
transport between Hamburg and Trieste, and would take
the goods on from Trieste at their own expense and risk,
provided that they could embark the goods with safety and
that they had the general protection of an armed vessel
cruising continually between Trieste and Manfredonia. Such
a vessel might be maintained by a subscription among all
the English merchants trading to Naples. Mr. Season's
letter closed with the warning : " If you entirely deprive
this country of your articles during the remainder of a war
whose termination cannot now be guessed at, by degrees
articles of the country manufacture and German goods will
be substituted in the place of yours, and, coming on cheaper

[1] *Proceedings of the Manchester Commercial Society*, 5th January,
1797.   [2] *Ibid.*, 2nd November, 1797.

terms, you may not be able at the Peace to establish so extensive a sale for your goods as before the War." [1]   Copies of the letter were circulated to all the English commercial societies, but the project was especially (though vainly) commended to the Manchester merchants, on the ground that their goods would best support the expense of land carriage across Europe.

Towards the end of 1798 British ascendancy in the Mediterranean began to be restored.   Nelson annihilated a French fleet at the Battle of the Nile in July, and Minorca fell into English possession in November.   On the 10th October Mr. Turnbull was able to assure the President of the Manchester Commercial Society that a strong fleet would be maintained in the Mediterranean, and that our naval supremacy there might be taken for granted.   Preparations were being made for the resumption of active trading, and for the reorganisation of a regular convoy system.   Pitt had already (in February, 1798) framed detailed proposals for the future protection of English commerce.   He suggested (a) that no ship should be allowed to leave a British port without convoy ; (b) that regular convoys should be appointed on all routes where possible ; (c) that, since commerce would be thus facilitated and insurance premiums reduced, the merchants ought to help to bear the cost of equipping and maintaining the convoys (2 per cent. ad valorem was suggested) ; (d) that heavy penalties ought to be inflicted on ships leaving the convoys ; (e) that neutral ships, especially those of America, might be given similar protection, so long as they conformed to the regulations binding British vessels. The London Committee of Merchants attempted to make the proposals more palatable by suggesting that the Government should insure goods against capture by the enemy, at a moderate premium.   The Ministers could then make such regulations for protection as they might think proper ; but " without this effectual security against the enemy, it cannot be expected that the proposed contribution should be given."

It may be imagined that Pitt and the British Government were not prepared to embark on the business of marine insurance, especially after the financial crisis of the previous year ; but in spite of the merchants' opposition

[1] *Proceedings of the Manchester Commercial Society*, 25th July, 1798 : letter dated 8th May, 1798.

the convoy proposals were carried.   By the Act 38 George III, c. 76, it was made unlawful for vessels to leave Britain without a convoy, or for ships' masters to separate from the convoy without leave ; and extra duties were placed upon exports to cover the cost.   Nevertheless, the naval convoys on both the Mediterranean and the Baltic routes continued to be inadequate, irregular, and unpunctual during the remainder of the war.   In 1799 the escort for the Mediterranean convoy consisted of a single frigate ; if this frigate were to be sent away on a special mission " all the Lisbon and Mediterranean trade must be stopped for want of convoy." [1]   Early in March, 1800, the Chairman of the Manchester Commercial Society had to call the attention of the members to " the irregularities which have lately taken place respecting your convoys, particularly that appointed to sail on the 26th December, which has not yet departed from Hull." [2]

By that time, affairs in the Mediterranean had once more taken an unfavourable turn.   Before the end of the year the Italian ports were again subject to France, and closed to English trade.   Spain was already under French control ; and even Portugal, the traditional ally of England, was forced to come to terms during the summer of 1801, by concluding a treaty which involved the closing of Portuguese ports to English ships.   Long before that time, however, the English merchants had apparently come to the conclusion that the Mediterranean trade was not likely to become profitable again so long as the war lasted.   The members of the Manchester Commercial Society had lost faith in the efficacy of petitions, memorials, and delegate conferences as methods of correcting the economic dislocation arising from military and naval vicissitudes.   Their hopes now centred round the conclusion of peace with Napoleon, the securing of compensation for their losses in the Mediterranean, and the re-opening of continental ports to English goods.   Even in these matters, however, the efforts of the associated commercial societies proved futile.   Although peace was temporarily patched up in 1802, the Manchester merchants did not get the compensation for which they had been asking since 1796, while the prohibition of imports from England, and the confiscation of English goods, continued unchecked in the countries subject to Napoleon. [3]

[1] *Hist. MSS.*, Fortescue, Vol. VI, p. 86 (24th December, 1799).
[2] *Proceedings of the Manchester Commercial Society*, 6th March, 1800.
[3] See Heckscher, *op. cit.*, p. 79.

CHAPTER IV.

THE DECLINE OF THE ASSOCIATED COMMERCIAL SOCIETIES, 1798–1801.

THE wartime dislocation of commerce and transport necessarily gave rise to many serious financial difficulties, concerned not only with compensation for goods confiscated by the enemy, but also with questions of marine insurance, losses caused by embargoes, and the repudiation of debts by foreign customers. With these financial problems the associated commercial societies wrestled strenuously, but not very successfully ; and the temporary decline of the movement towards commercial organisation, after 1798, seems to have been due largely to dissatisfaction with the financial results of collective action.

Disputes with marine underwriters involved the commercial societies in much tedious work and futile expense. In such disputes technical and legal knowledge was essential ; the cases had usually to be taken to the law courts for settlement, and counsel had to be engaged by the societies to plead on behalf of individual merchants. Even during the early years of the war, while the British navy was still in control of the Mediterranean, disputes arose between underwriters and merchants concerning the settlement of " averages." [1] The two main points at issue seem to have been (a) whether the underwriters should take over the entire contents of a partially damaged package, and (b) whether the damaged goods should be valued at the price they would have fetched, if sound, at the place of landing, or at the price agreed upon when the bargain was made between the English merchant and the foreign customer, a distinction being made between goods already sold and those still seeking a market. On the first point, the insured merchants claimed the right, when

---

[1] See Palgrave's *Dictionary of Political Economy*, 1901, Vol. I, pp. 74-5, *s.v.* " Average (Maritime)."

part of a package had been averaged, to sell the whole of the
package, sound and unsound together ; the underwriters
had in earlier years permitted this practice, but now objected
to it.   On the second point, the insured merchants insisted
on deducting the net proceeds of averaged goods from the
amount of the invoice (or value insured), and on claiming the
deficit from the underwriters as a loss ; this practice also
had been general in the past, but the underwriters now
wished the valuation to be made, not on the invoice or
insured value, but on the price which the goods would have
fetched at the port of landing, if they had been sound.

More serious causes of dispute arose when Leghorn was
occupied by the French in 1796 and when, in consequence,
the British Government placed its embargo on all English
ships about to sail for that port.   Several merchant ships
were already waiting at Falmouth and Portsmouth for the
next convoy, when the embargo was imposed.   Some loss
was bound to be incurred, through the goods aboard these
ships being unable to get to the markets for which they had
been manufactured ; but it was not clear whether the loss
should fall upon the shippers or the underwriters.   In
November, 1796, delegates were appointed by the Manchester
Commercial Society to meet the representatives of other
societies for the discussion of several questions of commercial
importance.[1]   Among other matters, the delegates were " to
consider what steps should be taken with regard to the goods
shipped in vessels bound to Leghorn, now under embargo,"
and to negotiate with the underwriters.   The point upon
which the merchants rested their hopes was that " the
insured have a right to abandon under the express words of
the policy—' Restraints of all Kings, Princes, or People '."
In this their claims were supported by legal opinion, but with
serious qualifications which weakened the merchants' case.
Messrs. Wood, Park and Erskine, whose expert opinions
were taken on the question, studied the observations made
by Lord Mansfield and Lord Kenyon on similar cases and
eventually agreed that the shippers had a right to abandon
to the underwriters.   Mr. Park was a little doubtful, however, whether compensation could be claimed for a total
loss or only for a partial one.   He pointed out that the
case of an embargo by the British Government was quite

[1] *Proceedings of the Manchester Commercial Society,* 3rd November,
1796.

different from detention by a foreign power, and also that insurance was on the goods, not on the ships. He thought that, if the goods were not perishable, only an average loss could be claimed : namely, the cost of carrying the goods back to the place whence they came, and of shipping them. Nevertheless, he advised that notice of total abandonment should be given and total loss claimed, without precluding the recovery of a partial loss. It was clear, in any case, that there could be no legal relief without abandonment.

On this advice, the delegates assembled in London maintained that the shippers had a right to abandon and claim for total loss. They resolved that the expenses in any law suits arising from this decision ought to be defrayed by " the Trade at large," according to the value of goods shipped from each town, and requested Mr. Bischoff of Leeds to commence an action and such other proceedings as counsel might advise in the case of the *Albion*, one of the ships detained under embargo at Portsmouth. The ensuing dispute turned largely on the question of abandonment. To secure compensation for a " constructive total loss " it was essential that the insured should give notice of abandonment immediately, before touching the goods. The goods would then become the property of the underwriters, who could take such steps as they might think fit in order to minimise the loss. Delay in giving notice of abandonment might prevent the insured from being able to claim for more than a partial loss ; and some delay had already occurred. The Manchester merchants were inclined, on this account, to be pessimistic concerning the issue of the case ; but their legal advisers assured them that nothing would have been gained by a more precipitate abandonment.

The dispute dragged on for a long time, and in the end the pessimism of the Manchester merchants seems to have been justified : for in May, 1797, the Court of King's Bench decided in favour of the underwriters, concerning the right of abandonment, and the merchants were left with the goods on their hands. Mr. Bischoff's suit concerning the goods on board the *Albion* was unsuccessful, and cost the associated merchants £525 2s., which was more than had been anticipated. The Manchester Commercial Society agreed to pay a share of the legal expenses, equal to the share paid by the Leeds Chamber of Commerce ; but some ill-feeling arose through the comparative niggardliness of the Birmingham and Exeter merchants, who were slow to recognise that the case was one of general interest to all shippers. The total sum involved seems very small to be the cause of such dissension ; but the financial resources of the societies had evidently been strained by their earlier efforts. As a result of this unfruitful legal expenditure, the Manchester Commercial Society not only exhausted its reserve funds, but had also to make a special levy of two guineas from every member.[1]

Equally important with the question of marine insurance was the difficulty of collecting debts due to English merchants for goods shipped to foreign ports. This difficulty became aggravated as the French gradually gained control, directly or indirectly, of most of the continental countries : for many foreign merchants welcomed the French occupation as an excuse for repudiating their English debts. Especially unwelcome to the Manchester exporters were the Acts [2] which forbade the settlement of bills drawn upon English merchants from places in the power or possession of the French. This, argued the merchants, would almost inevitably prevent their continental correspondents from paying for the goods they had received from England. The Manchester Commercial Society had, therefore, to spend much time in petitioning Government for a remedy against the injurious effects of the Acts. In July, 1796, the President of the Commercial Society was instructed to write to Mr. Pitt on the matter, informing him of " the alarm this Society is under on being informed that some Houses in London have refused to pay Bills drawn upon them from Leghorn, in consequence of that city being now in possession of the French." [3] In his letter, the President emphasised the serious consequences which would result from the action of the London merchants, and asked for a speedy remedy. " We therefore trust [he wrote] you will in your wisdom adopt such measures as will remove the evil, by issuing His Majesty's Royal Proclamation, or Licence, similar to the one issued on the invasion of Flanders and Holland, . . . as Leghorn and other parts of Italy are the only medium through which we can receive the returns of our exportations to that country." [4] An immediate reply was received from

---

[1] *Proceedings of the Manchester Commercial Society*, 5th January, 1798.   [2] 34 Geo. III, cc. 9 and 79.
[3] *Proceedings of the Manchester Commercial Society*, 27th July, 1796.
[4] *Ibid.*, 30th July, 1796.

Mr. Pitt, with a proclamation permitting the payment of bills drawn from Leghorn on or before the 27th June.[1]

This concession evidently did not satisfy the Manchester merchants, for some days later a further letter was sent to Mr. Pitt, complaining that the relief given was only temporary and partial, since Milan, Bologna, and other places occupied by the French were not covered by the proclamation. The gravity of the situation was emphasised in the same letter : " Leghorn has long been the emporium of the Italian trade, other places in the interior remit through its medium for goods exported from this country. . . . Consequently, considerable sums are successively becoming due to the exporters : the Italian merchants being debarred from drawing for the property they have in this country, has the effect of keeping British property in Italy, deprives the manufacturers of the use of their capitals, and leaves them exposed to the depredations of an enemy, whose career has already been marked by destruction and plunder, whilst the property of the Italian merchants in this country is perfectly secured." Therefore, to promote the returns of British property now on the Continent, it would be advisable to permit all bills to be paid, " drawn from places which now are, or hereafter may be, in possession of the French, payable to or endorsed to British subjects : the holders of such bills being required to declare by endorsement, or note affixed, that they have received them in payment for goods exported from this country." [2]

It is not certain how far this advice of the Manchester merchants was followed. Some such action seems to have been taken in the autumn of 1796 ; but the subject continued to cause difficulties, and when delegates from the associated societies met in London towards the close of the year, questions concerning the payment of bills and the recovery of foreign debts were prominent in the discussions. At a meeting between the delegates and Mr. Pitt, the Prime Minister promised that the facilities asked for would be granted, as far as this could be done without undue publicity ; the matter was evidently of some delicacy from the Government's point of view, because it was feared that the transference of British resources to merchants in Italy would merely help to maintain the French armies of occupation.

[1] *Proceedings of the Manchester Commercial Society*, 4th August, 1796.
[2] *Ibid.*, 8th August, 1796.

Early in January, 1797, the Manchester Commercial Society made the following recommendations to Mr. Pitt, as to the conditions under which bills should be allowed to be accepted and paid : (*a*) the holder of a bill was to endorse it before a magistrate, declaring on oath that he received the bill in return for goods exported, and an affidavit was to be filed at the office where the licences were granted ; (*b*) the bill thus endorsed was to be sent, along with the affidavit, to an office appointed by the Government for that purpose (preferably at the Bank of England).   It was there to be signed by the Government's representative, and called for on the following day.[1]   These resolutions were sent, through Mr. Turnbull, to be laid before the Privy Council ; they were then to be sent on to Mr. Carter (the private secretary to the Duke of Portland, the Home Secretary).   Mr. Carter was responsible for the granting of licences for the payment of bills, and it was hoped that he would try to make the regulations conform as closely as possible to the wishes of the merchants.   Later inquiries as to the reception of the resolutions, however, drew only the reply that " a licence shall be granted for the payment of any bill of exchange that may be accompanied with an affidavit saying that it has been remitted in payment for British manufactures."

Difficulties of this nature, affecting trade relations not only with Italy but also with Spain and other continental countries, continued to harass all the English commercial societies for the rest of the war ; and the recovery of foreign debts ranked with compensation for confiscated goods among the more prominent demands put forward by the English merchants during the peace negotiations of 1801.   A memorial of that year, drawn up at a delegate conference in London, suggested that each continental Government should issue a mandate to its subjects to satisfy within four or six months all the just claims made upon them, together with the accrued interest : that commissioners should be appointed to investigate the various claims : that the respective Governments should make good whatever debts their subjects were unable to meet : and that, in all cases, the creditor should be subject to no losses due to alterations in the exchange or to deterioration of paper money since the commencement of the war.   The delegates must have known,

---

[1] *Proceedings of the Manchester Commercial Society*, 5th January, 1797.

however, that these demands were not likely to be satisfied ; their real state of mind was probably reflected by Mr. Norman, the Manchester representative, when he said : " I dare not hope we shall get all we ask, but I think it right to ask for enough and to get as much as one can."

It will be evident that, in dealing with the complex financial and legal questions arising from continental warfare, the commercial societies of the 1790's met with little success ; and there can be no doubt that their failure to secure substantial and tangible benefits for their members contributed largely to the general decline of the movement after 1798. The growing apathy of the individual merchants can be traced very clearly in the records of the Manchester Commercial Society. During the first four years of the Society's existence the interest of the members was well maintained, and special meetings were frequent, in addition to the regular monthly meetings. In 1794 thirty-one meetings were held, at which the average attendance was about fourteen ; in 1795 the number of meetings was twenty-seven, and the average attendance ten ; twenty-nine meetings were held in 1796, twenty-three in 1797, and sixteen in 1798. In 1799, however, only eight meetings were held, at which the average attendance was six ; while in 1800 and 1801 only seven meetings were held in each year, with an average attendance of nine. Far more business was done at the frequent meetings of the earlier period than at those held during the last three years, in spite of the longer intervals between the meetings. At the annual meeting held on the 8th March, 1798, it was resolved that four quarterly meetings should be held, instead of the monthly meetings held in earlier years ; but the President was authorised to call special meetings at his own discretion, or at the request of five or more members. Even this less ambitious arrangement, however, did not work satisfactorily ; meetings were frequently called which were so sparsely attended that it was impossible to transact any business. An insufficient attendance of members prevented the conduct of business at two out of the sixteen meetings held in 1798, and the difficulty was more serious in the three following years. Out of the eight meetings held in 1799, three had to adjourn without doing any business, and the quarterly meeting held on the 2nd July was attended by only three members ; even at the annual meeting of that year no more than six members were present. Between the 26th June and the 11th December, 1800, no meeting of any kind was held, and the meeting on the former date was prevented from doing business because only four members attended.

The most annoying feature of the situation was that a group of members would often request the President to call a special meeting and then, when the meeting had been called, would themselves fail to attend it. As early as June, 1798, it was resolved that all members who signed a requisition for a special meeting should be present at the meeting, otherwise it should be at the option of the members who did attend, to decide whether the business should be dropped. At the annual meeting held in March, 1799, a special clause was added to the rules of the Society : " That it will be deemed incumbent on every person signing a requisition to attend the said meeting " ; but the cases of default continued. On the 12th February, 1800, a formal requisition was sent to the President of the Society, asking him to call a special meeting for the purpose of considering Mr. Foden's dis-covery of a substitute for flour " in sizing and making paste, used in the manufactures of this kingdom, which has been submitted to Government and recommended to be left to the Commercial Committee of Manchester." This was evidently an important matter, having regard to the war-time scarcity of flour ; yet, although the requisition was signed by nine members, only six attended the meeting.[1]

Attendance at the Society's meetings became so unsatis-factory that, at the annual meeting held on the 6th March, 1800, a letter was read from the retiring Chairman, Mr. Silvester, warning the members against allowing the Society to pass out of existence, and appealing for better support. Mr. Silvester's letter enumerated the objects for which the Society had been founded, and added : " It is not the shadow or merely the name of a Commercial Society that will be productive of advantage ; it is only from a regular attendance and frequent intercourse of its members, a laudable spirit to encourage and communicate useful information, and a minute attention to all the advantages and general objects of its institution, that they can be answered. . . . At meetings regularly called, on subjects of great commercial importance, frequently the proposers of

[1] *Proceedings of the Manchester Commercial Society,* 22nd February, 1800.

the question have absented themselves on the day requested by them for discussion, and, at special meetings called by the Chairman, it has sometimes occurred that I have not had a single member to advise with. . . . I wish to impress on your minds that, as the objects of this Society are not of a trivial or visionary nature, you will give it your support by a regular attendance ; that a proper system may be adopted and adhered to in future, for the purpose of giving more energy and effect to all your proceedings."

Mr. Silvester was thanked by the Society for his " necessary and sensible letter," but it had little practical effect ; the attendance of members remained as poor as ever, and meetings were held very infrequently.   During the last few years of the Society's activities, indeed, Mr. Silvester seems to have been the mainstay of its existence.   He was elected President in March, 1798, and remained the leading member of the Society until its meetings ceased in December, 1801. A rule had been made in 1798 that, in the absence of the President, the President of the previous year should act as Chairman.   This rule had soon to be applied, for Mr. Potter, who was elected to succeed Mr. Silvester as President for the year 1799, declined the appointment altogether ; Mr. Silvester had therefore to act as Chairman throughout the year.   In 1800 Mr. John Entwistle was elected President ; but Mr. Silvester still had to support the main burden of leadership. It was evident that this state of affairs could not go on indefinitely ; at the annual meeting held in March, 1801, it was therefore proposed by Mr. Brandt (the first President of the Society) and seconded by Mr. Lawrence Peel, that the meetings of the Society should be suspended.   Three members were in favour of the resolution, and three against ; the decision was accordingly left to the Chairman, Mr. Silvester, who gave his casting vote in favour of suspension.   Thereupon the balance of cash in the hands of the Treasurer was ordered to be lodged in his name in Jones's Bank, to be held on behalf of the Society.   Considering the apathy of the members during the preceding three years, it is a little surprising to find that the Society had a balance in hand of £146 5s. 10d., which did not include the twelve guineas " deemed collectable " as subscriptions from six defaulting members.   Against this satisfactory balance, however, must be reckoned £4 10s., owing to Mr. Harrop (presumably for notices and advertisements in his *Manchester Mercury*) ;

while the sum of £45 14s. was later paid out as expenses of the Manchester delegates who attended the conference of commercial societies held in London during the latter part of 1801.

The ordinary affairs of the Commercial Society might now be considered to have been settled ; but the position of Mr. Silvester remained peculiar. Although no ordinary meetings were held after March, 1801, special meetings were called on several occasions later in the year ; moreover, letters for the Society continued to be received, and had to be answered by Mr. Silvester, though he no longer held any official position in the Society.   When Lord Spencer resigned office in 1801, Mr. Turnbull proposed to thank him for his services to the trade of the country, and hoped that the Manchester merchants would also express their grati-tude.   Mr. Silvester had to reply that, however much he would like to subscribe to Mr. Turnbull's address, he was unable to take such action, since he was no longer Chairman of the Manchester Commercial Society, the meetings of the Society having been suspended for the time being.   On another occasion, when Mr. Turnbull wrote urging the Manchester society to send representatives to the delegate conference of the various commercial associations in London, Mr. Silvester replied that he was unable to call a meeting, but would send round letters to the members ; later he reported that he had handed over the correspondence to J. Thackery, the boroughreeve of Manchester, who was the official responsible for calling public town's meetings.

Fortunately for Mr. Silvester's peace, the activities of the other commercial societies had also fallen off by this time, and Mr. Turnbull's own organising functions were coming to an end.   During the early years of the war there had been very active correspondence between the commercial organisations of London, Manchester, Birmingham, Leeds and Exeter, which also co-operated, though less actively, with the merchants of Liverpool, Halifax and Norwich. The Manchester Commercial Society was founded on the model of the Chamber of Commerce which was already in existence at Leeds ; and in its turn the Manchester society served as a pattern for the Commercial Society founded in the same year (1794) at Exeter.   The Birmingham Commer-cial Committee of the 1780's had broken up in 1790 as the result of a somewhat obscure dispute concerning the manufacture and testing of sword blades ; [1] but the Birmingham merchants quickly responded to a suggestion from the President of the newly-founded Commercial Society at Manchester, and the Birmingham Commercial Society played a quite active part in the commercial negotiations of the next few years.   There was as yet no general Commercial Society or Chamber of Commerce at Liverpool ; [2] but the merchants of both Liverpool and Halifax sent delegates on several occasions to confer with the representatives of the associated commercial organisations.   The case of Halifax was rather peculiar, and of some interest to the student of early industrial organisation.   In March, 1797, the President of the Manchester Commercial Society wrote to Messrs. Lees, of Halifax, suggesting that a Commercial Society should be formed there.   To this suggestion Messrs. Lees replied that they had no such society at Halifax, " nor could have, from the nature of the trade in these parts ; the merchants, though numerous, being dispersed through an extensive tract of country, a parish of sixteen miles, and very few residing in the town."

Co-ordination between the various commercial organisations depended to a great extent upon the efforts and influence of Mr. Turnbull, whose position as a leader of the London merchants may call for some explanation.   No general Commercial Society or Chamber of Commerce had yet been established in London, but there was an informal organisation known as the London Committee of Merchants, of which Mr. Turnbull was Chairman.   The London Committee, like the Manchester Commercial Society, was composed largely of merchants interested in the Mediterranean trade, and Mr. Turnbull's own business interests seem to have lain mainly in that direction ;   in 1797 his firm (Turnbull, Forbes & Co.) was receiving considerable remittances from Cadiz, while from a later letter it appears that the firm was in partnership with a commercial house at Leghorn, and had suffered heavy losses by the confiscation of goods after the French occupation. [3]   In a letter written by Mr. Brandt in October, 1794, Mr. Turnbull was referred to as the " Chairman of the General Committee of Merchants." [4]

[1] G. H. Wright, *op. cit.*, pp. 26-38.
[2] See above, Chap. II, p. 19.
[3] *Proceedings of the Manchester Commercial Society*, 4th May, 1797, and letter dated 21st January, 1800.
[4] *Ibid.*, 1st October, 1794.

The exact meaning of the title remains obscure ; though the phrase may suggest that the organisation of the General Chamber of Manufacturers of 1785-87 was still fresh in Mr. Brandt's memory.   More probably, however, the direct reference of the phrase is to Mr. Turnbull's chairmanship of the Merchants' Conference in October, 1793,[1] when delegates from Manchester, Birmingham and Halifax had met in London to discuss convoy questions with five London representatives.   Whatever his official title may have been, during the next seven years Mr. Turnbull acted not only as the leader of the London merchants, but also as the co-ordinator and spokesman of the associated commercial organisations in the provincial towns.   The burden of his correspondence with the societies and with the Government must have been considerable, but his services were given without payment ; the provincial societies sent monetary contributions to him only when a meeting of their delegates in London had involved him in additional clerical expenses.   Mr. Turnbull's task in organising the collective action of the commercial societies was not always easy ; friction arose on many questions, especially concerning the working of the convoy system. Yet only once is Mr. Turnbull recorded as having protested against the amount of work demanded from him, and that was in November, 1794, before he had properly adjusted himself to the strain.

Though it is natural to regard the " General Committee of Merchants " as in some sense related to the earlier General Chamber of Manufacturers, there was not really much similarity between the two organisations ; it is clear that the commercial movement of the 1790's never possessed the driving force and close-knit organisation achieved by the General Chamber in 1785-86.   During the active existence of the General Chamber, regular monthly meetings had been held in London by an elected committee representative of the principal industrial and commercial districts ; there was no such regular and central organisation of the commercial interest during the 1790's.   The delegates of the provincial commercial societies attended only two conferences in London: the first in 1796-97, soon after the French occupation of Leghorn, and the second in 1801, during the progress of the peace negotiations which led to the Treaty of Amiens.   The

---

[1] *Manchester Mercury*, 29th October, 1793.

weakness of the movement may be deduced, perhaps, from the long interval between the two conferences, as well as from the friction which arose at the first, and the apathy with which the second was attended ; the initiative in calling the conferences was taken in each case by Mr. Turnbull. In November, 1796, the Manchester Commercial Society received a letter from Mr. Turnbull, in which he proposed that the various commercial societies should send delegates to London to consult together concerning the damage done to English property in Italy and Spain. This plan was supported by the Leeds Chamber of Commerce, the Birmingham Commercial Society, and the Halifax merchants. On the other hand, the merchants of Norwich declined to co-operate, on the ground that they " did not think it advisable at the present juncture to interfere in a matter that might raise difficulties during the pending negotiations for peace with France." [1]

Despite this chilly warning from Norwich, the Manchester merchants decided to take part in the conference, and appointed Messrs. Brandt and Richardson as their representatives. The other commercial societies were informed that the Manchester delegates would be at Varley's York Hotel, Bridge Street, Blackfriars, on Sunday the 20th November, and invitations were also sent from Manchester to the merchants of Chester, Rochdale and Liverpool. On the 23rd November Messrs. Brandt and Richardson reported that delegates from Liverpool, Leeds, Halifax and Birmingham had arrived, but not the Exeter delegates, whose " extraordinary action " in publishing their memorial to the Government was adversely criticised. When the Exeter representatives eventually appeared at the conference they were received rather coolly, though they denied any knowledge of the publication of the memorial, and assured the other delegates that they had no intention of appearing in a political light, but were merely stating the situation of their trade, as commercial men. This was an unpromising start, and further delays arose because Mr. Pitt was occupied " in preparing the budget and in considering the proposals of France for reciprocal compensation." In the end, however, the conference was able to transact a considerable amount of

---

[1] The Norwich Chamber of Commerce was not formed until 1797. (See *Proceedings of the Manchester Commercial Society*, 2nd November, 1797.)

business on a wide range of commercial topics ; and the
Manchester representatives reported that they were satisfied
as to " the general utility of a general association of merchants
from different places." This opinion was evidently shared
by the other delegates, for at one meeting of the conference
it was resolved (*a*) that the various societies and bodies of
merchants should communicate one with the other as much
as possible, to counteract any attempts at chicane or any
other impositions on English merchants (*b*) that delegates
from the manufacturing towns should meet for any matter
of general interest, and to attain general objects.

Encouraged by these resolutions in favour of closer co-
operation, the Exeter Chamber of Commerce subsequently
proposed that the various mercantile associations should
join together in a general organisation, to be called " The
United Commercial Societies of England," and that arrangements should be made for further delegate conferences in
London. Regulations for the benefit of trade in general
were drawn up, and circulated to the commercial organisations
of Exeter, Manchester, Halifax and Leeds ; from Leeds they
were to be returned to Mr. Turnbull, who was evidently to
continue his organising work, as Chairman of the new association. The regulations, which were to be printed in the
main European languages, provided that

(*a*) An English House, having shipped the goods, was to
be no longer responsible for any subsequent delay.
(*b*) Where no specific agreement was made, contracts
were always understood to be made in English
money and English weights and measures.
(*c*) No delay or abatement could be admitted from a
variation in exchange or a detention of vessels.
(*d*) No forced payment of debts to hostile armies or to
Governments should be admitted as partial or
total acquittal of such debts.
(*e*) The commercial societies of England were to communicate to each other the names of any houses
abroad acting contrary to the honour expected
among merchants.

The general temper of the United Commercial Societies may
be reflected in a letter circulated by the Exeter merchants,
in the form of a proposed addition to the rules : " That this

Union is formed by the societies in justice to themselves and to such of their correspondents abroad whose honourable dealings have entitled them to full confidence, and to every advantage the Trade can afford, and who must have been equally injured with the exporters by the chicaneries complained of, the persons practising them having been thereby enabled to undersell the fair dealers in any market where a competition prevails."

With this temper, and these definite regulations, the foundation of the Union might have been expected to inaugurate a period of more active commercial co-operation. It is therefore surprising to find that no further conference of delegates from the societies was held, either in London or elsewhere, until the later months of 1801. Such a meeting might have been expected to take place early in 1800, when the French had been driven out of northern Italy by the Austrian and Russian armies. The Manchester Commercial Society, indeed, did suggest at this time that more active co-operation would be desirable on the questions of debt recovery and compensation for confiscated goods; and letters inviting such co-operation were sent from Manchester to London, Leeds, Halifax, Exeter, Liverpool, Birmingham and Norwich. Mr. Turnbull's response, however, showed him to have little hope that this action would yield satisfactory results. In his reply to the Manchester merchants he mentioned, among other reasons for inaction, that the London merchants were but little interested, and that he had as yet received no communication on the subject from the other associated societies.

It was not until the negotiations preceding the Peace of Amiens were in train, during the later months of 1801, that Mr. Turnbull was able to call the delegates of the provincial commercial societies to a conference in London. By that time the regular meetings of the Manchester Commercial Society had been suspended, and the Manchester merchants were at first disinclined to take any part in the conference. They had, however, appointed a committee in March, 1800, to discuss the questions of debt recovery and compensation for confiscated goods. A special meeting of the Commercial Society was held on the 28th October, 1801, to receive the report of this committee; and at the special meeting Mr. Norman was appointed to " proceed immediately to London and to co-operate with the delegates from the various towns

and cities in Britain now assembled in London." A committee of nine was formed to correspond with Mr. Norman,
and his expenses were to be paid out of the Society's funds.
At the London conference Mr. Norman met nine other delegates from the provincial commercial societies : two each
from Leeds, Birmingham, Exeter and Norwich, with one
from Halifax. Mr. Norman dutifully assisted the conference
in its attempt to secure the insertion of favourable commercial
clauses in the peace treaty, and prepared a report on the
conference's activities, for presentation to the Manchester
Commercial Society. How little interest the Manchester
merchants took in the matter may be gauged from the circumstance that, when a special meeting was called to receive
Mr. Norman's report, not a single member appeared. Mr.
Norman had therefore to send in his report in the form of
a letter, along with a list of his expenses, which amounted
to £38 7s. In the end, however, a special meeting of
the Society was successfully held on the 17th December,
1801, and Mr. Norman was thanked for his services in
London.

How far the moribund apathy of the Manchester Commercial Society reflected the general condition of the other
provincial organisations cannot be directly ascertained, for
the records of the other societies have apparently not sur-
vived. Early in 1801 Mr. Turnbull had described himself
(in a letter to Lord Spencer) as " Chairman of the respective
bodies of the merchants and manufacturers of England
trading with the southern ports of Europe and with South
America." [1] After the delegate conference of that year,
however, Mr. Turnbull seems to have recognised that the
provincial merchants' enthusiasm for collective action had
evaporated, at any rate for the time being. No doubt there
were various factors contributing to cause the decline of the
provincial commercial societies, and of the wider movement
towards commercial co-operation. Many merchants appear
to have considered that the results achieved by collective
action were not worth the expense of time, trouble and
money. Certainly, as the war with Napoleon became more
intense, the requests of the commercial societies could hardly
be expected to exert much influence upon the harassed and
over-worked Ministry, especially as many of the merchants'

[1] *Proceedings of the Manchester Commercial Society,* 5th March, 1801.

demands were such as the British Government had no power to grant.

Moreover, the export trade in English manufactures was still increasing rapidly, in spite of the war. " Mercator," writing to the *Manchester Mercury* in 1801, felt bound to admit that " during a war which hath continued nine years, our Trade hath suffered less, perhaps, than any other manufacture in the Empire, and is even far more extensive than it was at the commencement of that period " ; though he did not consider that this fact justified any relaxation of collective efforts for the defence of trade.[1] Difficulties were placed in the way of direct intercourse with some parts of the Continent; but other lines of approach remained open, and English goods still made their way in large quantities, by circuitous routes, even into the interdicted markets. Even more remarkable was the system of government licences, by which some trade between the principal belligerent countries was officially permitted. The continued expansion of the English export trade was achieved largely by its diversion from the Mediterranean to the countries of northern and central Europe. The official values of the exports to Italy and Spain declined markedly after 1796 ; but this was much more than counterbalanced by the expansion of the export trade to Germany, while a similar expansion (though on a smaller scale) was taking place in the trade with France, Holland, Portugal, Prussia, Poland and Russia. This may have been why the chief aim of the commercial societies, during the last few years of their existence, was not that the Government should assist the revival of the Mediterranean trade (for which the societies had been primarily organised), but merely that the Government should help them to get compensation for the confiscation of their property, and to obtain payment for the goods they had already exported to Mediterranean markets.

As the movement towards the closer organisation of the commercial interest was already moribund, the conclusion of peace in 1802 gave Mr. Turnbull a convenient opportunity to terminate his connection with the provincial merchants, and to seek more profitable employment under the Crown. One of the last recorded actions of the Manchester Commercial Society was a resolution of thanks to Mr. Turnbull ; and, as

---

[1] *Manchester Mercury*, 3rd November, 1801.

a tribute to his long and important services to the commercial interests of the country, the Manchester merchants resolved to give their full support to Mr. Turnbull's application to be appointed one of the Commissioners for disposing of the Crown lands in the island of Trinidad.[1]   Nothing more was heard concerning the United Commercial Societies of England.

[1] *Proceedings of the Manchester Commercial Society*, 24th December, 1801.

CHAPTER V.

THE BEGINNINGS OF THE MANCHESTER CHAMBER OF COMMERCE.

AFTER the suspension of the Manchester Commercial Society's regular activities, the collective efforts of the Manchester merchants and manufacturers came to depend once more on the calling of special town's meetings, and the appointment of temporary committees for specific purposes. The movement may, in this fashion, have become more truly representative of the public opinion of the town ; and the apathy of the Commercial Society towards the peace negotiations with France, in 1801, may have arisen from a general feeling that the problems involved were so complex as to be outside the scope of a small organisation of merchants, concerned primarily with one section of the export trade of the district. As we have already seen, the Manchester Commercial Society held a special meeting on the 28th October, 1801, and appointed Mr. Norman to represent the society at the conference of merchants, which was to meet in London for the purpose of safeguarding British commercial interests during the negotiations. On that same day the following letter was addressed to the Boroughreeve and Constables of Manchester :

" GENTLEMEN,
      " As the pending negotiations for peace will, of course, embrace many regulations of the utmost importance to the manufacturing and commercial interests of this town and neighbourhood, we, the undersigned, request that you will call a MEETING of those interested, as early as possible, to consider of this and such other commercial arrangements as may then be submitted to the meeting."

The letter was signed by eighteen members of the Commercial Society, and the first signature was that of the Society's Chairman, J. Silvester.[1]

    [1] *Manchester Mercury*, 3rd November, 1801.

In consequence of this requisition, a " General Meeting of the Merchants, Manufacturers, and other Inhabitants of the Town and Neighbourhood of Manchester " was duly held on the 3rd November at the Bull's Head Inn, with the Borough-reeve in the chair ; and it was resolved unanimously

> " That the negotiations now depending with France and other countries being of great importance to the commercial interests of this Town and neighbourhood, it is expedient that a Committee be formed and a sub-scription entered into, for the purpose of attending to and promoting the welfare of the different branches of our Manufactures, with full powers to add to their own number, chuse sub-committees, appoint delegates, and take such other measures as may, from time to time, appear to them most expedient to promote the desired end."

Every subscriber of five guineas was to be entitled to become a member of the committee, and over eighty names were at once submitted for election ; books of subscriptions were to be prepared immediately, and arrangements were made for the first meeting of the General Committee.[1]   The list of persons nominated for immediate election seems to show once more the influence of the Manchester Commercial Society, for the first two names are those of C. F. Brandt (the first President of the Society) and J. Silvester (its last Chairman).   Among the other well-known merchants and manufacturers in the list were George and Francis Philips, John and William Douglas, Samuel and Peter Marsland, Lawrence and Robert Peel, Thomas Richardson, Joseph Seddon, Samuel Oldknow, Thomas Satterthwaite, Charles Wood, William Dinwiddie, Benjamin, Thomas and James Potter, James Touchet, John and Thomas Drinkwater, and James Norman (the Commercial Society's delegate to the London Conference).   Altogether, a more representative list of Manchester business men could hardly have been framed, though it must be added that not all the persons nominated were present at the meeting.   It is fairly evident that the members of the Manchester Commercial Society, after the appointment of this influential General Committee of Merchants and Manufacturers, considered that the Society

---

[1] *Manchester Mercury*, 10th November, 1801.

was absolved from taking any further action for the protection of local commercial interests during the peace negotiations.

Various other temporary committees for specific purposes were formed during the short Peace of Amiens and the ensuing struggle against Napoleon. Thus in February, 1803, a public meeting was called to organise resistance to the import duties on raw cotton, which had been imposed during the preceding parliamentary session. The meeting denounced the cotton duties as " unpolitic in principle and dangerous in consequences " ; the committee appointed once more included such important merchants and manufacturers as William Douglas, Samuel Marsland, Robert Peel, Samuel Greg, William Dinwiddie, Samuel Oldknow, and James M'Connel.[1] Again, in May of the same year, a public town's meeting was called " to take into consideration the proposed Consolidated Duty Bill now before Parliament, as far as it respects the introduction of East Indian Silk Goods for Home Consumption, which are at present prohibited." The proposed relaxation was duly denounced, a committee was appointed " to co-operate with the committee on this business in London," and a petition was prepared, for presentation by the members of Parliament for the county.[2]

When action was taken, in 1802, to prevent the handloom weavers from securing " the enlargement of the powers of a late Act of Parliament " (the Cotton Arbitration Act of 1800),[3] it was the members for the county who took the initiative ; but otherwise the procedure followed the customary rules. The Boroughreeve and Constables called a public meeting at the Bull's Head Inn ; the meeting declared that the proposed enlargement of the Act should be opposed, " and were it practicable even the Act itself should be immediately repealed." Another special committee was appointed, and the first person nominated was once more C. F. Brandt ; the long list of names which followed Mr. Brandt's differed only slightly from the lists of other contemporary committees among the Manchester merchants.[4] A year later, " the renewed application of the weavers to

[1] *Manchester Mercury*, 8th February, 1803 ; *Cowdroy's Manchester Gazette*, 26th February, 1803.
[2] *Ibid.*, 14th May, 1803.
[3] 39 and 40 George III, c. 90.
[4] *Manchester Mercury*, 23rd February and 2nd March, 1802.

Parliament for an amendment and enlargement of the powers of the Act,[1] lately passed in consequence of their petition," led to the reconstitution of the Manchester committee, which was instructed to enter into communication with other towns engaged in the cotton industry.[2] During the next twelve months this committee opposed the weavers vigorously, and incurred an expenditure of over £2000, " by delegates to London, the attendance and examination of witnesses in Parliament, the fees of the House, and other incidental and yet unpaid charges, which the funds subscribed are greatly insufficient to defray." [3] They therefore called another public meeting, presented their report and accounts, received a vote of thanks, and were instructed " to continue for the present " but without taking any further action. Eventually, after some months' delay, their accounts were paid, and the committee (" in concurrence with their own sentiments ") were discharged.[4] It may be surmised that the expense of collective action had once more surprised and discouraged the Manchester business men. When the weavers' petition for the settlement and regulation of wages came up again three years later, the public meeting decided " that at present the occasion will not render expedient the appointment of any delegate to London " ; the committee appointed was therefore merely for the purpose of corresponding with members of Parliament.[5]

Meanwhile, various sectional organisations were springing up among the local manufacturers, in spite of the Combination Acts of 1799 and 1800. In October, 1803, the master spinners of Manchester had met at the Bridgewater Arms to frame a common policy in dealing with their rebellious operatives. It appeared to the meeting " that the Working Mule Spinners in this town and neighbourhood have entered into a dangerous and wicked combination, to compel the master spinners to raise their wages." The meeting, therefore, resolved " that for the purpose of defeating this dangerous and unjust combination it is highly expedient that the master

[1] Presumably 44 George III, c. 87. For a general account of the Cotton Arbitration Acts of 1800 and 1803, see J. L. and B. Hammond, *The Skilled Labourer* (2nd edition, 1920), pp. 62-9.
[2] *Cowdroy's Manchester Gazette*, 22nd February, 1803.
[3] *Manchester Mercury*, 21st February, 1804: the total expenses amounted to £2031 6s. 2d., the subscription to £1540 17s. 6d., leaving a deficit of £490 8s. 8d.
[4] *Ibid.*, 5th June, 1804.   [5] *Ibid.*, 10th and 12th March, 1807.

spinners form themselves into an association and raise a fund to defray the expenses of prosecuting the persons engaged in such combinations, and to indemnify the individual masters who suffer therefrom, and for the encouragement of masters who shall instruct apprentices in the art of spinning." The amount of the fund to be raised was fixed at £20,000, and each member of the association was to contribute in proportion to the number of spindles employed. The members pledged themselves not to employ any person " who shall be discovered to join in, or be guilty of aiding, abetting or assisting in any such unlawful combination," but on the contrary to take such legal proceedings as might be recommended by counsel, for the suppression of the combinations.[1] Another instance of sectional organisation among industrial employers occurred in the following year, when plans were circulated of an Association of Master Printers, which was to be founded for the ostensible purpose of taking apprentices, providing for aged workers, and dealing with " turn outs." This project arose out of a dispute between the master printers and the journeymen calico printers' combination, which was one of the strongest labour unions of the period.[2]

The only organisation of this period bearing any resemblance either to the earlier Manchester Commercial Society or to the later Manchester Chamber of Commerce was a Society for the Protection of Trade, which seems to have been brought into existence by the joint efforts of the Commercial Society and the Society for the Prosecution of Felons. The Commercial Society had become alarmed at the seduction of British artisans to foreign countries, and at the exportation of machinery ; the " Prosecution of Persons for exporting Machinery and inveigling Mechanicks " was the special function of the Committee for the General Protection of Trade, which was appointed early in 1799 under the chairmanship of Mr. J. Silvester.[3] This committee seems to have shared the inactivity of the Commercial Society after 1800, but was revived in 1803 as the Society for the Protection of Trade. The new Chairman (Joseph Seddon) commended " the vigilance some time ago exerted by the Merchants and

---

[1] *Cowdroy's Manchester Gazette*, 15th October, 1803.

[2] *Ibid.*, 8th June, 1804, 2nd March, 1805, 16th August, 1806 ; and see Webb, *History of Trade Unionism* (1920 ed.), pp. 56-7, 75-6, etc.

[3] *Proceedings of the Manchester Commercial Society*, 27th December, 1798 ; *Manchester Mercury*, 8th and 15th January, 26th February, 5th and 19th March, 1799.

Manufacturers of Manchester and of the several towns acting concurrently with them," and hoped that much might yet be done " by renewing the Powers of the Society for the Protection of Trade." [1]

The special importance of this Society is as a possible link between the Manchester Commercial Society and the later Manchester Chamber of Commerce. At an early meeting of the Chamber of Commerce it was reported that a sum of about £172 was being handed over to the Chamber by the executors of Richard Yates, and that the money had belonged to a Society for the Protection of Trade " long since dissolved." [2]   It has been generally assumed [3] that this was the fund which the Manchester Commercial Society had in hand when it suspended its meetings in 1801 ; the sum handed over in 1821 would agree fairly well with the sum deposited in 1801, assuming accumulation at interest during the intervening twenty years. If this assumption is correct, it is perhaps reasonable to suppose that the Society for the Protection of Trade was regarded as a potential successor to the Commercial Society, and that Joseph Seddon, in 1803, may have been attempting to " renew the powers " of the earlier Society under another title. If the assumption is not correct, an awkward question may arise as to what became of the Commercial Society's funds and the accrued interest.

The Society for the Protection of Trade, like the Manchester Commercial Society, failed to withstand the shocks and strains of the French wars.[4]   During the later phases of the struggle against Napoleon, and in the immediate post-war years, collective action among the Manchester merchants and manufacturers still depended upon the calling of public town's meetings, the appointment of temporary committees for specific purposes, or the maintenance of sectional associations such as have already been mentioned. The lack of a continuous central organisation must have increased the difficulties of wartime commerce ; and the necessity for

---

[1] *Manchester Mercury*, 3rd and 10th May, 1803 ; *Cowdroy's Manchester Gazette*, 7th May, 1803.

[2] *Proceedings of the Manchester Chamber of Commerce*, 14th November, 1821.

[3] *E.g.* by Helm, *Chapters in the History of the Manchester Chamber of Commerce*, p. 60.

[4] Joseph Seddon was still Chairman of the " Society for the General Protection of Trade " in 1807 (*Manchester Mercury*, 25th August, 1807).

collective action certainly did not decrease in the later stages of the war. The records of Lloyd's show that the organisation of convoys and the abnormal risks of marine underwriting became even more thorny problems during the period of Orders in Council, Napoleonic Decrees, and General Embargoes ; to the very end of the wars the Committee of Lloyd's was protesting loudly against the inadequacy of the naval protection given to British shipping.[1] Manchester merchants still found it difficult to deliver goods to their foreign customers, and even more difficult to get paid for the goods delivered.[2]

In the years immediately after the return of peace, Manchester commerce and industry suffered exceptionally severe reverses ; and the necessity for making a concerted inquiry into the depressed state of local trade was one of the reasons for the foundation of the Manchester Chamber of Commerce in 1820. The immediate stimulus to this momentous step seems to have come from the contemporary revival of enthusiasm for the free trade movement among merchants and manufacturers throughout the country. On the 8th May, 1820, Mr. Alexander Baring presented to the House of Commons the famous " Petition of the Merchants of London in favour of Free Trade," [3] which had been drafted by Thomas Tooke ; ten days later a similar petition was presented from " the Merchants, Manufacturers and other Inhabitants of the Towns of Manchester and Salford, and their immediate neighbourhood." [4] Only eleven days after the presentation of this latter petition the foundation of the Manchester Chamber of Commerce was formally decided upon, by a public meeting held at the Police Office, with the Boroughreeve in the chair. The meeting resolved " to establish a Chamber of Commerce for the purpose of guarding and promoting, in the most effectual manner, the commercial interests of the town and neighbourhood," and appointed a provisional committee to draw up a code of rules and regulations. By the following November the constitution of

[1] C. Wright and C. E. Fayle, *History of Lloyd's* (1928), Chapters VIII-XIII, especially pp. 231-2, 279-80.

[2] See evidence given by Manchester merchants (G. W. Wood and S. Philips) on merchants' petitions against the Orders in Council (reported in *Wheeler's Manchester Chronicle*, 26th March, 1808).

[3] Full text printed in Tooke and Newmarch, *History of Prices*, Vol. VI (1857), Appendix I.

[4] *Manchester Chronicle*, 27th May, 1820.

the Chamber had been framed, and its first Board of Directors appointed.[1] In the meantime, the provisional committee had not been inactive ; only a month after the first meeting, petitions on China and the East India trade had been sent to Parliament in the name of " the Committee of Commerce of Manchester." [2]

The aims and characteristics of the new Chamber of Commerce were expressed in the resolutions of a meeting held in January, 1822, " to consider the most effectual means of giving increased support and more extended utility " to the organisation.[3] The meeting resolved

" 1. That a union of the merchants and manufacturers of Manchester and its neighbourhood, for the protection of their commercial interests, would be attended with great practical utility.

" 2. That an Association formed for this object should be open to every individual of good character, who would conform to its regulations.

" 3. That the duty of the Association should be to attend to proceedings in Parliament affecting the commercial interests of Manchester and its neighbourhood, and to promote, at proper seasons and by proper means, the removal of existing regulations injurious to the freedom of trade, and not requisite for purposes of necessary revenue.

" 4. That party objects and party feelings should be rigidly excluded from the proceedings of the Association.

" 5. That its ordinary affairs should be conducted by a limited number of individuals, annually chosen by the Members at large from their own body, at a stated general meeting publicly convened for the purpose ; and that other general meetings of the members should be held for special business as often as may be requisite.

" 6. That the Manchester Chamber of Commerce and Manufactures, established in 1820, for these objects and on these principles, has rendered material service to the commercial interests of the town."

[1] *Manchester Mercury*, 19th December, 1820.
[2] *Ibid.*, 27th June, 1820.
[3] *Report Book of the Manchester Chamber of Commerce ;* the First Annual Report of the Chamber is prefaced by a printed report of the public meeting held on the 30th January, 1822.

According to its original constitution [1] the Chamber of Commerce was to be managed by a Board of twenty-four Directors, chosen by annual elections in which all the members had votes ; six of the Directors were to retire annually, and to be ineligible for one year or until a vacancy occurred. Business partners might become members of the Chamber either individually or collectively.   Meetings of the Directors were to take place once a week ; in addition, regular quarterly and annual general meetings were to be held, as well as special general meetings at other times, if called for by a sufficient number of members.   " Personal communications from members of the Chamber to the Board of Directors . . . relating to the general interests of trade in this district " were to be " entitled to the early consideration of the Board." General meetings were empowered " to exclude any member whose conduct may have been such as, in the opinion of a majority present, to render him unfit to continue a member of the Chamber."

The main framework of the Chamber's constitution remained intact for more than one generation ; but minor changes were necessary from time to time, and in 1835 an interesting alteration in the method of electing new Directors was made, at the instance of Mr. Richard Birley.   At that time the Board of Directors still numbered twenty-four, of whom six were elected each year ; the six Directors with the least number of attendances during the year retired automatically at the Annual General Meeting in February, and six new Directors were chosen by the direct vote of a majority of the members present at the meeting.   Mr. Birley's amendment to the constitution replaced this democratic method of direct election by a somewhat ingenious mixture of nomination and ballot.   According to the system introduced in 1835, nine gentlemen were chosen by the Board in the first instance.   The first of the nine was nominated by the President, the second by the Vice-President, and the remaining seven by those seven Directors who had served longest and most continuously on the Board.   If the President or Vice-President (or both) were absent, the Chairman and eight other Directors nominated.   Only Directors present had the right to nominate, and if two Directors had an equal right to nominate, the decision between them was made by ballot.

[1] A copy of the original code of regulations is pasted in at the back of the first volume of *Proceedings* of the Chamber.

Nine gentlemen having been chosen in this way, their number was reduced to six by ballot of the Board, and the six thus chosen were submitted as the nominees of the Board to the General Meeting for acceptance or rejection.   In the absence of both the President and Vice-President, the Directors present nominated a Chairman for the day, and he had full presidential powers, including a casting vote.[1]

Needless to say, after the Chamber of Commerce had adopted this elaborate system of nomination by the Board, the actual election of the new Directors by the annual general meeting tended to become not much more than a polite formality, except at times when feelings ran high, as in the Anti-Corn-Law crisis.   The adoption of a less democratic system of choosing new Directors does not appear to have impaired the efficiency of the Board in the conduct of business ;   during the later 'thirties and the earlier 'forties, the Manchester Chamber of Commerce became a most influential body dealing with a wide variety of questions, concerning fiscal and financial policy, foreign and imperial trade, company law, and many other aspects of commercial life.   During the 1830's the Chamber of Commerce had between 230 and 320 yearly subscribers ;   the Manchester Commercial Society of the 1790's never had more than sixty members.   The difference in size rather understates the difference in strength of the two organisations :   though it must be remembered that the great influence exercised by the Chamber of Commerce during the second quarter of the nineteenth century arose partly from the tremendous growth in the population and trade of Manchester, and of the surrounding industrial districts.

By 1801 the boroughs of Manchester and Salford contained 94,876 inhabitants ;   twenty years later, just after the foundation of the Chamber of Commerce, the two boroughs had a population of 161,635, and in 1831 they numbered 237,832 inhabitants.   The increase of population during the first thirty years of the nineteenth century had thus amounted to more than 143 per cent. ;   and more than half of this increase had occurred in the ten years after 1820.   In that same decade the number of cotton mills in Manchester and Salford increased from sixty-six to ninety-nine, the number of silk mills from three to fourteen, and two new flax-spinning

---

[1] *Proceedings of the Manchester Chamber of Commerce,* 7th October, 1835.

mills were established.[1] Meanwhile (reported the Manchester
Chamber of Commerce to the Board of Trade) " an enormous
increase has taken place in the productive energies of this
district, and of course the means of employment have kept
pace with it. Various circumstances have combined to
create this increase, amongst which, the constant improvement in machinery, the increased demand for our manufactures both at home and abroad . . . and the placid course of
commercial operation, arising from the preservation of peace
in Europe, may be placed in the foremost rank." [2] After the
stupendous burst of town-growth in the 'twenties, the *rate* of
increase tended to fall off ; but the actual *amount* of growth
was fairly steadily maintained, decade by decade, throughout the next half-century.[3]

[1] There were also three woollen or worsted mills in the town. For
fuller details, see Appendix A, pp. 237-9 below.

[2] *Proceedings of the Manchester Chamber of Commerce*, 27th April,
1833.

[3] See E. Cannan, " The Growth of Manchester and Liverpool, 1801-91,"
in *Economic Journal*, Vol. IV (1894), p. 112.

CHAPTER VI.

THE VICISSITUDES OF MANCHESTER TRADE, 1820-58.

THERE have been few periods in which more substantial commercial progress has been made than in the forty years after 1820 ; yet " the placid course of commercial operation " contained many treacherous whirlpools, and the commercial instability of that post-war generation would have appeared sufficiently disquieting even to Manchester merchants of the present day. During the years immediately after the Napoleonic wars the cotton trade remained in a very un-settled condition, and there was terrible suffering in the industrial districts round Manchester.[1] The social unrest, which led to the " March of the Blanketeers " in 1817, and to the " Peterloo Massacre " of 1819, found expression in demands for radical political reforms ; but it derived its main force from the economic distress of the working classes during the post-war slump. One of the first acts of the Manchester Chamber of Commerce was to organise a detailed inquiry into the distressed state of local trade ; and this was followed by a series of similar investigations carried out dur-ing the winter of 1820-21.[2] That the social distress persisted is evident from the petitions which were still being received by Parliament from Manchester and elsewhere ; but it is also evident that the commercial distress was already abating. Even at the beginning of 1820 the *Manchester Mercury* reported that prices were rising, and that merchants predicted a period of prosperity on a firmer and more

[1] See G. W. Daniels, " The Cotton Trade at the Close of the Napoleonic War," in *Transactions of the Manchester Statistical Society*, 1917-18, pp. 1-28.
[2] *First Annual Report of the Manchester Chamber of Commerce*, January, 1822.

permanent basis than during the preceding twenty years.[1] Early in 1821 Mr. Thomas Wallace, in moving the appointment of a Select Committee on Foreign Trade, stated that a great improvement in the cotton trade had recently taken place ; " and it gave him pleasure to state, that the cotton manufacturers in England and Scotland were generally employed." [2] Before the end of 1821 the *Manchester Chronicle* could report that " Peace, Cheerfulness and Industry, with their estimable train of advantages," had returned to " the extensive towns of Manchester, Salford, and their widespread neighbourhood." [3]

The years between 1821 and 1825 proved to be a time of steadily increasing prosperity. At the beginning of 1823 the Manchester Chamber of Commerce prepared for the Government a statement concerning the condition of trade, and reported that the cotton industry had been carried on to a greater extent in 1822 than in any former year.[4] With the exception of the fustian cutters and the dyers, workers in the cotton industry were fully employed ; the cost of food had decreased, while wages had (with few exceptions) been maintained at the same level or raised. The official value of cotton goods exported from Great Britain increased from £23,541,615 in 1821, to £30,155,901 in 1824 ; though the increase in the declared value was much less, owing to the fact that prices had fallen. This fall in prices was not indicative of trade depression, however, but was caused partly by currency deflation, partly by improvements in machinery and methods of production, and most of all by the increasing cheapness of raw cotton, which was being grown in the United States more extensively. The low prices caused an extension of demand which stimulated production ; but the rate of profits remained low, and the increase of production was kept within the bounds of reason and caution. According to the report of the Chamber of Commerce, the demand for cotton goods was barely equal to current production, and the trade forecast was correspondingly cautious : a gradual increase of trade might be expected from a continuance of low prices, if the purchasing

[1] *Manchester Mercury*, 4th January, 1820.
[2] Hansard, New Series, Vol. IV, col. 425 (6th February, 1821).
[3] *Manchester Chronicle*, 27th October, 1821.
[4] *Proceedings of the Manchester Chamber of Commerce*, 30th January, 1823.

power of the consumer remained the same. This caution persisted until 1824 ; trade continued to be good, but was still carried on with " prudence and sobriety, without any apparent resort to an undue extension of credit." [1]

Towards the end of 1824, however, there were reports that the supplies of raw cotton and silk would be inadequate to meet the demands of the manufacturers, and a reckless burst of speculation ensued.   Cotton doubled in price during the winter of 1824-25,[2] and speculative activity affected the prices of most other commodities, in varying degrees.   The inevitable reaction set in during the spring of 1825, and prices continued to droop for the rest of the year.   Several important cotton firms in the United States collapsed, and the wave of commercial discredit soon spread to this country. Early in 1826 the Manchester Chamber of Commerce reported that many spinners and manufacturers were overstocked with goods for which no market could be found, and that even the goods for which there was a demand were being sold at a ruinous loss, because of the excessive competition among manufacturers, who were being forced to sell at any price in order to meet pressing engagements.[3]   Many employers had been compelled to stop their factories wholly or in part, the number of bankruptcies had increased, and the severe distress among the working classes was leading to alarming riots.   Several mills in the Manchester district were attacked, and hundreds of power looms were destroyed ; nearly £20,000 (part of which was raised in London) was spent in providing food and clothing for the unemployed.

Meanwhile, the " pecuniary embarrassment and general distrust which paralysed the operations of manufactures and commerce " had compelled the provincial towns to seek temporary financial assistance from the Government and the Bank.   Early in 1826 the Manchester Chamber of Commerce co-operated with the merchants of Liverpool and Glasgow in urging the Government to relieve the monetary stringency by issuing Exchequer Bills.   The memorial, presented to the Treasury by a deputation from the Manchester Chamber, called attention to the distressed state of

---

[1] T. Tooke, *History of Prices*, Vol. II, p. 142.

[2] *Ibid.*, Vol. II, p. 157.

[3] *Proceedings of the Manchester Chamber of Commerce*, 18th February, 1826 : Memorial to the Treasury regarding a temporary Issue of Exchequer Bills.

the manufacturing districts, and declared that even a moderate amount of financial assistance would restore confidence, which was the chief factor needed for recovery. The merchants pleaded, not for " the rash and improvident speculator, but for the steady and industrious manufacturer and the workpeople dependent on him." [1] The Government believed, however, that to issue Exchequer Bills would be offering a bonus to speculators, and referred the deputation to the Bank of England, by which the required assistance was eventually given in the form of loans.

In the negotiation and administration of these loans the Chamber of Commerce performed a useful service to Manchester trade. It was arranged that the Directors of the Chamber of Commerce should represent the Bank of England in Manchester ; they were to make investigations into the circumstances of the applicants for loans, and were to keep in close touch with the Bank, submitting all records of investigations " until such a system shall have been established as to induce the Governors and Directors to waive any of their interference anterior to the advance." Seven members of the Chamber of Commerce were appointed as a Board of Assistance to manage all the administrative business arising from the scheme. Loans were to be made to Manchester merchants and manufacturers in sums varying from £500 to £10,000, on either personal security or the security of imperishable goods, at a rate of interest of 5 per cent. per annum, the principal to be repaid in four months' time.[2] Actually the Bank, on the recommendation of the Board of Assistance, agreed to renew the loans to the full amount, in cases where adequate security could be given.[3] In May, 1827, the Board of Assistance reported that it had received, in all, eighty-eight applications for loans amounting in the aggregate to £216,440 ; of these applications, forty-one were approved, and loans were made to the extent of £114,040, mainly on personal security. All the loans were repaid within eleven months, and some within two months ; the borrowers had paid £2914 11s. 1d. in interest, and commercial confidence had been completely restored.

From this severe depression Manchester trade recovered comparatively quickly, and by the summer of 1827 the

---

[1] *Proceedings of the Manchester Chamber of Commerce,* 10th and 25th February, 1826.
[2] *Ibid.,* 6th and 8th March, 1826.   [3] *Ibid.,* 26th July, 1826.

economic condition of the district was becoming more nearly normal.   On the 22nd May, 1827, the *Manchester Mercury* reported that " last Tuesday, the market for manufactured goods was the briskest which there has been for a very long time.   Better prices obtained in leading articles, and some further advance has, in particular instances, been made to the wages of the weavers."   Not only had trade revived at Manchester, but it was reported (later in the summer) that " the manufacturers of the West Riding of Yorkshire have attained to a steady and prosperous condition on the woollen cloth, worsted stuff, linen and cotton branches, . . . while the prospects from abroad, particularly in North and South America, are of the most favourable kind." [1]

Notwithstanding this partial recovery, trade remained more or less stagnant for the next five years, and some sections of the working classes continued to feel the pinch of hunger ; there were many serious industrial strikes in the districts round Manchester, and the whole country was for some time in a state almost bordering on revolution.   Yet (as we have seen) the population of Manchester and Salford continued to grow with extraordinary rapidity, and the number of factories still went on increasing after the crisis.   The imports of raw cotton increased by 85 per cent. between 1821 and 1831, and there was an almost comparable increase in the exports of cotton manufactured goods.   Meanwhile, important technical improvements had been made in the industry.   The fly-frame and the tube-frame had been introduced at Manchester during the post-war years, and were patented in the later 'twenties.   In 1825 a patent for the self-acting mule was taken out ; in the same year the Manchester Chamber of Commerce was trying to obtain some public remuneration for Messrs. Radcliffe & Ross, whose dressing machine had " brought the whole process of manufacture from the raw material to the cloth into one connected series of operations," and was considered by contemporaries to be the most important improvement since the invention of the fly-shuttle.

The contrast between continued industrial progress and the persistent social distress which accompanied it is striking enough to call for some special explanation.   The trade of Manchester was undoubtedly prosperous, in spite of tem-

---

[1] *Manchester Mercury*, 14th August, 1827.

porary checks caused by such crises as that of 1825 ; yet it is equally indubitable that the social condition of a considerable proportion of the Manchester working classes was deplorable. Many of the streets were narrow, congested, ill-paved, and badly ventilated ; the lack of sewers, and of the most elementary sanitary devices, led to the formation of numerous stagnant pools and the accumulation of huge heaps of evil-smelling refuse. The houses of the working classes in these streets were correspondingly squalid ; they were badly drained, damp, and often dilapidated. In the district appropriately known as Little Ireland (between Oxford Road and the river Medlock) a large proportion of the inhabitants lived in cellars, nine or ten feet square, which in some cases housed ten or more persons. In many of these cellar dwellings the people had no bed, and kept each other warm by " close stowage " on straw or shavings ; many of the back rooms in which they slept had no other means of ventilation than from the front rooms. Little Ireland was also subject to frequent flooding by the river Medlock ; it was usually covered by a blanket of smoke, and was an ideal breeding ground for diseases, such as the cholera of 1832.

In such conditions it was natural that both health and morality should be at a low ebb. Drunkenness was spreading rapidly, among both men and women ; it was not only a symptom, but also a contributory cause of improvidence, squalor and ill-health. Dr. J. P. Kay, who was at that time a medical practitioner in Manchester, calculated that in 1830-31 about one-fifth of the population of the town received direct medical treatment through the Infirmary, the House of Recovery, and other public medical charities. The abnormally high death-rate in Manchester at this period is a most searching commentary upon the relation between industrial progress and social welfare.[1] Yet the Manchester factories were paying wages which compared favourably with those paid to industrial workers elsewhere, and which were often three or four times as high as the wages paid to agricultural labourers in the southern counties. According

---

[1] On the social condition of Manchester in the early 'thirties, see Dr. J. P. Kay's account of *The Moral and Physical Condition of the Working Classes Employed in the Cotton Manufacture in Manchester* (1832) ; on urban death-rates in the early nineteenth century, with special reference to Manchester, see Barbara Hammond, in *Economic Journal*, Economic History Supplement No. 3 (January, 1928), pp. 419-28.

to the elaborate investigations made by the Manchester Chamber of Commerce in 1832-33, men cotton spinners were earning an average of from 20s. to 25s. a week, clear of deductions, and some were making as much as 32s. Dressers were earning between 28s. and 30s., men power-loom weavers between 13s. and 17s., mechanics between 24s. and 26s., machine-makers between 26s. and 30s., iron-founders between 28s. and 30s.[1] In all these grades of labour, the best workers were receiving higher wages than the rates quoted. It is true that the hand-loom weavers of cambrics and common checks were earning only 6s. or 7s. a week, and that even the highly skilled hand-loom weavers of " fancy nan-keens " were not getting more than 15s. a week ; but the Secretary of the Chamber of Commerce was careful to add that " Hand-loom Weaving has ceased, except in a few of its branches or under peculiar circumstances, to be the work of Adults." It has also to be remembered that a large and increasing proportion of the hand-loom weavers in Manchester were recent Irish immigrants, who would have thought themselves lucky if they had been able to earn as much as 7s. a week at home in Ireland.[2]

By 1833 there were some indications that trade had once more turned the corner, and it was hoped that the business world had learned enough wisdom from the bitter experience of the preceding years to check any recurrence of reckless speculation. The trade of Manchester was reported to be particularly sound and to be increasing in volume, though profits and wages remained low. This healthy condition was thought likely to continue ; there were signs, indeed, that the foreign demand would increase, especially the demand from America for manufactured goods. On the other hand, the Manchester merchants were seriously concerned at the growth of foreign competition in the cotton industry. By 1833 the United States were consuming nearly as much raw cotton as Great Britain had consumed twenty years previously, and there was already considered to be a danger that the American cotton supply might eventually be no more than sufficient for the American factories. American competition was beginning to interfere

[1] *Proceedings of the Manchester Chamber of Commerce*, 27th April, 1833.
[2] See Redford, *Labour Migration in England, 1800-1850*, 1926, Chapter IX, especially pp. 131-4.

with the British export trade in Mexico, Brazil and the whole of South America, and was even threatening to encroach upon the Mediterranean trade. France and Switzerland were also becoming rivals to Lancashire ; the cotton manufacture was expanding in Germany, Austria and Italy. Wages in the continental countries were much lower than in England, and the Manchester merchants declared that " we cannot maintain our footing in their markets unless we meet them on such terms as will prevent them from investing their capital in buildings and machinery."[1]

Alarming reports concerning the growth of foreign competition continued to be made at frequent intervals ; nevertheless, British trade and industry was remarkably prosperous during the years 1834 and 1835, and remained healthy. Early in 1836, however, it became evident that the supplies of such raw materials as cotton and silk were again running short ; speculative interest was therefore aroused, and prices began to rise sharply. From this and other causes a serious financial crisis occurred before the end of the year, comparable with the crisis of 1825, and a most disastrous depression of trade developed during 1837. Many business firms went bankrupt, thousands of workers were suddenly thrown out of employment, and severe distress was reported from all the manufacturing districts.

The Lancashire cotton trade experienced the full force of this renewed commercial depression, and the Liverpool merchants were obliged to seek special assistance from the Government and the Bank of England. On the 1st April, 1837, a public meeting was held in Liverpool to discuss what steps should be taken in the alarming state of commercial affairs ; a memorial to the Government received within the space of an hour the signatures of 191 commercial firms, and was forwarded to London with a special deputation.[2] In this application for financial assistance the Liverpool merchants sought the co-operation of Manchester, and on the 8th April a special general meeting of the Manchester Chamber of Commerce was called to discuss the matter. The draft memorial to the Chancellor of the Exchequer, which was submitted to the meeting, declared that the mercantile

[1] *Proceedings of the Manchester Chamber of Commerce,* 13th March, 1833 : Memorial to the Treasury.
[2] *Ibid.,* 2nd April, 1837 : report by the President (Mr. Macvicar) to a special Board meeting.

distress then extant was unexampled, and was spreading irretrievable ruin among all classes. The previous high prices were held partly responsible for this state of affairs, but it was thought likely that the more recent fall in the price level would in time attract sufficient capital to relieve the pressure. The memorial asked only for a measure of temporary relief, without which there was a danger that members of all classes would be ruined, the public peace would be destroyed, and the revenue would be adversely affected. Strangely enough, however, the Manchester merchants were disinclined to give their unqualified approval to these melancholy prophecies, and Mr. Richard Roberts eventually carried an amendment to the draft memorial : " That the present condition of commerce in Manchester does not necessitate assistance, but looking to the heavy calamities sustained by the Liverpool merchants, and their probable effects, the application of that body for aid should be supported by a deputation from this Board." [1]

The Manchester deputation proceeded at once to London, and on the 11th April interviewed Lord Melbourne (the Prime Minister), Mr. Spring Rice (the Chancellor of the Exchequer), and Mr. C. Poulett Thomson (the President of the Board of Trade) ; but no satisfactory response was made by either the Government or the Bank of England.[2] Acting on a suggestion made by the Chancellor of the Exchequer, the Liverpool and Manchester deputations tried to persuade the Bank to issue Exchequer Bills, but the Court of Directors refused to allow it ; nor would the Bank agree to discount the acceptances of Liverpool brokers of acknowledged standing and property. The Chancellor of the Exchequer supported his refusal to grant the relief desired by the Liverpool merchants (namely, an advance of £1,000,000 on the security of goods) by maintaining that the stocks of goods in hand were not excessive, whilst foreign orders were considerable, and the prices of public securities were such as to enable the holder to convert them advantageously into money. Moreover, as the advance was sought on the security of raw materials, it would raise the price of raw materials and thus throw the pressure from the importer on to the manufacturer. This would make it more difficult for

[1] *Proceedings of the Manchester Chamber of Commerce*, 8th April, 1837.
[2] *Ibid.*, 26th April, 1837.

British goods to compete in the foreign markets, industrial unemployment would be increased, and the distress of the labouring classes would be more widely diffused. Thus the object for which the aid was sought would be nullified.

This ingenious reasoning would doubtless have been more convincing to the Liverpool and Manchester merchants if it had not been known that the Bank of England (with the consent of the Government) was making large uncovered advances to some of the biggest Anglo-American firms to save them from ruin. The truth is that the financial mechanism of Anglo-American commerce had been thoroughly disorganised by the crisis of 1836, and that the market in raw cotton was affected with especial severity by Mr. Nicholas Biddle's attempt to " corner " the whole of the American cotton crop. In 1837 Mr. Biddle (who was the President of the United States Bank of Pennsylvania) drew bills on England for £3,000,000 against cotton which was to be consigned from America to his agents in Liverpool. These transactions in cotton continued during the years 1838 and 1839, and imposed a severe strain on the financial houses of both America and England. Eventually Mr. Biddle overreached himself, the price of cotton fell rapidly, and the market slowly resumed a more normal appearance ; but it may be imagined that, in the interval, the Liverpool cotton merchants must have carried on their business in a constant nightmare of uncertainty.[1] During the early part of 1838 trade showed some signs of recovery, both at Manchester and in other parts of the country ; but before the end of the year the financial situation was once more critical, and in 1839 the credit of the Bank of England itself was in grave danger for some months. After this renewed shock, business confidence could not be expected to recover quickly ; and gradually the depressed 'thirties merged into the hungry 'forties.

Trade and industry continued to fluctuate alarmingly throughout the succeeding generation, in spite of constant efforts to minimise the evil by means of legislative and administrative reforms. There were commercial crises in 1847 and 1857, quite comparable in intensity with those of

[1] On Biddle and his financial operations, see C. A. Conant's *History of Modern Banks of Issue* (4th edition, 1909), p. 628 ; N. S. Buck's *Anglo-American Trade, 1800-1850*, 1925, pp. 93-96 ; and R. C. H. Catterall's *The Second Bank of the United States*, 1903.

1825 and 1836 ; and the importance of financial instability, as an underlying cause of this almost regular fluctuation of trade, will require fuller discussion in a later chapter.[1] Here it must suffice to emphasise once more the precarious basis upon which the prosperity of Manchester was built in that generation ; Manchester merchants and manufacturers whose business life was passed between 1820 and 1860 cannot for long have been free from the fear of commercial collapse lurking behind each temporary revival of trade.

[1] See Chapter XII, below.

CHAPTER VII.

FOREIGN TRADE AND TARIFF PROBLEMS:
(i) EUROPEAN COUNTRIES.

AMONG the general factors which unsettled and distorted the development of Manchester's export trade during the earlier nineteenth century, foreign tariffs were unquestionably the most prominent. This, of course, was no new problem ; European commercial policy during the seventeenth and eighteenth centuries had consisted of an almost continuous series of economic blockades, by which the various states had attempted to restrict their imports whilst stimulating their exports, their manufacturing industries, and their shipping.[1] The principles underlying this " Mercantile System " were so deeply ingrained in the minds of all classes that even Adam Smith thought it inconceivable that they should ever be eradicated. " To expect, indeed, that the freedom of trade should ever be restored in Great Britain," he wrote, " is as absurd as to expect that an Oceana or Utopia should ever be established in it. Not only the prejudices of the public, but what is much more unconquerable, the private interests of many individuals, irresistibly oppose it." [2]

Each country realised that its economic development was being hindered by the tariff policy of its neighbours ; but no country was willing to forgo the special advantages which it derived from the restrictive character of its own tariff, though the mercantile classes often favoured the negotiation of commercial treaties which would bring about the reciprocal reduction of customs duties. One of the declared objects of the General Chamber of Manufacturers, in 1785, had been to obtain information about the prohibitions laid upon the importation of British goods into foreign countries, and also

[1] See Heckscher, *The Continental System*, 1922, pp. 9-15.
[2] *The Wealth of Nations*, Bk. IV, Chap. III.

about the duties imposed on foreign produce imported into England ; one of the ultimate aims of the Chamber was to secure equitable commercial reciprocity with foreign states.[1] At that time the merchants of Manchester observed with alarm " the successive and rapid exclusion of our manufactures from almost every one of our best foreign markets . . . in all the extensive dominions of the Empress of Russia, and in the territories subject to the Emperor of Germany, in Prussia, Brandenburg, and Spain, the manufactures of Great Britain are either excluded by absolute prohibitions, or loaded with enormous imposts ; . . . within the compass of a very few months, the like exclusions have taken place in France, in the Venetian territories, and in the United States of North America."

If Manchester merchants found their export trade hampered by foreign tariffs and prohibitions in 1785, it may readily be imagined that the difficulty would be greatly increased during the generation of European warfare which followed the outbreak of the French Revolution. High tariff walls obstructed the entrance of British manufactured goods even into those markets which did not fall under the direct control of the French ; in the territories subject to Napoleon there arose the more formidable obstacle of the Continental System. Political changes, even in eastern Europe, were anxiously watched by the Manchester merchants; in particular, the second Partition of Poland caused them to seek the co-operation of the other industrial centres of England in asking for commercial negotiations with the partitioning Powers.[2] The Manchester Commercial Society reminded the Government that British textile goods had a regular sale in Poland, and that goods going to the fairs of Frankfort and Leipzig were largely intended for the Polish market. Thus the dismemberment of Poland would rob the Manchester manufacturers of important markets, unless the British Government could come to some amicable arrangement with the Emperor of Germany, the Empress of Russia and the King of Prussia. The merchants further begged leave to observe that, " previous to the year 1785, considerable sales of their cotton manufactures were made in Austria, Bohemia and Hungary, but since that period they have been

[1] *Manchester Mercury*, 29th November, 1785.
[2] *Proceedings of the Manchester Commercial Society*, 22nd September, 1795.

either wholly prohibited, or subject to such enormous duties as in effect amount to a prohibition." [1]

Similar attempts were also made to secure commercial negotiations with such widely different dignitaries as the Sultan of Turkey and the Pope ; but all these wartime suggestions of commercial reciprocity proved unsuccessful. The general tone of European opinion, concerning trade with Great Britain, may be gathered from the Austrian Minister's reply ; he declared that the proposed agreement would be subversive of the commercial regulations of Austria, and would (from the superiority of British goods, and the taste that existed for them) entirely ruin the Austrian cotton manufacture.[2] While the wars lasted, the advocates of commercial reciprocity could not hope to gain any considerable success ; even during the short Peace of Amiens the markets of the Continent remained (officially) closed to British goods, behind a barrier of prohibitive tariffs which were asserted to be more ruinous than open warfare.

Manchester merchants hoped to find freer markets in the continental countries when the wars were over ; but even this hope proved vain. In the whole of the Mediterranean, Naples was the only reasonably open market for Manchester goods ; and the unsettled political condition of Naples in the post-war period hindered the development of steady trading relations.[3] In 1823 the uncertainty of the trade was still further aggravated by vexatious tariff changes. On the 13th July, the Neapolitan Government issued an edict increasing by 50 per cent. the existing duties of 13 per cent. to 18 per cent. on British manufactures. The edict was to take effect from the day following its issue ; but British merchants had no chance of clearing their goods, because the Custom House (in which the merchants' warehouses were situated) was closed on the 13th July. A month later a second edict was issued, by which considerably increased duties were to be levied on British goods on and after the 1st January, 1824. These duties, it was stated, would fall with particular severity on cotton goods, " under the plea that they are not enumerated in a late treaty between Naples and Great Britain,

[1] *Proceedings of the Manchester Commercial Society*, 22nd October, 1795 : Memorial to the Committee of Privy Council for Trade.
[2] *Ibid.*, 4th March, 1796 : copy of a letter from Sir Morton Eden to Lord Grenville.
[3] *First Annual Report of the Manchester Chamber of Commerce*, 30th January, 1822 ; *cf. Proceedings*, 6th February, 1822.

whereas the treaty in question is represented as not enumerating a third of the articles usually imported at the time the
treaty was framed." Such duties would have a disastrous
effect on Manchester's export trade to Naples; and this un-
friendly treatment of British merchants was considered to be
most unfair, since Great Britain was the chief market for the
oil, silks, wine and other products of Naples. They therefore
urged the Foreign Secretary to lodge a formal protest against
such interference with a trade which was "important to British
manufactures and beneficial to the Neapolitan Government."[1]

Canning complied with the request of the Manchester
merchants, and secured the withdrawal of the additional
duties, which the Neapolitan Government admitted to be an
unfair burden contrary to the terms of the treaty.[2] With
this, however, neither the merchants at Naples nor the
Manchester Chamber of Commerce were satisfied; they now
claimed compensation from the Neapolitan Government for
the losses sustained through the unfair impositions. A
memorial to this effect was sent to Canning in 1825, through
the Manchester Chamber of Commerce, from the British
merchants at Palermo. They considered that a firm note
from the British Government "to his Neapolitan Majesty
upon this subject would be attended with general salutary
effects at this moment when it would appear that the influence
of our Government has become insufficient to protect us from
a variety of serious encroachments and petty vexations,
which have been lately practised upon us by the several
departments of this administration."[3] The memorial from
Palermo was sent by Canning to the British Minister at
Naples "to be used to put further pressure on the Neapolitan
Government," and it apparently served its purpose; a year
later the Manchester Chamber of Commerce was informed
that the Neapolitan Government had agreed to indemnify
British merchants for the extra taxation to which they had
been subjected.[4]

Even after this sharp rap over the knuckles, the Sicilian
Government continued to show some laxity in interpreting
its treaty obligations. In 1839 there were again complaints

---

[1] *Proceedings of the Manchester Chamber of Commerce*, 31st December, 1823.
[2] *Fifth Annual Report of the Manchester Chamber of Commerce*, 18th February, 1826.
[3] *Proceedings of the Manchester Chamber of Commerce*, 8th June, 1825.
[4] *Ibid.*, 29th June, 1825, and 26th July, 1826.

that the treaty of 1816 was being violated, this time by the grant of a sulphur monopoly to French merchants; and during the next few years the state of trade with Sicily came up repeatedly for discussion before the Board of the Manchester Chamber of Commerce. Negotiations for a new commercial treaty made very slow progress, and the Manchester merchants were by no means satisfied that their interests were being adequately safeguarded. They considered that Messina should be a " Porto Franco," with a nominal duty of 1 per cent.; this concession had been proposed and discussed, but was subsequently abandoned. Complaints were also made about the exaction of " canna and pesa " dues; bonding, moreover, was not free, for no return was made on the re-export of goods on which entrance dues had been paid. The merchants also complained of the unsatisfactory methods of assessing the duties on imported textiles; the Sicilian customs authorities did not assess on area but on length, and this meant that specially wide pieces had to be woven for the Sicilian market, so that the burden of the duties might be minimised. All these points were raised in communications between the Manchester Chamber of Commerce and the British Government during the protracted Anglo-Sicilian negotiations in the early 'forties; and many of the difficulties seem to have been settled by the commercial treaty of the 25th June, 1845, which was very favourably received by the Manchester merchants.[1]

Difficult as it was to arrange satisfactory trading conditions between England and the Sicilian Kingdom, British merchants found it even more difficult to sell their goods in the other countries of southern Europe. During the postwar years both Spain and Portugal imposed such high tariffs that the importation of Manchester goods was practically impossible.[2] It is true that the British merchants confidently expected that this prohibitory system would soon be broken down; it was known that many of the Spanish merchants were opposed to the new tariff, and it was considered impossible for the Portuguese to do without British manufactures, " their own being so much inferior to those of

[1] *Proceedings of the Manchester Chamber of Commerce*, 12th December, 1839; 26th August, 1840; 26th April, 1843; 25th Annual Report, 9th February, 1846.

[2] *Manchester Observer*, 23rd September, 1820; *Manchester Chronicle*, 13th November, 1821.

Great Britain." [1]   Nevertheless, in 1834, the merchants of Glasgow and Manchester complained that British cotton goods were still excluded from the Spanish markets, and that the opportunities for negotiation provided in the treaties of 1809 and 1814 had not been used.   In a memorial sent to Lord Palmerston in January, 1834, the Manchester merchants not only asked for the negotiation of an Anglo-Spanish commercial treaty, but suggested that Gibraltar should be given the privileges of a British port, so that British goods could be imported there as if they came direct from England. Sympathetic consideration was given to this and other communications on the subject ;   but after two years of suspense the negotiations had to be abandoned, on account of the civil war which was then raging in Spain. [2]

In the eastern Mediterranean, trade was hindered not only by the peculiar organisation of economic affairs in the Turkish Empire, but also by the vexatious regulations of the moribund Levant Company.   No English merchant was allowed to trade with the Sultan's dominions (which included Egypt) without first being admitted to the freedom of the Levant Company ;   and even when he had purchased his freedom to trade, the merchant had still considerable dues to pay on his merchandise. [3]   In general, the regulations of the Levant Company were so framed as to confine membership to traders living in or near London, and to keep the bulk of the trade in the hands of a few wealthy merchants who were members of the Court of Assistants of the Company.   Complaints had frequently been made against the restrictive policy of the Court of Assistants, even in the eighteenth century, and after the Napoleonic wars the continued existence of the Company could no longer be justified.   In 1825 a Bill " to repeal certain Acts relating to the Governor and Company of Merchants of England trading to the Levant Seas " passed safely into law, [4] and the Levant Company was abolished, to the great relief of the Manchester merchants and manufacturers.

[1] *Manchester Mercury*, 19th December, 1820 ;   *Manchester Chronicle*, 3rd November, 1821.

[2] *Proceedings of the Manchester Chamber of Commerce*, 8th and 15th January, 1834 ;   27th February, 1834 ;   Annual Reports, 9th February, 1835, and 8th February, 1836.

[3] *Ibid.*, 9th February, 1825.

[4] *Journals of the House of Lords*, 10th June, 1825 ;   *Statutes at Large*, 6 Geo. IV, c. 33.

It still remained necessary to establish satisfactory trading relations with the Turkish authorities, but this was eventually achieved by means of a commercial treaty signed in 1838. By this treaty, freedom to trade throughout the Ottoman Empire was granted to all British subjects and their agents, who were to pay only those duties paid by the most favoured class of Turkish subjects engaged in the internal trade of Turkey, " whether Mussulmans or Rayahs." Moreover, all rights granted by the Sublime Porte after this time were to be enjoyed equally by Great Britain. The importance of these concessions to British traders in Turkey has to be considered also in relation to the Anglo-Austrian Commercial Treaty of 1838, which allowed Austrian ships to bring " enumerated " European goods (such as grain and timber) from Turkish river ports to England.[1] That these treaties were favourable to the growth of Manchester's trade with the Levant may be presumed from the very glowing terms in which the Board of the Chamber of Commerce expressed their gratitude to the Prime Minister, the Foreign Secretary, the President of the Board of Trade, the Austrian and Turkish Ambassadors in London, and the British Ambassadors at Vienna and Constantinople.[2]

In the Baltic trade, British merchants had to pay vexatious Sound Dues to Denmark, as well as high customs duties in Russia and the other northern countries. The Danish Sound Dues dated from the fifteenth century, and were levied on all foreign vessels and merchandise entering the Baltic, with the exception of Hanseatic ships and certain other privileged classes. In the nineteenth century the Sound Dues were an irksome anachronism, but the Danish Government showed a natural reluctance to abolish an immemorial custom which produced a steady revenue. The merchants and manufacturers of Manchester complained in 1821 that the dues on cotton yarn (of which large quantities were then being exported to the Baltic countries) were $3\frac{1}{2}$ per cent. *ad valorem*, a much heavier duty than on any other article.[3] The protest of the Manchester Chamber of Commerce was immediately effective in securing a reduction of the duty, from thirty to eighteen stivers on every 50 lb. of cotton

[1] *British and Foreign State Papers*, 1837-38, Vol. XXVI, 1855, pp. 677-94.
[2] *Proceedings of the Manchester Chamber of Commerce*, 26th January and 6th February, 1839 ; 18th Annual Report, 11th February, 1839.
[3] *Manchester Chronicle*, 16th June, 1821.

yarn ; but, even so, the Manchester merchants remained dissatisfied with the situation.[1]

Another aspect of the problem arose from the incon-venience and delay caused by the collection of the dues ; this was emphasised in a memorial which the Board of the Manchester Chamber sent to Canning in 1823.[2] All ships passing through the Sound had to report in turn on arrival at Elsinore. If there were adverse winds the ships ac-cumulated under the Scaw, and arrived at Elsinore all at the same time. In such a case they might have to wait a considerable time, as they were not allowed to leave Elsinore until they had reported at the Customs House, and even then they might be prevented by a contrary wind from leaving port ; such delays had serious consequences upon the Baltic trade. The Manchester Chamber of Commerce suggested that delay might be prevented by making not the ship's captain but " the house in Elsinore to which the ship was addressed " answerable for the Sound Dues. It was also pointed out that some relaxation of the Baltic Quarantine Regulations might usefully be made ; the regulations were considered to be unnecessary in the case of English ships, and were in any case ineffective, because a Quarantine Pass was always granted as a matter of course. The system acted only as a restraint upon trade (since captains were forbidden to land anywhere except at Elsinore) and merely put money into the pockets of the foreign consuls. In these demands for freer access to the Baltic, the Manchester Chamber of Commerce had the co-operation of most of the industrial and commercial centres of Great Britain, including London, Liverpool, Glasgow, Hull and Leeds ; [3] but their combined efforts were unavailing, and it was not until 1857 that strong pressure from the United States of America (involving some danger of reprisals against Danish possessions in the West Indies) resulted in the remission of the dues, in return for monetary compensation paid to Denmark by a group of associated Powers, including Great Britain.

British trade with northern Europe had in the post-war period to contend against the determined rivalry of the Netherlands, which at that time included Belgium. The Dutch were at nearly the same stage of economic develop-

---

[1] *Proceedings of the Manchester Chamber of Commerce*, 26th October, 1821 ; 30th January, 1822 ; 10th April, 1822.
[2] *Ibid.*, 26th March, 1823.   [3] *Ibid.*, 2nd April, 1823.

ment as the English; they imported their own raw cotton, and were industrial competitors, though Dutch industrial technique had not kept pace with English during the generation of warfare. In Holland, as in France, there existed " a vulgar opinion that the true motive of our (British) persevering courage and conduct is to be sought in our commercial spirit ; and that our Government is still seeking to advance our commerce and manufactures at the expense of all other nations." [1] Partly because of this antipathy, no commercial treaty was concluded with Holland during the post-war years, although between 1823 and 1830 England was able to secure the benefits of commercial reciprocity with many other continental countries. From this movement Holland stood obstinately aloof, and Canning's famous rhyming despatch—

> " In matters of commerce the fault of the Dutch
> Is offering too little and asking too much "

reflected but faintly the rivalry between the two countries. At the time of this despatch, the Dutch had just imposed increased import duties on Manchester goods ; after the beginning of 1826, every 200 lb. of British cotton goods imported into the Netherlands was to pay £10 duty instead of the former duty of 6 per cent. *ad valorem*. [2]

Throughout the earlier nineteenth century Manchester merchants were practically excluded by protectionist tariffs from legitimate trade with France. Immediately after the return of peace, pressure was put upon the restored French monarchy to break down the Napoleonic prohibitions of British goods ; but the French manufacturers protested very vigorously against any relaxation, and demanded an " eternal prohibition of all foreign yarns and fabrics." The protectionist interest won a decided victory ; Article 59 of the law of 18th April, 1816, declared that " as from the publication of this law, cotton yarn, cotton and wool fabrics and hosiery and all other prohibited foreign fabrics shall be sought out and seized throughout the kingdom." [3] Protectionist feeling was especially strong in the linen industry, which was suffering not only from the more rapid introduction of improved

---

[1] *The State of the Nation*, 1822, p. 101.
[2] *Proceedings of the Manchester Chamber of Commerce*, 21st December, 1825, and 21st August, 1826.
[3] See J. H. Clapham, *Economic Development of France and Germany, 1815-1914* (2nd edition, 1923), pp. 71-5.

machinery in the British linen industry, but also from the widespread substitution of cotton for linen fabrics through-out the world. It is not surprising, therefore, to find the Manchester Chamber of Commerce memorialising the Treasury, in 1838, with the object of preventing any increase in the duties levied on the import of linens into France and Belgium ; but it was evident that the protest was not likely to be effective.[1]

The question of the linen duties led to the appointment of a sub-committee of the Chamber, which discussed Belgian tariff policy more generally, and reported in favour of send-ing further memorials to the Board of Trade and the Secretary for Foreign Affairs. In these later statements the Chamber of Commerce referred to " systematic attacks upon the British manufacturing industry," which had " seriously injured the trade between this country and Germany in past years," and had now spread to Belgium. The aggres-sive measures (the Chamber declared) were not imposed by the will of the Belgian Government, but were the work of the Chamber of Deputies. The tariffs imposed were so heavy as to be prohibitive, and would have been even more extensive if the Chamber of Deputies had not feared opposi-tion from the agricultural population, who were afraid of losing one of their best markets, through retaliatory measures adopted by Great Britain. The memorialists further advo-cated an appeal to the Belgian Senate, on the ground that Britain allowed the importation of some classes of Belgian goods at a merely nominal rate of duty, whereas the first article in the new Belgian scale raised the duty on British woollens by more than 30 per cent. Needless to say, the logic of the Manchester merchants did not prove convincing to the Belgian Government, Senate, or Chamber of Deputies.[2]

The reference of the Manchester Chamber of Commerce to Germany's " systematic attacks upon the British manu-facturing industry " may call for some special explanation : Germany had for a long time been the best northern European market for British textile goods. In a memorial sent to the Admiralty by the Manchester Commercial Society in Feb-ruary, 1795, it was pointed out that the manufacturers and merchants of Manchester " constantly export considerable

---

[1] *Proceedings of the Manchester Chamber of Commerce*, 7th February, 1838.　　　　　　　　　　[2] *Ibid.*, 28th February, 1838.

quantities of manufactured goods to Germany . . . through the ports of Kingston-upon-Hull and Hamburgh." [1] Most of these manufactured goods were sold at the great German fairs, of which Reinhard, writing in 1805, gives a most graphic description. " The produce and manufactures of Great Britain exported to Germany " (he writes) " with the exception of consignments to particular mercantile houses, are sold at the great fairs held, at certain seasons of the year, at Frankfort, Leipzig, Brunswick and Nuremberg. The Easter fair at Leipzig is justly celebrated for the immense quantities of British manufactures sold there. Towards the latter end of March, numberless bales of printed and other coloured cottons, of the finest cambrics, and of the most beautiful muslins, are sent from Glasgow, Paisley, Rutherglen, and other manufacturing places to Hamburgh. The manufacturers proceed themselves or send their agents forwards to Leipzig. . . . The Manchester manufacturers also transmit large quantities of their cottons, etc., to Humphries, their principal agent, besides whom several other merchants go themselves with their goods to the fair." [2]

It was from such fairs that British manufactured goods penetrated (often in defiance of hostile tariffs) into the numerous separate states of central Germany, as well as into Austria, Poland, Russia, and even Turkey. After the Napoleonic wars, however, the movement towards the economic unification of Germany gradually reduced the accessibility of the central European markets. By 1834 the Prussian Customs Union (or *Zollverein*) had established its predominance over the tariff policy of the German states, and was already threatening to close the few remaining free inlets to British trade. It was the fear of commercial exclusion which prompted the Manchester Chamber of Commerce, in 1836, to oppose the further extension of the Zollverein, and in particular to oppose its absorption of Frankfort. The Manchester merchants thought that this latter object could be achieved by a refusal to cancel the treaty obligations between Great Britain and Frankfort ; but Lord Palmerston pointed out that only by a modification of the treaty could Frankfort be preserved as an open

---

[1] *Proceedings of the Manchester Commercial Society,* 10th February, 1795.
[2] Charles Reinhard, *The Present State of the Commerce of Great Britain,* 1805, p. 7, note.

market for British manufactures. It was clearly impracticable for the British Government to interfere with the
actions of an independent state (Frankfort was a free imperial
city) ; and, in point of fact, it seemed to Lord Palmerston
doubtful whether the Zollverein had done any substantial
injury to British trade.[1]   On this latter point the Manchester
merchants themselves seem to have been as yet uncertain.
In 1838 the Chamber of Commerce appointed a sub-committee to inquire into the effect of the Prussian Customs
Union upon the trade of Manchester ; and a lecture on
the subject by Dr. Bowring, who had recently attended
the Congress of the Prussian Union, was listened to " with
the deepest interest " by the Board of the Chamber in 1839.[2]

   The most obvious and ordinary method of evading tariff
barriers was by smuggling ; it was as a smuggling base
that Frankfort was particularly important to Manchester
merchants in 1836.   Other smuggling routes went through
Leipzig into Bohemia and Russian Poland.   Further to the
south-east, Cracow was (until its seizure by Austria in 1846)
an important smuggling base for goods going by way of the
Vistula and the Danube into Austria-Hungary and the
Turkish Empire.[3]   But smuggling was a precarious business
at all times.   A much more satisfactory method of combating
tariff restrictions was by developing new markets faster than
the old ones were closed.   During the French wars important
new outlets for British cotton goods were opened in South
America and elsewhere ; and from that time the *proportion*
of Manchester goods exported to European countries tended
to decline.   By the middle of the nineteenth century the
great bulk of the cotton manufactured goods exported went
to non-European markets.   Of the cotton goods exported to
the Continent, twist and yarn formed a rapidly increasing
proportion ; and Manchester merchants viewed with grave
apprehension this change in the character of the trade.[4]

[1] *Proceedings of the Manchester Chamber of Commerce*, 20th January,
1836, *et seq.*
[2] *Ibid.*, 28th March, 1838, and 14th November, 1839.
[3] *Ibid.*, 2nd and 23rd December, 1846, and 10th February, 1847.
[4] *Ibid.*, 20th December, 1838.

CHAPTER VIII.

FOREIGN TRADE AND TARIFF PROBLEMS: (ii) AMERICAN STATES.

THE Manchester merchants of the earlier nineteenth century paid great attention to the possibility of opening up new markets for cotton goods in South and Central America ; in the records of the Manchester Chamber of Commerce Brazil, Mexico, Colombia and Buenos Ayres figured much more largely than Canada, the West Indies, or even the United States. The infrequency with which the Chamber discussed questions arising from trade with the United States is, indeed, somewhat surprising ; for the United States was one of the best customers for British manufactured goods, as well as being an increasingly important source of raw material for Lancashire manufacturers. Between 1820 and 1850 British goods accounted for nearly 40 per cent. of the total value of all merchandise imported into the United States. At the beginning of that period British importers took about one-third of the total value of merchandise sold abroad by the United States ; by the middle of the century they were taking more than one-half of the rapidly increasing stream of exports.[1]

The Manchester merchants more often referred to the United States as an increasingly serious competitor in the export of cotton goods, than as a growing market for British manufactures. It is true that the American cotton industry had received a great stimulus during the later phases of the Napoleonic wars, when British goods were prevented by embargo or naval operations from entering the United States. Moreover, after the wars the American manufacturers were able to secure the protection of a high tariff wall against

---

[1] N. S. Buck, *Anglo-American Trade, 1800-1850*, 1925, p. 2.

British goods, and the cotton industry of the United States continued to expand, after the temporary setback of the post-war slump.   In 1803 there are said to have been only four cotton mills in the United States ; by 1832 there were about eight hundred factories, employing 62,000 workers, and consuming annually 77,000,000 lb. of raw cotton.   Yet although the United States could manufacture enough plain cotton cloth for their own needs, American merchants still purchased increasing quantities of English dyed and printed cottons, and were especially important customers for the new mixed fabrics of cotton and wool.   The exports of these " Orleans cloths " increased from   2,400,000   yards   to 42,115,000 yards during the 'forties, and the United States bought nearly a half of the total.[1]   The rapid and con-tinuous increase of Anglo-American trade throughout the earlier nineteenth century makes it difficult to explain the infrequency with which North American trade was discussed by the Manchester Chamber of Commerce.   A partial ex-planation may, perhaps, be found in the long-established character of the trade ; it is possible also that its most troublesome problems were dealt with by the Liverpool merchants and shippers, who are said to have been strengthening their position in both the importing and the exporting branches of Anglo-American commerce.[2]

The special interest with which the Manchester merchants regarded the trade with South and Central America arose partly from the fact that it was a new trade, carried on under very unsettled conditions.   During the eighteenth century British trade with Latin America had been hindered by the restrictive character of the Spanish and Portuguese colonial systems ; English textile goods destined for South America had been exported in the first instance to Spain or Portugal, Cadiz being important as an entrepôt in this triangular trade.   The revolt of the Spanish colonies during the Napoleonic wars opened up the possibility of a large direct trade with England after 1808 ; and the commercial crisis of 1810 was largely caused by reckless speculation in the South American markets.   Latin America had become once more an El Dorado ; and British merchants were naturally anxious that the new markets which had been opened up during the wars should not be closed on the

[1] See J. H. Clapham, *Economic History of Modern Britain*, Vol. I, p. 482.   [2] See Buck, *op. cit.*, pp. 30-2.

return of peace. A petition sent by the Birmingham Chamber of Commerce to the Prince Regent, in 1814, declared that the commercial and colonial regulations enforced by the Spanish Government had previously operated almost as a prohibition to the consumption of British manufactures in the South American colonies. The Chamber feared that " in the settlement of affairs in the Mother Country—unless some provision were made to the contrary by the British Government—such regulations might be restored or adopted as would prove highly prejudicial to the manufacturing interest of the country." It was reported " that the merchants of the United Kingdom had latterly suspended their orders for the Spanish Colonies, under the apprehension that their property might be liable to confiscation on the return of the Mother Country to the old Colonial system." To remove this fear, and to secure the continuance of " the great export of British manufactures to the Spanish Colonies which had been experienced during the intercourse then already established," the Birmingham merchants prayed that any treaty with Spain should include more liberal commercial regulations than had existed hitherto.[1]

For some years revolution and counter-revolution alternated in the rebellious colonies, and their political future remained uncertain; but the renewal of political disturbances in Spain and Portugal after 1820 made the virtual independence of the colonies more secure, and a rapid expansion of their trade with England was confidently prophesied. It was pointed out that the South American exports to Spain, even at a time when there was civil war among the various colonies, exceeded fifteen millions, and that the imports would have been comparable in value if Spain had not maintained a system of " injudicious monopoly." [2] South America was already an important source of supply of raw cotton for Lancashire; in 1819 about a quarter of the total imports of cotton wool came from Brazil, in 1820 about a third.[3] Henceforth it seemed likely that these imports of raw cotton could be paid for by the export of cotton manufactured goods, for which there was said to be a steady and

---

[1] G. H. Wright, *Chronicles of the Birmingham Chamber of Commerce*, 1913, pp. 65-6.
[2] *The State of the Nation*, 1822, pp. 96-7.
[3] *Proceedings of the Manchester Chamber of Commerce*, 27th April, 1833.

increasing demand. Lord Lansdowne noted with gratification that in 1821, " the very first year in which the trade with the South American colonies could be said to be fairly opened," British exports thither had amounted to £3,227,560 ; in the following year they had increased by £640,000. It might reasonably be hoped that the trade would expand still further, having regard to the improvement that had taken place in British trade with the United States after they had won their independence.[1] By 1823 the South American markets had become so important to the Lancashire cotton trade that the Manchester Chamber of Commerce, considering this trade to be " of the first magnitude and involving the safety of capital to an immense amount," persuaded the Government to appoint British consuls in all the chief commercial towns of Mexico, Colombia, Peru, Chile and Buenos Ayres.[2]

The rapid growth of British trade with South America strengthened the movement in favour of giving official recognition to the political independence of the new republics. Even while the states were still struggling for their existence, some merchants had urged the British Government to give practical assistance instead of maintaining strict neutrality ;[3] now that their independence was established *de facto*, the British Government was strongly pressed to give them formal recognition, in spite of the Spanish Government's persistence in claiming sovereignty over them. A petition drawn up by the Manchester Chamber of Commerce, in 1824, pointed out the " varied nature, steady growth, great extent and expanding prospects " of the South American trade, and asked for " an early and formal acknowledgment . . . of the freedom and sovereignty of the *de facto* independent South American states."[4] The Chamber of Commerce upheld the principle that " as soon as the power or will to protect a colony ceases, the duty of allegiance ceases. . . . To deny the existence of these states and to continue to withhold from them the distinctions usually allowed between friendly civilised states, whilst secretly courting their commercial friendship,

---

[1] Hansard, New Series, Vol. X, cols. 986-7 (15th March, 1824).
[2] *Proceedings of the Manchester Chamber of Commerce*, 30th July, 1823, and 3rd Annual Report, 12th February, 1824.
[3] *State of the Nation*, 1822, pp. 92-5.
[4] *Proceedings of the Manchester Chamber of Commerce*, 17th June, 1824.

is unbecoming to the dignity of a great State and may lead to serious consequences." Similar petitions were being sent from the other main industrial districts at the same time,[1] and appear to have succeeded in influencing the policy of the Government; before the end of 1825 most of the new republics had received the diplomatic recognition of the United Kingdom.[2]

The hopes of a rapid expansion of trade were not without foundation. A correspondent writing in 1824 from Callao said : " All the trade with Europe almost is in our hands, and they like our manufactures. An immense trade is likewise carried on between Chili and Peru now almost wholly in our cottons."[3] But South America was soon glutted with cotton goods, and Lancashire was heavily involved in the subsequent collapse of business credit. Throughout the succeeding generation Manchester merchants had to fight hard to retain their footing in the South American trade ; tariff difficulties soon appeared, and were aggravated by the persistent recurrence of civil warfare, which caused violent fluctuations of rates, arbitrary discriminations, and sometimes even lack of uniformity between different ports of the same state.

The connection between tariff difficulties and civil warfare in South America may be seen in the dispute which arose in 1827 concerning import duties at Monte Video, the chief town of Uruguay (" Banda Oriental "). Uruguay was at that time a bone of contention between the Empire of Brazil and the Argentine Republic, and had been seized by the Brazilian forces. British manufactures paid a duty of 15 per cent. in the Brazilian ports, whereas at Monte Video a duty of 24 per cent. had been regularly levied ; the Manchester merchants therefore claimed that the duties at Monte Video should be reduced to the general Brazilian level. The injustice of the existing arrangement was aggravated by the fact that French and Portuguese goods could be imported at Monte Video on payment of a duty of $16\frac{1}{2}$ per cent.[4] The complaints of the Manchester Chamber of Commerce led the British Foreign Office to instruct its representative

---

[1] For the Birmingham petition, see G. H. Wright, *op. cit.*, p. 91.
[2] See Page, *Commerce and Industry*, Vol. I, p. 69.
[3] *Manchester Chronicle*, 5th April, 1824.
[4] *Proceedings of the Manchester Chamber of Commerce*, 31st January, 1827.

at Rio to inquire into the difficulty, " and to take such steps as may appear justifiable from the circumstances of each case, both for the purpose of checking the practices of undue exaction, and of establishing the claims of British merchants who may have suffered from it." [1] As a result of this inquiry, the Brazilian Government ordered its customs authorities to discontinue the exaction of more than 15 per cent. on goods imported into Monte Video ; but it may be presumed that this concession was not very fruitful, as Uruguay became an independent republic before the end of the year.

Other tariff disputes between British merchants and the Brazilian Government arose from the arbitrary methods of valuation adopted by the customs authorities in some of the Brazilian ports. The Anglo-Brazilian commercial treaty of 1827 provided (Article XIX) that in the formation of future *pantas* the current market price of goods should be taken as the principal basis, and laid down rules for the settlement of valuation disputes " after the manner observed in the Custom Houses of Great Britain." [2] Nevertheless, the merchants of Liverpool and Manchester had reason to complain repeatedly between 1828 and 1831 concerning the excessive valuations imposed on British goods by the farmers of the customs at Pernambuco. The British Consul protested to the Junta, and was referred by the Junta to the Emperor ; but the grievances remained unredressed. In 1831, after renewed applications had been made, the Brazilian Government issued a circular to all the Chambers of Commerce of the northern provinces, enjoining them to assess the *ad valorem* duties according to the prices current at each of the ports, and *not* according to the *panta* of Rio de Janeiro ; but the duties which had been unjustly levied were not repaid, and unified regulations covering all the Brazilian Customs Houses were not put into operation until 1844. [3]

It has to be remembered that between 1828 and 1831 the political condition of Brazil did not encourage administrative efficiency or the scrupulous observance of customs regulations. In 1828 fighting was still going on between Brazil and Buenos Ayres ; it was reported that in consequence of the insecurity

---

[1] *Proceedings of the Manchester Chamber of Commerce*, 2nd May, 1827 : letter from Lord Stanley.
[2] *Ibid.*, 11th February, 1829 : Memorial to Lord Aberdeen.
[3] See Macgregor's *Commercial Statistics*, 1848, Vol. IV, pp. 233-8.

arising from the war, British trade to the River Plate was almost suspended. Viscount Strangford declared that £150,000 worth of goods was lying ready to be shipped off to the Brazils, waiting for the return of peace. English capital amounting to £2,000,000 was locked up in the Brazils, and the merchants could not remit it, owing to the disastrous fall in the exchanges.[1] The financial situation of the Brazilian Government went from bad to worse, and in the end the Emperor was forced (under pressure from the British Government) to acquiesce in the separation of Uruguay from Brazil ; popular distrust of the Emperor's absolutist tendencies led eventually to open rebellion, and in 1831 Pedro I was obliged to abdicate the Brazilian Crown.

Meanwhile, trade with the Spanish republics of South and Central America still remained insecure, owing to the persistence of civil warfare, which may have been aggravated by the Spanish Government's refusal to recognise the independence of the new states. In 1829 the Manchester Chamber of Commerce was moved to present a memorial to Lord Aberdeen, urging the British Government to interpose its good offices with the Court of Spain on behalf of the republics of Mexico, Colombia, Buenos Ayres, Chile and Peru, with the object of " putting an end to all pretext for those petty hostilities, which, though of no national importance, are exceedingly mischievous in their effects on the peaceful pursuits of trade." [2] From later correspondence it becomes clear that British merchants were seriously alarmed at the preparations which were being made in Spain for the invasion of Mexico, and the British Government was urged to make a definite pronouncement on the matter. Peel argued, however, that the British Government had all along maintained strict neutrality towards the struggle between Spain and her former colonies ; and, in point of fact, Spain did not recognise the independence of the South American republics for another thirty years. Throughout that period (and even beyond it) the political condition of Mexico remained chaotic, and trading conditions remained correspondingly unsettled.

Many of the Mexican commercial questions with which the Manchester Chamber of Commerce was concerned were

[1] *Manchester Mercury*, 25th March, 1828.
[2] *Proceedings of the Manchester Chamber of Commerce*, 22nd April, 1829.

customs disputes arising from such practices as the unjust exaction of duties on goods which had not been shipped, or the arbitrary confiscation of goods as a penalty for trivial and involuntary breaches of customs regulations. A more serious grievance was exposed in October, 1836, when the question of forced loans levied on British subjects in Mexico was raised in a letter from the Mexican and South American Association of Liverpool. A guarantee against the exaction of forced loans had been given in the Anglo-Mexican commercial treaty of 1825, which provided (according to the English version): "That the subjects of His Britannic Majesty, and the citizens of Mexico, respectively, shall be subject to the local laws and regulations of the dominions and territories in which they may reside. No forced loans shall be levied upon them ; nor shall their property be subject to any other charges, requisitions or taxes, than such as are paid by the native subjects or citizens of the contracting parties in their respective dominions." The Mexican authorities, however, declared that the English and Spanish versions did not coincide on this point ; and in the succeeding decade several attempts had been made to levy forced loans on British subjects in Mexico. The British residents there had made voluntary contributions rather than admit the Mexican Government's right to exact forced loans ; but Mexican Presidents and Dictators followed each other in such rapid succession that the necessity for repeated " voluntary " contributions became not merely onerous upon the British residents, but injurious to British trade. The merchants of London, Liverpool, Glasgow and Manchester co-operated in bringing this and other difficulties of the Mexican trade to the notice of the British Government ; but, although Lord Palmerston and the Foreign Office were sympathetic, no substantial redress was obtained.[1]

Trading conditions in South and Central America took a decided turn for the worse in 1838, when the French blockaded both Mexico and Buenos Ayres to secure more adequate protection for French residents and traders. Once again the Manchester Chamber of Commerce followed the initiative of the Liverpool Mexican and South American Association in urging Lord Palmerston to use the influence of the British

---

[1] *Proceedings of the Manchester Chamber of Commerce*, 5th and 26th October, 1836, and 16th Annual Report, 13th February, 1837.

Foreign Office to secure the raising of the blockade, which was crippling British trade. The French had declared that they would capture all vessels coming to Mexico from ports which had been notified of the blockade ; they had even refused admission to British ships bringing quicksilver, though this was necessary for the extensive mining operations which were being carried on by British companies in Mexico.[1] To a combined deputation of merchants from Liverpool, Manchester, Glasgow and Belfast, Lord Palmerston explained that he had twice offered his mediation to the French Government. On the first occasion the offer was definitely refused ; on the second, however, the French attitude had been more conciliatory, and the British Mission in Mexico was doing its best to promote a friendly settlement. Partly as a result of these efforts, the Mexican blockade was raised in November, 1838 ; but the French blockade of Buenos Ayres continued to hinder British trade with the Argentine and Brazil for the next two years.[2]

In the 1840's the causes of commercial dislocation in Latin America multiplied. The Mexican Government doubled its customs duties in 1842, and made further vexatious changes in 1845. In 1846 war broke out between Mexico and the United States concerning the annexation of Texas, and hostilities continued for the next two years, causing serious losses to British traders, and also to British capitalists who had invested money in Mexican stock.[3] Meanwhile, renewed warfare between Buenos Ayres and Monte Video was once more hindering trade to the River Plate, and a combined blockade of Buenos Ayres by the British and French fleets was necessary before the navigation of the Paraná was re-opened.[4] A new aspect of Lancashire's interest in South American trade was seen in 1846, when the Manchester Chamber of Commerce gave considerable attention to the domestic politics of Ecuador, and took some small share in stopping the proposed expedition of General Flores,

[1] Quicksilver from European mines was extensively employed in South and Central America in the extraction of gold and silver from their ores. See Ure's *Dictionary of Arts, Manufactures and Mines* (4th edition, 1853), Vol. II, *s.v.* " Mercury."
[2] *Proceedings of the Manchester Chamber of Commerce*, 27th June, 13th September, and 17th October, 1838, etc.
[3] *Ibid.*, 13th January, 1847 : Memorial to Lord Palmerston.
[4] *Ibid.*, 9th January and 6th February, 1845.

the former President and Generalissimo.[1] It is improbable that the Manchester merchants had any strongly partisan feelings about Ecuadorian politics ; in all such cases of civil warfare, their main concern was to secure a peaceful settlement, in the interests of trade. Every South American revolution or rebellion (whatever the issue) caused serious commercial losses, for which compensation could not usually be obtained ; in 1842 the Manchester Chamber of Commerce was still vainly urging the Government to demand compensation for losses sustained by British merchants at Para during a Brazilian insurrection which had occurred seven years earlier.[2]

A more serious Brazilian question began to trouble the Manchester merchants in 1845, when the British Government took steps to check the extensive slave trade between West Africa and Brazil. By " Lord Aberdeen's Act " (8 & 9 Vict. c. 122) the British Government reserved to itself the right to seize any vessel found to be engaged in the slave trade ; it may be imagined that the practical execution of this policy at the expense of Brazilian slavers would not promote amicable trading relations between the two countries. In 1849 the Manchester Chamber of Commerce petitioned Parliament to repeal the Act, on the grounds that it was hampering trade and fostering ill-feeling, as well as being ineffective in checking the slave trade.[3] The Manchester Commercial Association expressed similar views, and co-operated with the Liverpool Brazilian Association and the Glasgow Chamber of Commerce in putting pressure upon the Foreign Office.[4] On this point, however, Lord Palmerston stood firm; the agitation continued spasmodically for at least seven years, but the Act remained unrepealed until 1869.[5] Nevertheless, the average annual exports of cotton piece goods to Brazil increased by more than 50 per cent. between 1850 and 1860, though it is only fair to state that the exports of piece goods to other South American States were increasing at an even quicker rate.

[1] Proceedings of the Manchester Chamber of Commerce, 26th Annual Report, 8th February, 1847.
[2] Ibid., 20th April and 25th May, 1842.
[3] Ibid., 29th March, 1849.
[4] Proceedings of the Manchester Commercial Association, 18th September and 17th November, 1851.
[5] Ibid., 2nd March, 1853, and 6th February, 1856; cf. W. L. Mathieson, Great Britain and the Slave Trade, 1839-1865, 1929, pp. 73-4, 136, and Chap. IV, passim.

In general, the European continental countries were by this time taking a decreasing proportion of the British exports of manufactured goods, and this was especially true of cotton piece goods.[1] Manchester merchants were pushing their way into hitherto undeveloped markets, and the New World was being called in to " redress the balance of the Old," commercially as well as politically.

[1] See Mr. Thomas Bazley's *Table of the Declared Value of British and Irish Cotton Manufactures*, 1853, in Appendix B, p. 243 below ; and *cf. Encyclopædia Britannica*, 9th edition, 1877, article on " Cotton " by Isaac Watts.

CHAPTER IX.

TRADE WITH THE FAR EAST.

In the Far East the success of the Manchester merchants in opening up new markets for cotton goods depended largely on the abolition of the East India Company's commercial privileges. Opposition to the East India Company as a trading body had been vigorously maintained in Manchester during the eighteenth century; but the grounds of opposition gradually shifted as the technical supremacy of British manufacturing industry began to dominate the situation. When the renewal of the East India Company's charter came under discussion in 1791, Manchester opinion was strongly against any renewal; but this was not the outcome of pure zeal for freedom of trade. At that time the East India Company was disliked because it brought to England fine Indian textiles with which the Lancashire manufacturers did not yet feel able to compete on equal terms. On the 20th January, 1791, the " Muslin and Cotton Manufacturers and Cotton Spinners " of the Manchester district discussed the East India Company's competition, and resolved:

" That the cotton and muslin manufactures are of the greatest consequence to this kingdom, giving employment to nearly half a million of his Majesty's subjects.

" That by means of the mills and other machinery which have been lately invented and erected at a very great expense, these manufactures are now brought to great perfection; and those concerned in them are enabled to supply the whole consumption of *Great Britain* on very reasonable terms.

" That the British manufacturers . . . are exposed to continual danger and immense losses by the importation of muslins and cotton goods from the *East Indies*, manufactured by persons—the price of whose labour does not exceed even the amount of taxes paid to Government by individual labourers in *Great Britain*. That such importation of manufactured goods is highly injurious to the nation, by transferring the price of labour from this country to the inhabitants of the East." [1]

Two years later, the renewal of the East India Company's Charter was still under discussion, and was still being opposed by both the cotton and the woollen manufacturers.

Indian competition was even more serious in the silk industry, which was at that time of growing importance in the Manchester district. Indian silk handkerchiefs were being smuggled into England in large quantities, and " clandestinely sold by Drapers and Others, contrary to an Act of Parliament passed in the 11th and 12th years of the reign of King William III,[2] intituled ' an Act for the more effectual employing the Poor, by encouraging the Manufactures of this Kingdom '." Manchester silk manufacturers complained in 1788 that this widespread smuggling had resulted in unemployment, in injury to the British silk manufacture, and in loss to the revenue; they therefore offered a substantial reward for information against offenders.[3] Eleven years later the manufacturers and weavers of silk goods were still urging the Government to take effective action against the smuggling of Indian silk goods, and their agitation had the support of the Manchester Commercial Society. In a memorial presented to the Treasury in 1799, the Commercial Society stated that India silk handkerchiefs, though prohibited except for purposes of re-exportation, were being sold in this country as if no such prohibitive law existed. These handkerchiefs were being supplied to retail dealers throughout the country by the big London houses, who took orders for them despite the heavy penalties. The English silk manufacturers were thus considerably injured, for they had to pay a duty of seven shillings on every pound weight of raw material, as well as $4\frac{1}{2}d$. on every square yard of the manufactured goods when printed ; the manufacturers in India bore no such burdens, and were therefore in a stronger competitive position.[4] There was apparently little difficulty

[1] *Manchester Mercury*, 25th January, 1791.
[2] 11 & 12 Will. III, c. 10.
[3] *Manchester Mercury*, 6th May, 1788.
[4] *Proceedings of the Manchester Commercial Society*, 27th April, 1799.

in getting the handkerchiefs into this country ; a later communication from the Manchester society referred to " the
illicit trade carried on by smugglers who bring these goods
from Holland, Germany, and other ships in the East India
trade, besides those of our East India Company." [1]

The Commissioners of Excise suggested that the evil
might be partially remedied if all silk handkerchiefs were
distinctively marked, according to whether they were of
British or foreign manufacture, any unmarked pieces being
confiscated ; [2] but the English manufacturers found it
difficult to agree upon the kind of mark to be adopted, and
continued to nurse their grievance. Although they seem to
have been convinced that the existing prohibition of Indian
silks was quite useless, they were equally clear that any
removal of the prohibition would ruin the English silk
industry. The Manchester merchants were loud in their
condemnation of the Consolidated Duty Bill of 1803, which
proposed to admit Indian silk goods into this country for
home consumption, on payment of customs duties. A
public Town's Meeting, held on the 11th May, 1803, declared
" That the silk manufactures of this country would un-
avoidably experience the most destructive consequences from
the proposed admission, under certain duties, of silk handkerchiefs, manufactured in India, which have hitherto been
wholly prohibited " ; it was resolved unanimously that the
introduction of such handkerchiefs should be vigorously
opposed, that a committee should be appointed to effect
such opposition, and that they should be requested to co-
operate with the committee on this business in London. [3]

Further instances are hardly necessary to show that,
down to the end of the eighteenth century, Lancashire
merchants and manufacturers still felt the necessity for
protection against the competition of Indian textiles. There
is, indeed, some superficial justification for Mr. G. B. Hertz's
contention that in Manchester, at the end of the eighteenth
century, all classes interested in the cotton trade accepted
every principle which was abhorred, forty years later, by the
" Manchester School " of free-trade enthusiasts. " No part
of England then asked more than did Lancashire for help

---

[1] *Proceedings of the Manchester Commercial Society*, 6th March, 1800 :
letter dated 13th March, 1800.
[2] *Ibid.*, 22nd February, 1800.
[3] *Cowdroy's Manchester Gazette*, 14th May, 1803.

from the state." [1] Before the end of the French wars,
however, the commercial relationship between England and
India had profoundly changed; and nowhere was the
change more profound than in the cotton trade.   Lancashire
manufacturers were now convinced that they need not fear
the competition of Indian cotton goods in the English
market, and were eager to develop the export trade in cotton
goods *to* India.   This could not be expected so long as the
East India Company retained its monopolistic control of
Indian trade; the import of fine Indian textiles was one of
the oldest branches of the company's trade, and was not to be
relinquished lightly at a time when the difficulty of arranging
" remittances " from the East was constantly increasing.

The changed outlook of the rising textile districts of
Great Britain may be clearly seen in the controversy preceding the renewal of the East India Company's Charter in 1813.
There were petitions to Parliament from Glasgow, Manchester,
Blackburn and other textile towns, all to the effect that
" Freedom of commerce is one of the birthrights of Britons,"
and that openings could undoubtedly be found for English
cotton goods in the East, if free trade were allowed.[2] Similar
petitions were also received from the manufacturing towns of
the West Riding of Yorkshire, which contended that the
renewal of the East India Company's commercial privileges
would be injurious to the woollen and worsted industries.[3]
On the other hand, the older clothing districts of the West
Country and East Anglia, whence the Company obtained
camlets, long ells and broadcloths for export (often at a loss)
to India and China, maintained that the conduct of the
Company's trade was perfectly satisfactory, and that a free
trade would ruin their industry.[4]

In the end, the midland and northern manufacturers
secured a substantial (though not complete) victory over the
Company and the older industrial districts.   The Government
agreed to renew the Company's Charter for a further twenty
years, and the Company was to retain its monopoly of the
China trade.   All other outward trade (including the trade
with India) was " to be opened to all ports of the Empire
generally, and homeward commerce to other ports than

[1] G. B. Hertz, *The Manchester Politician*, 1912, p. 23.
[2] *Journals of the House of Commons*, Vol. LXVIII, pp. 113, 114, 332,
etc.
[3] *Ibid.*, p. 245 (Leeds).   [4] *Ibid.*, pp. 245, 273, 308.

London, if provided with warehouses and docks." [1] The trade with India was now open to the independent merchants ; though it is true that their activities were still hampered by many vexatious restrictions. The Company's licence, for which a fee had to be paid, was still required for the Indian trade, and no ships of under 350 tons could take part in that trade. The Company still retained the exclusive right to export goods to the European mainland, to engage in the Indian coasting trade, and to conduct all other kinds of traffic in the Far East, in addition to its monopoly of the China trade. These surviving relics of the Company's commercial power contained the germs of much future controversy ; but for the time being the independent merchants were well pleased with the concessions they had gained, and looked forward confidently to a great expansion of their export trade with the East.

The expectation of a rapidly expanding trade was strikingly fulfilled ; and it was in the export of cotton piece goods that the expansion was most remarkable. In 1814 only 818,208 yards of manufactured cotton goods were exported from Great Britain to India and the East Indies ; by 1832 the annual total had risen to 57,568,161 yards. The Select Committee which inquired into the affairs of the East India Company in 1832 asked the general question : " To what extent has trade with India increased since 1814, and, with regard to exports from Great Britain, to what degree has the

BRITISH EXPORTS OF COTTON PIECE GOODS TO ALL PLACES EAST OF THE CAPE, EXCEPT CHINA, 1814-32 (IN YARDS).[2]

Date.	1814.	1817.	1820.	1823.	1826.	1829.	1832.
Calicoes, etc., white or plain . .	82,638	938,680	3,764,843	9,325,970	11,200,282	26,218,516	34,084,224
Calicoes, printed, checked, dyed, etc. . . .	597,595	2,842,993	7,496,771	9,391,188	9,624,730	11,107,429	17,907,088
Muslins, white or plain . .	130,770	1,529,344	2,719,413	3,721,747	4,048,499	6,675,415	5,192,287
Muslins, printed, etc.	7,205	5,712	12,229	40,512	125,346	108,314	384,562
Totals . .	818,208	5,316,729	13,993,256	22,479,417	24,998,857	44,109,674	57,568,161

[1] Hansard, Vol. XXV, col. 22 et seq. (22nd March, 1813) ; and Vol. XXVI, col. 1207.
[2] See Wheeler's *Manchester*, 1836, p. 176.

increase consisted of British staples ? " [1] In the answers
to this question there was general agreement that an unprecedented expansion had taken place in the volume of
exports from Great Britain ; and in particular the Manchester
Chamber of Commerce declared that " the increase in the
staples of Lancashire is believed to be without parallel." [2]
By the 1830's it was reported that " Even the Dacca muslins,
which were considered to be unapproachable in beauty, have
been superseded by Manchester goods ; the shawls of Cash-
mere are pushed from the market, and employ now only
about 6000 looms instead of 30,000 as in bye-gone days." [3]
It is true that the British Government exacted a duty of
30 per cent. on Indian cotton goods imported into England,
while only 2½ per cent. was levied on English cottons imported into India ; but Manchester goods were now beating
the Indian cotton goods, not only in England and India, but
also in the neutral markets of the East Indies, where they
enjoyed no differential advantage of tariff and were handicapped by heavier transport charges.

The possibility of opening up wider markets in such
places as Java and the Philippines stimulated the Manchester
merchants to further agitation against the surviving privileges of the East India Company in the trade with " countries
east of the Cape of Good Hope." If Manchester could
strengthen its hold on the markets of the East Indies, these
in turn would serve as important bases for a further attack
upon the East India Company's monopoly of the China trade.
It was even conjectured (in 1821) that in a few years " the
whole of the Eastern Archipelago will be clothed from Great
Britain ; and I see no reason why Ava, Siam, Cochin China,
and even a large portion of China, may not follow the
example." [4] One of the first acts of the provisional " Committee of Commerce of Manchester " set up in 1820 was to
petition Parliament concerning the East India and China
trades.[5] The petitioners urged that " the countries east of
the Cape of Good Hope, especially China, would become
important markets for cotton manufactures of this district
if some of the existing restrictions on our commerce with

[1] *Report of the Select Committee of the House of Commons on the Affairs
of the East India Company*, 1832 : *Commercial Appendix*, App. 4, p. 506.
    [2] *Ibid.*, p. 515.   [3] Wheeler, *loc. cit.*
    [4] *Manchester Chronicle*, 9th June, 1821.
    [5] *Manchester Mercury*, 27th June, 1820.

that rich and populous portion of the globe were removed";
and that, while the traders of Manchester were anxious
not "to urge the adoption of measures inconsistent with
the strictest good faith to the Honourable the East India
Company," they felt that it was only fair to admit them
to such parts of the eastern trade as the Company had
not taken up. The restrictive regulations concerning the
size of ships engaging in the eastern trade were declared
by the Manchester Chamber of Commerce, in 1822, to be
injurious because they "totally precluded the export of
British manufactures in that class of vessels which is best
calculated for the successful extension of our highly important
commerce with India, the Persian Gulf and the Oriental
Islands." [1] The Chamber of Commerce was satisfied "that
the trade might be pursued with more economy and dispatch
in vessels of smaller size than is allowed by law," and without
any increased risk of smuggling.[2]

For this point of view there was already strong parliamentary support. In 1821 the House of Commons Committee
on Foreign Trade had remarked upon "the inexpediency of
continuing the restriction on the tonnage of vessels, if it can
be done away with without interfering with the rights of
the East India Company," and expressed their "hope and
confidence that the other restrictions which the system of
1813 imposes may be put into force . . . with a constant
recollection of the inconvenience of all commercial restriction,
and the necessity of alleviating it wherever it cannot be
removed." The considered judgment of the committee was
"That it is expedient to permit his Majesty's subjects to
carry on trade and traffic, directly and circuitously, between
any ports within the limits of the East India Company's
charter (except the Dominions of the Emperor of China) and
any port or ports beyond the limits of the said charter belonging to any state or countries in amity with his Majesty." [3]
These recommendations bore fruit in an important Act of
1823,[4] which declared that "It shall be lawful for any of his
Majesty's subjects, in ships or vessels registered and navigated
according to law, to carry on trade and traffic in any goods,

---

[1] *Proceedings of the Manchester Chamber of Commerce*, 17th April,
1822.

[2] *Ibid.*, 2nd Annual Report, 10th February, 1823.

[3] For provincial comments on the Committee's Reports, see
Manchester Chronicle, 24th November, 1821, and Wright, *op. cit.*, pp. 82-4.

[4] 4 Geo. IV, c. 80.

wares or merchandise, except tea, as well directly as circuitously, between all ports and places belonging either to his
Majesty, or to any prince, state or country, at amity with his
Majesty, and all ports and places whatsoever situate within
the limits of the Charter of the Company, except the dominions
of the Emperor of China, and also from port to port and
from place to place within the said limits, except the said
dominions of the Emperor of China." That this extension
of commercial liberty was considered beneficial to English
trade and industry may be gathered from the favourable
comments of witnesses before the Select Committee on the
Affairs of the East India Company, in 1832 ; in particular, the
Manchester Chamber of Commerce described it as " a measure
of great moment."

Encouraged by their success in securing freer trade with
India and the East Indies, the provincial merchants continued
to press their demands for the opening up of the China trade.
In this aspect of the controversy the Liverpool importers of
tea were even more directly interested than the Manchester
exporters of cotton goods or the Birmingham exporters of
hardware. The East India Company had taken advantage
of its monopolistic position in the China trade to keep the
price of tea much higher in the English markets than in
the markets of the continental countries ; the Dutch and
American traders were selling tea at 48 per cent. advance
on the prime cost, while the East India Company sold at
92 per cent. over the same original price at Canton. " The
consequence is that 28,300,000 lb. of tea of all kinds, which
are assumed as the annual average for some years past, have
been sold to the retail dealers at the Company's sales for
£3,686,682 sterling, while at the rate of continental profits
the same quantity would have been disposed of to the public
at £2,950,178, leaving an excess of £736,504 as the surcharge
of the Company's monopoly." [1] Such a surcharge was not
only an unfair burden on the tea-drinkers of England, but
was contrary to the conditions on which the Company held
its Charter ; for the exclusive privilege of trading with China
had been granted on condition that " The Company shall,
with a view to keep the price of tea in this country upon an
equality with the price thereof in other neighbouring countries
of Europe, import such quantities from any other part of

[1] *Manchester Mercury*, 29th April, 1828.

Europe as may be necessary for this purpose, and that if the Company shall at any time neglect to keep this market supplied with a sufficient quantity of tea at reasonable prices to answer the consumption of Great Britain it shall be the duty of the Lords Commissioners of the Treasury to grant licences to any other persons whatsoever, to import teas on the same conditions for the same purpose." [1]   The provincial merchants, led by the Liverpool East India Association, considered that the Company should be regarded as having forfeited its exclusive privileges by not fulfilling its contract to furnish an adequate supply of tea at reasonable prices. One consequence of the Company's restrictive policy was that the consumption of tea in England remained almost stationary, although wealth and population were increasing rapidly ; another consequence was that Dutch and American traders were growing wealthy from the profits of a trade from which the independent merchants of England were excluded.

Early in 1829 the Liverpool East India Association invited the co-operation of the merchants of Birmingham, Bristol, Glasgow and Manchester in an attempt to free the China trade ; the East India Company's Charter was due to be renewed in 1833, and there was reason to hope that the united efforts of the provincial merchants might induce the Government to abolish the Company's remaining commercial privileges.   The request of the Liverpool merchants for co-operation met with a ready response.   The Birmingham Chamber of Commerce decided to petition both Houses of Parliament " to take into their consideration during the present session the restrictions which impede the commerce of this country with China, for the purpose of facilitating and extending a more beneficial intercourse with those vast regions," and looked forward to " the eventual removal of every existing obstruction to our intercourse with British India, China, Southern Asia and the Eastern Islands." [2] The Manchester Chamber of Commerce caused the Borough-reeve and Constables to call a public Town's Meeting, at which several resolutions were passed and a petition to the House of Lords was framed, praying that the trade to the interior of India and China might be thrown open at the

---

[1] *Manchester Mercury*, 29th April, 1828, quoting from *The Times*.
[2] Wright, *op. cit.*, p. 103.

earliest practicable moment, and that the monopoly in tea might be abolished.[1] Both Birmingham and Manchester appointed deputations to meet the representatives of other towns in London, and the united deputation of "nearly twenty persons" was permitted to state its case verbally to the Duke of Wellington, with whom were the Chancellor of the Exchequer, the President of the Board of Control, and the President of the Board of Trade. Wellington declined to make any declaration as to the Government's policy on the subject, but the deputation retired with the conviction that it had received the "most implicit and satisfactory attention of the Ministers present during an audience of nearly an hour's duration."[2]

For the next three years the provincial merchants kept up a steady pressure on the Government, by means of petitions, memorials, deputations and pamphlets. Early in 1830 the united deputation of the provincial merchants, which now included representatives from Leeds, resumed its work in London, and became very active in producing evidence before Select Committees of both Houses which were then investigating the affairs of the East India Company.[3] According to the report of the deputation, the parliamentary inquiry had brought out clearly "The commercial disposition of the Chinese people, their willingness to trade with all nations, their taste for the productions of England, and the extraordinary facilities offered both to mariners and merchants by the port of Canton. . . . The great opening existing in China for the sale of British manufactures and the prospect of a vast increase of the demand in that country for metals and for wrought goods of all descriptions. . . . The certainty of a great diminution in the price of tea to the English consumer from the cessation of the monopoly. . . . The indisposition of the East India Company to increase the importation of British goods into China and to benefit the commercial and shipping interests of the Empire. . . . From all which it results, that unless the monopoly in the tea trade with China possessed by the East India Company be removed, the commerce of the Empire with the East must continue paralysed."[4]

---

[1] *Proceedings of the Manchester Chamber of Commerce*, 15th, 25th, 27th, 29th and 30th April, 1829.   [2] Wright, *op. cit.*, pp. 104-5.
[3] *Proceedings of the Manchester Chamber of Commerce*, 13th and 26th March, 1830.   [4] *Ibid.*, 28th May, 1830.

The struggle, however, was not yet over; the parliamentary inquiries continued throughout 1831 and 1832, and the provincial merchants could not afford to relax their efforts. In order to maintain continuity and co-ordination in the movement, it was considered desirable that " one gentleman from the principal towns should remain all through the inquiry, from beginning to end, others coming up for a day or two, on occasion of interviews with Ministers ";[1] such a standing committee would also be useful in securing the presentation of the numerous petitions which continued to be sent from all the principal commercial and industrial centres. In the end the merchants gained their objective. The parliamentary investigation resulted in a recommendation against any renewal of the East India Company's monopoly of the China trade, and this recommendation was carried into effect by the Company's new Charter of 1833.[2] Henceforth it was ordained that " it shall be lawful for any of His Majesty's subjects to carry on trade with any countries beyond the Cape of Good Hope to the Streights of Magellan ";[3] the way seemed clear for a great expansion of British trade with the Far East.

The independent British merchants soon found, however, that the establishment of peaceful and profitable commercial relations with the Chinese was no easy task. In some respects the task had been made harder by the abolition of the East India Company's monopoly; for Chinese external trade was organised under the control of a quasi-medieval Gild of Merchants (the Co Hong) which was much better adapted to deal with a corporate organisation like the East India Company than with a great number of independent and irresponsible traders. Moreover, the abolition of the East India Company's monopoly had been accompanied by the appointment of British commercial superintendents in China, to act as agents of the British Crown for the regulation of British trade and the protection of British traders; but the Chinese Government had always been unwilling to enter into any political relations with foreigners. Lord Napier, who had been appointed as Chief Superintendent of Trade with China in 1833, evidently failed to appreciate the delicacy

---

[1] *Proceedings of the Manchester Chamber of Commerce,* 17th December, 1830 : statement of Mr. K. Finlay of Glasgow.

[2] See 3 and 4 Will. IV, cc. 85 and 93.

[3] 3 and 4 Will. IV, c. 93, § 2.

of his position, and outraged Chinese sentiment by demanding recognition as the accredited representative of the British Crown. The Chinese authorities ordered that trade with the English should be suspended until Lord Napier withdrew to Macao; but even after his withdrawal and death the position of British merchants in China remained precarious. It was this condition of uncertainty which led the Manchester Chamber of Commerce, in 1836, to present a memorial to the Prime Minister and the Foreign Secretary, asking for the establishment of the China trade on a sounder basis, and for an embassy to Peking to achieve this object.[1]

Other commercial troubles soon followed in 1838 and 1839, when the Chinese authorities took energetic measures to suppress the illegal import of Indian opium in English ships. A Chinese Commissioner appeared at Canton and shut up all the foreign traders in their factories, without provisions, until all the opium chests on the Chinese coast had been surrendered. This high-handed action was followed by the outbreak of open warfare, which dislocated Anglo Chinese trade for about three years (1839-42). The loss of over 20,000 chests of opium led the Chambers of Commerce of Bombay and Calcutta to request compensation, and to ask for the help of the Manchester Chamber in securing redress. From the point of view of the English merchants, however, the loss of the opium was a minor evil compared with the general dislocation of the China trade which resulted from the incident; it was this wider aspect of the question which received most emphasis in the memorial sent by the Manchester Chamber to Lord Palmerston in November, 1839.[2] One great barrier to Anglo-Chinese trade had arisen from the difficulty of inducing the Chinese to accept foreign manufactured goods in exchange for their tea and silk. On the other hand, there was a ready market in China for Indian opium, although its importation was forbidden; moreover, the opium was always paid for in silver, and the illicit traffic was thus regarded (even in the days of the East India Company's monopoly) as an indispensable factor in the mechanism of exchange. Nevertheless, the history of the opium dispute does not reflect much credit upon the British and Indian merchants of that generation, and they

[1] *Proceedings of the Manchester Chamber of Commerce*, 10th February, 1836.
[2] *Ibid.*, 22nd August and 7th November, 1839.

must be regarded as having fared better than they deserved ; not only were the authorities at Canton forced to pay £1,125,000 as compensation for the opium destroyed, but the Treaty of Nanking of 1842 provided for the further payment of £4,375,000, as well as for the opening of four new treaty ports.

Peace on such terms was not likely to make the Chinese more friendly to British traders ; nor were the Chinese authorities who had " lost face " in the struggle likely to maintain order efficiently. Complaints continued to reach England of outrages committed on British residents in China, and within a few years the East India and China Association of Liverpool was seeking the co-operation of the Manchester Chamber of Commerce in an attempt to reduce the insecurity of life at Canton.[1] The Manchester merchants received further information concerning the activities of " organised bands of murderers " in China, and suggested to Lord Palmerston that the presence of one or two warships in Chinese waters might be useful ; [2] but the British Foreign Office was not in one of its truculent moods. Lord Palmerston replied that while ill-feeling existed between the English traders and the Chinese people, no amount of protection could be effective ; the best protection English merchants could have would be their own moderate conduct. If the Manchester Chamber of Commerce would urge its correspondents to avoid collisions with the natives, it would be doing a great deal for the cause of peace.[3]

These sentiments were undoubtedly commendable ; but they hardly reflected a clear understanding of the critical condition of Anglo-Chinese trade. According to a subsequent memorial from the Manchester Chamber, the China trade was stagnant ; only freer access to the interior could avert a complete collapse. Under existing conditions, the British merchants had no idea what became of their goods once they were sold to the Chinese merchants on the coast, and had no means of finding out what charges were put on the goods when they were sent to the interior.[4] The most serious factor in the situation, however, was the continued hostility of the Chinese, which the English merchants believed to be fostered by the authorities at Canton. In a memorial of

[1] *Proceedings of the Manchester Chamber of Commerce*, 8th July, 1847.
[2] *Ibid.*, 9th March, 1848.   [3] *Ibid.*, 6th April, 1848.
[4] *Ibid.*, 12th October, 1848, and 1st February, 1849.

1849 the Manchester Chamber of Commerce complained that
the Chinese authorities were disregarding the Treaty of Nanking, and that the Cantonese merchants were attempting
to re-establish the monopolistic organisation of trade which
had been broken up in 1842. The native traders had combined, and had resolved not to buy at any public auction ;
penalties had been fixed for non-compliance with this decision.
One Chinese, who had bought goods, had been assaulted,
robbed, and then put in prison by the authorities ; in consequence, not a single buyer had appeared at the public
auctions.[1] Once more the British Foreign Office declined
to be drawn into drastic action ; and its attitude remained
unshaken throughout the next few years, although commercial complaints multiplied, especially from Shanghai.[2]

The trouble came to a head in 1853, when rebellion in
North China dislocated the Chinese customs organisation,
and caused the Manchester Chamber to urge upon the Earl
of Clarendon the necessity of providing a stronger protective
force at Shanghai.[3] For the next three years the customs
arrangements at Shanghai caused frequent interchange of
acrimonious correspondence between the Manchester merchants and the British Foreign Office ; [4] and the dispute was
still going on, when a more serious threat to commercial
stability arose from the outbreak of open warfare between
England and China in 1856. This was occasioned by an
attack made by Chinese naval officers on the *Arrow*, a
Chinese boat sailing under British colours. The British
Government's demand for an apology met with evasive
replies from the Chinese authorities ; thereupon the British
retaliated by seizing an imperial junk, and preparations were
made for a blockade of Canton. The Chinese still remained
obdurate against the threat of war, and in the end Canton
was occupied by the British. The British Government
seized this opportunity to secure more favourable conditions
for British merchants in China. By the Treaty of Tientsin
of 1858, the British Government gained the right to appoint

[1] *Proceedings of the Manchester Chamber of Commerce*, 19th July, 1849.
[2] See *ibid.*, 13th June and 28th October, 1850, 26th June, 1851,
and 13th May, 1852 ; *cf. Proceedings of the Manchester Commercial
Association*, 19th December, 1850.
[3] *Proceedings of the Manchester Chamber of Commerce*, 14th April,
1853.
[4] *Ibid.*, 29th December, 1853 ; 19th July, 9th November and 27th
December, 1854 ; 12th September, 1855 ; 24th July, 1856. *Cf. Proceedings of the Manchester Commercial Association* during the same years.

a British Minister at Peking, British subjects were permitted to travel to all parts of the interior, British ships were allowed to enter three ports on the Yangtse, certain other Chinese towns were thrown open to British residents, and the Chinese tariffs were fixed on a new and uniform basis. Now at last the Manchester Chamber of Commerce could, for the time being, cease from troubling the Foreign Secretary with its requests for the more effective protection of British residents in China.[1]

It may well appear surprising that the Manchester merchants should have taken so much interest in the opening up of a country where the precarious tenure of law and order made the establishment of settled trading relations seem improbable ; what is much more surprising to note, however, is that Manchester's trade with China went on extending even during the troubled decade of the 1850's. The annual value of British cotton goods exported to China almost doubled between 1849 and 1852 ; the trade suffered a temporary set-back during the critical years 1853 and 1854, but thereafter expanded steadily and rapidly.[2]

Meanwhile, the provincial merchants had found that the East India Company was still a force to be reckoned with in the control of English trade with the Far East, even after the Company's trading privileges had been withdrawn. One of the main reasons why the Company had wished to continue its trading activities was the necessity for making large periodical remittances to England from its surplus administrative revenues in India, to provide for its English expenditure and to pay dividends on its stock. Owing partly to the steady absorption of bullion by India (a process which seems to have been going on since the time of the Romans) the East India Company's remittances to England could most conveniently be made in goods, that is by trading operations ; and such " remittance " trading had often been carried on without any particular regard to the question of commercial profit or loss. This might cause serious injury to the private traders, both in India and England. In India, the Company's purchasing power was great enough to rule the market ; in England, the private trader's chances of profit were largely determined by the prices ruling at the Company's sales.

---

[1] The requests were still being made in 1857 ; see *Proceedings of the Manchester Chamber of Commerce*, 5th March, 1857.

[2] See J. A. Mann, *The Cotton Trade of Great Britain*, 1860, p. 119.

The independent merchants considered that the Company ought to make its remittances through the ordinary financial channels, by bills of exchange or by the transmission of specie. This would cause an initial difficulty through the stronger demand for bills drawn in India on Great Britain than for bills drawn in Great Britain on India ; but if Anglo-Indian commerce were allowed to find its own level, free from the disturbing influences of the Company's trading operations, the Manchester merchants were confident that the problem would be simplified. " The necessity on the part of the Company to have such remittances made, combined with the resolution of the private merchants not to trade knowingly at a loss, would (it is believed) overcome the difficulty by operating conjointly on exchange and prices, and so produce that related correspondence of markets which admits of and stimulates to active business." With regard to possible losses by bad bills, the Company should be prepared to take the risk. This risk, like others dependent on mercantile operations, resolved itself into a moderate average loss, and would necessarily be less embarrassing in the operations of a great Company, possessing international standing, than in the operations of private traders.[1]

The cessation of the Company's trading activities after 1833 was not a final solution of the problem. The Company had now to make its remittances by means of financial rather than commercial transactions ; but its financial operations inevitably reacted on the trading operations of the independent merchants. The Company was still able to exercise a strong control over English trade with the Far East, by manipulating the exchanges and by granting or withholding advances on the shipment of produce. The Manchester Chamber of Commerce lost no time in attacking this new form of the evil. The Board of the Chamber appointed a sub-committee to inquire into the financial operations of the East India Company, requested the co-operation of the merchants of Liverpool, Glasgow and Leeds, and sent a delegate to open parliamentary negotiations in London.[2] In

---

[1] The question is discussed at length in information supplied by the Manchester Chamber of Commerce to Mr. Hyde Villiers, the Secretary of the India Board, for submission to the Committee on the Affairs of the East India Company in 1832 (*Proceedings of the Manchester Chamber of Commerce*, 11th and 18th April, 16th and 23rd May, 1832).

[2] *Ibid.*, 9th February, 1833.

subsequent memorials to the Treasury, the Manchester merchants attributed special blame to the East India Company for making advances on the security of eastern produce at Calcutta, consigned to Leadenhall Street, at different rates of exchange from those then existing in London and those which the cost of transmitting bullion would justify. It was asserted that by these operations the Company was depressing the English rate of exchange, and making British merchants pay higher rates than their Indian competitors.[1]

At Canton, also, the Company had set up a Finance Committee to conduct exchange operations and control the course of trade. Hitherto the China trade had been conducted on arrangements which practically amounted to barter, with smuggled opium as a balancing factor ; but the financial facilities now advertised by the East India Company at Canton caused the " expectation of an abundance of money for investment in tea, silk, etc., and have had the effect of raising prices to the advantage of the Chinese," while British goods had decreased by 25 per cent. in value. At any moment, moreover, the Company could constrict and cripple the trade by refusing to discount bills or make advances. To the Manchester merchants this seemed quite contrary to the spirit of the Company's charter of 1833 ; they therefore proposed that the Treasury at Canton should be closed, and that trade with the Far East should be financed from Leadenhall Street, at fair rates of exchange. As a result of this change it was considered likely that the Company would be applied to for numerous bills on Bengal and Bombay, by which British merchants could place funds in China for the purchase of tea and silk ; such bills would also be a means of making remittances from China to India in payment for Indian cotton and opium.

Late in 1838 the Manchester Chamber of Commerce appointed a committee to report on the financial system at Canton, and drew up a memorial to the Court of Directors of the East India Company. These financial operations, declared the memorial, were " uncalled for by any necessity for the remittance to this country of the surplus Indian revenue to pay home charges, as British merchants will readily pay their money into the Leadenhall Street Treasury as the readiest means of sending remittances

[1] *Proceedings of the Manchester Chamber of Commerce*, 3rd February, 1836, etc.

to China, even at a rate of exchange exceeding the cost of the transmission of bullion." The memorial was never despatched, however, for at this point the East India Company announced its decision to limit the negotiation of bills for the remittance of revenue through China to the sum of £300,000 for the season 1839-40, and afterwards to suspend them altogether; the independent merchants had gained their point.[1]

There remained the financial grievances arising from the East India Company's practice of granting very long credits to merchants in India, who became virtually the commercial agents of the company. English merchants in the India trade accepted sixty days sight bills, whereas the Company in India was offering to discount ten months date bills; this practice was very bitterly denounced by the Manchester Chamber of Commerce in 1848, as tending to withdraw Indian custom from the independent English merchants.[2] The question had evidently become more urgent in the light of the financial crisis of 1847; in that breakdown of business confidence many firms engaged in eastern trade had collapsed, and there were indications that some of the independent merchants had over-reached themselves in attempting to compete with the Company's agents in the granting of long credits. The question of the most desirable terms of credit was, of course, highly technical, and the provincial merchants were not in complete agreement on the subject even among themselves. The East India and China Association of Liverpool considered that six months date bills and four months sight bills should be the limits of credit; the Manchester Chamber of Commerce thought that sixty days sight bills were long enough,[3] but did not press the point. Eventually, the long struggle between the East India Company and the provincial merchants was ended abruptly by Lord Derby's India Act of 1858, when the last remaining functions of the Company were transferred to the Crown.

[1] *Proceedings of the Manchester Chamber of Commerce*, 5th to 26th December, 1838.

[2] *Ibid.*, 14th February and 28th September, 1848; *cf. ibid.*, 24th September, 1846: Memorial to Lord John Russell.

[3] They were employed, as a general rule, in remittances from England to India.

CHAPTER X.

THE STRUGGLE FOR FREE TRADE : (i) ORIGINS AND EARLY STAGES, 1785–1828.

As the prosperity of the Lancashire cotton industry was already dependent on the expansion of the export trade, it was natural that the Manchester merchants should be actively in favour of universal freedom of trade. The general acceptance of free-trade principles in the middle period of the nineteenth century has been rightly regarded as a triumph of the " Manchester School " ; and many of the earlier victories of the " Manchester School " had been gained at meetings of the Manchester Chamber of Commerce. Even among the merchants of Manchester, however, the advantages of complete freedom of trade were recognised somewhat tardily, and the programme of the commercial reformers went through many vicissitudes before reaching its final shape.

Some approach to a policy of commercial liberalism had been made, both in England and France, before the end of the eighteenth century. France had not only benefited from the fiscal reforms made during Turgot's short ministry of 1774-75, but had concluded commercial treaties with Great Britain, Holland and Russia during the ten years which followed the American War of Independence. In the same decade Pitt had tried, with only partial success, to re-model the tariff system of Great Britain in conformity with the new economic doctrines. His attempts to secure commercial reciprocity with Ireland and France have already been mentioned ; [1] but the history of the General Chamber of Manufacturers, between 1785 and 1787, suggests that the industrial interests were not yet united or consistent in their principles of commercial policy.

[1] See Chapter I, pp. 9-13 above.

The dissensions within the General Chamber, concerning the Eden Treaty with France in 1786, may be explained as a cleavage between the newer large-scale industries of the provinces and the older handicraft industries of the metropolis ; but while the older industries clung to the protection which they enjoyed under the Mercantile System, even the newer industries were not altogether consistent in their demands for greater freedom of trade.   The northern and midland industrialists (the manufacturers of textiles, hardware and pottery) who were in favour of commercial reciprocity with France and other countries, were violently hostile to commercial reciprocity with Ireland ; and even when they supported proposals for freer trade, their declarations had often a narrower application than might appear at first sight. When the representatives of the Birmingham Commercial Committee expressed their wish for commercial reciprocity with France, they were asked whether a similar arrangement with Spain would be advantageous.   They replied " Yes— with all the world " ; and in this sentiment they were supported by the representatives of the Lancashire and Staffordshire manufacturers.[1] It must not be imagined, however, that the provincial industrialists were in favour of any unconditional or unilateral relaxation of the customs tariff ; their willingness to grant increased trading facilities extended only to such countries as were willing to grant reciprocal privileges to British goods.   In the northern manufacturers' opposition to Pitt's scheme for commercial reciprocity with Ireland an even narrower application of free-trade principles may be seen ; for the opponents of the scheme asserted that English manufacturers would be unfairly handicapped by the proposed changes, since in Ireland labour was cheaper and taxes were lower than in England, while Irish manufactures were encouraged by the payment of bounties.   From this it may appear that the English manufacturers of the later eighteenth century were in favour of commercial reciprocity rather than commercial freedom, and of commercial reciprocity only with countries where industrial conditions gave the English manufacturers a favourable chance of establishing their superiority.

One of the general aims of the " United Commercial Societies," during the last years of the eighteenth century,

---

[1] Bowden, *op. cit.*, p. 200.

was to secure most-favoured-nation treatment for British goods in foreign ports. In 1797, when there was a general expectation that negotiations for peace were to be renewed, Mr. Turnbull reported a resolution of the London Commercial Committee that the manufactures of England would increase if English goods were allowed to enter foreign ports on the same terms as the goods of the most favoured nation, and that reciprocal privileges might be granted by England, " without much danger of inconvenience," to all the foreign European countries. Agreements of this sort would simplify the commercial treaties, " which have been hitherto so complicated as to be rendered useless," and " must essentially promote the trade and manufactures of England, of which the capital, ingenuity, industry, and machinery, give her a decided superiority over every other country of Europe." It may have been a consideration of the concluding phrases which prompted Mr. Turnbull, in writing to the Manchester merchants, to add the warning : " If it be judged expedient to carry the plan suggested by this letter into effect, it would be for various reasons necessary to keep it as private as possible." [1]

In the paper eventually delivered to Lord Liverpool, Lord Grenville and Mr. Pitt, the merchants prayed that Lord Malmesbury (the British representative in the peace negotiations) would " endeavour to stipulate that commercial treaties shall be hereafter formed between England and France, Spain, and such other countries, with whom he may negotiate, on the basis of an unlimited and reciprocal admission of importation into each of the respective countries of the produce and manufactures of the other, of whatever nature or description they may be ; the duties on importation, and the internal duties, thereafter to be at the discretion of the Government into whose country the goods may be introduced, with the only provision that they shall not exceed the duties required to be paid on similar articles and similar qualities when imported from the most-favoured nations." [2]

Similar representations were made when negotiations were once more proceeding in 1801, just before the Peace of Amiens. The Manchester merchants were, indeed, inclined to make more ambitious proposals, with the avowed conviction that it was right " to ask for enough, and to get as much

[1] *Proceedings of the Manchester Commercial Society*, 1st June, 1797.
[2] *Ibid.*, 11th July, 1797.

as one can." Mr. Norman, the delegate of the Manchester Commercial Society, declared that it was his intention to "impress upon the minds of Ministers the great glory they will acquire if, in the definitive treaty or in any new treaties of commerce with France, Spain or Portugal, they can obtain a free admission of cotton goods into those countries, or even with a small *valorem* duty."[1] All these hopes, however, were to be disappointed; the Peace of Amiens embodied no treaty of commerce and, instead of the extended facilities which the commercial societies expected, the continental markets remained closed to British goods, "with a system of prohibitive tariffs more ruinous than war."

While the Manchester merchants were anxious to secure freer access to foreign markets for Lancashire cotton goods, they were not yet prepared to admit all classes of foreign textile goods to the English markets ; reference has already been made to their jealousy of the Irish textile industries, and to their long struggle against the importation of Indian silk and cotton goods.[2] That protectionist ideas still had a strong foothold in Lancashire may be seen also from the bitter disputes which took place within the Manchester Commercial Society concerning the exportation of cotton twist. The Manchester merchants and manufacturers of cotton piece goods, while they wished their finished products to have free entry into the continental markets, wished to prevent the exportation of twist or yarn ; on the other hand, the spinners naturally wished to find for their twist as wide a market as possible, whether at home or abroad. The merchants and manufacturers argued that the cost of weaving was dearer in England than in Germany ; therefore the German manufacturers, by using yarn imported from England, were able to market their manufactured goods at lower prices than the English. The natural consequence was that many English workmen were thrown out of work, since "the spinning of cotton does not constitute one-third in many articles, nor in others one-fifth, of the price of weaving and preparing the cloth." It was therefore to the interest of the state to keep up the numbers of the weavers, who paid taxes and brought up large families, rather than to encourage the

---

[1] *Proceedings of the Manchester Commercial Society*, 17th December, 1801.   [2] See Chapter IX, pp. 108-110 above.

employment of women and children in spinning. It was asserted that, owing to the facilities for importing yarn into Germany, the import of muslinets into Berlin had been prohibited, and the fear was that there might soon be a prohibition placed on the entry of such finished goods into Brandenburg and other German states. The Manchester merchants and manufacturers therefore lent favourable ears to suggestions from their London friends, that either prohibition or heavy protective duties should be imposed on the exportation of cotton yarn, the duties to be "something higher than the difference in the cost of workmanship in England and Germany." [1]

A long discussion on the subject took place at an extra-ordinary meeting of the Commercial Society, called at the request of the Holywell Spinning Company in September, 1794. The manufacturers of cotton goods, in addition to the arguments already brought forward, urged that neither a protective duty nor even prohibition would seriously injure the spinners ; the production of English manufactured goods would increase, and this increased home production would consume more yarn than was taken by the foreign manufacturers, since the latter required British cotton twist for warps only, and spun their own weft. Without British cotton twist the foreign manufacturers would be unable to compete with the British piece goods. On the other hand, the representative " gentlemen spinners " who attended the meeting pointed out that they had expended large sums in erecting machinery, and that it was impossible to regulate the production of yarn to the home demand. The possession of machinery entailed a double loss if work was interrupted, since capital was left standing idle and the machinery deteriorated with non-usage. They argued that the manufacturers' grievance was not so serious as had been made out, because cotton twist was not exported except when its price had fallen very low through the failure of home demand ; as soon as the home demand became brisker, the export of twist would cease. Moreover, the spinners con-tended that from their point of view cotton twist was a manufactured article, and that they had as much right to export it as any other class of manufactured goods. If the export of cotton twist were prohibited, the foreign manu-

[1] *Proceedings of the Manchester Commercial Society,* 19th August, 1794.

facturers would be induced to build spinning mills, and this country would be deprived of its overseas markets both for cotton twist and for finished goods.[1]

A similar conflict of interests, obscuring the gradual growth of free-trade enthusiasm, may be seen in the long struggle concerning the exportation of machinery; in this case, however, the cotton spinners, manufacturers and merchants were in alliance for the maintenance of prohibition, their common enemies being the new class of machinery-makers. The opposition of English industrialists to the export of machinery, and the comprehensive body of legislation passed in the later eighteenth century for the purpose of preventing such export,[2] are too generally known to call for detailed treatment; it is interesting, however, to find that organised attempts to prevent the export of machinery were still being made in both Manchester and Birmingham, even in the second quarter of the nineteenth century, when in most other respects free-trade principles were becoming predominant in the minds of the manufacturers and merchants. In 1824, when these questions were formally investigated during Francis Place's attack on the Combination Laws, the Manchester Chamber of Commerce became the centre of an organised agitation, which included not only Birmingham but also Liverpool, Glasgow, Leeds, Huddersfield and other towns. At a special general meeting of the Manchester Chamber, held on the 15th March, it was declared that the one great reason for the supremacy of England in manufacturing industry lay in the fact that she was always the first to adopt new mechanical inventions; if machinery were exported and artisans allowed to emigrate, this advantage could not be maintained. Foreign capitalists would be willing to pay higher prices for the new machinery than British manufacturers could afford; but any consequent stimulus to British trade would be short-lived, as the foreigners who bought British machines would soon learn to make their own on the same models.[3]

When, in February of the following year, it became known that the parliamentary committee on the exportation of

---

[1] *Proceedings of the Manchester Commercial Society*, 4th and 11th September, 2nd October, 6th November and 18th December, 1794.
[2] See *e.g.* Statutes 14 Geo. III, cap. 71; 21 Geo. III, cap. 37; and 22 Geo. III, cap. 60.
[3] *Proceedings of the Manchester Chamber of Commerce*, 3rd, 10th and 15th March, 1824.

machinery was to be revived, the provincial merchants lost no time in reorganising their defences. Circulars, embodying the views of the Manchester Chamber, were sent to the principal manufacturing towns, inviting their co-operation in a general assembly of delegates to meet in London; old arguments against the exportation of machinery were re-iterated, and new arguments put forth. The export of machinery, it was conceded, might give a temporary stimulus to the growing industry of machine-making, but " to confer a bounty on one class to the detriment of the whole is partiality and favouritism, not substantial justice." English mechanics " would for a time be almost exclusively employed in supply-ing the foreign market with machinery of the newest and best construction, while we should be obliged to work on with our old machines." This was considered to be manifestly unjust and even suicidal; " the improvements in our machinery having been effected by slow degrees and at great expense, by the reiterated and combined efforts of many individuals, we should, by exporting it, put our rivals in a short time and comparatively at a small cost in possession of what has, with us, been the result of so much ingenuity and perseverance." Here are several arguments which cannot easily be brought into line with later free-trade doctrine; and the Chamber's references to the Corn Laws (which it was already attacking) do not sound particularly orthodox. The Corn Laws kept labour costs high as compared with those of other countries. This comparative disadvantage had been balanced by the " superior perfection " of British machinery. " If we part with this compensation, what substitute shall we find for it ? " [1]

From later references it appears that the Manchester merchants were conscious of some shadow of inconsistency in pressing for general freedom of trade whilst opposing the free exportation of machinery; but, they held, the growing threat of foreign industrial competition gave a special justification for a restrictive policy as regarded machinery —" the race is begun, and we would not wantonly throw away any advantage." [2] Very much the same line of defence was taken by the Birmingham Chamber of Commerce a month or two later; at a meeting held on the 25th January, 1827, the Birmingham merchants reiterated many of the

[1] *Proceedings of the Manchester Chamber of Commerce,* 19th February and 18th March, 1825.   [2] *Ibid.,* 8th and 11th November, 1826.

already familiar arguments, and resolved " That whilst this Chamber is not disposed to question the correctness of those principles of free trade which have been adopted, it contends that these principles cannot under existing circumstances be justly applied to the machinery of the country (by which the effects of heavy taxation and a high price of subsistence are chiefly counteracted), but that especial care should be taken not to afford other nations, not subject to similar disadvantages, any facilities by which the processes for abridging and perfecting its manufacturing operations could be transferred from this kingdom." [1]

By the Customs Regulation Act of 1825 (and a later Act of 1833) schedules of prohibited machines were drawn up and enforced ; but the Board of Trade retained the power to issue licences for the export of the articles on the schedule.[2] Thenceforward the efforts of the Manchester Chamber were directed to preventing evasion of the schedules and abuse of the licensing system ; the investigation of suspicious shipments of machinery went on throughout the later 'twenties and the earlier 'thirties, together with persistent pressure upon the Board of Trade to tighten its licensing system and enforce the law more strictly. The Board of Trade, however, was becoming increasingly unsympathetic to all such restrictions upon trade, and the laws relating to machinery were notoriously evaded with impunity ; but the activities of the Manchester Chamber may have been partly responsible for the fact that, even in the early 'forties, licences for the exportation of spinning and weaving machinery were still being withheld, though they were being freely granted for all other kinds of machinery.

Restrictions on the exportation of cotton twist and textile machinery appear to the modern mind to be as protectionist in intention as restrictions on the importation of foreign goods. The persistent efforts of the Manchester merchants to maintain these export restrictions may most charitably be explained as arising from an irrational reluctance to surrender the advantages which British industrialists had gained by their own ingenuity and enterprise, at a time when the British agricultural interest was still sheltering behind the Corn Laws. In almost all other respects, Manchester merchants and manufacturers were already convinced advocates of commercial freedom, and were taking an increasingly prominent part in the fiscal controversies of the period.

Opposition to the Corn Laws of 1815 began before the laws were actually passed. In 1814 the Glasgow Chamber of Commerce called the attention of the Birmingham Chamber to the proposed alterations in the Corn Laws, and the Birmingham merchants " long and anxiously debated upon a question so momentous and of so complicated a nature." As a result of this discussion, several important resolutions were passed, declaring that the proposed alteration, " by imposing additional restraints on importation is calculated to effect a permanent advance in the price of grain, which, as the value of corn ultimately regulates the prices of all kinds of provisions, the wages of labour, and every article of native produce or manufacture, must essentially involve the interests of the community." The Birmingham Chamber considered that no additional legislative encouragement to agriculture was necessary, and decided to petition Parliament that " no immediate extension may be made to the prices at which importations of grain are permitted under the Act 44th of George III." [1]

In Manchester there was at that time no general Commercial Society or Chamber of Commerce. Action was therefore taken in the traditional manner ; a group of prominent citizens, headed by the first Sir Robert Peel, requested the Boroughreeves and Constables of Manchester and Salford to call a public Town's Meeting, which was held on the 27th February, 1815, in the dining room of the Exchange Buildings. The resolutions of the meeting were very closely similar to the conclusions of the Birmingham merchants. In particular, it was asserted " that the proposed restrictions on the importation of corn must materially raise its price, and consequently that of every other species of provisions ; and as a great proportion of labour in the manufacture is and *must* be manual, it will be utterly impossible to carry on competition with the Continent for any length of time, if the projected measure be adopted." [2]

It is to be noted that neither at Manchester nor at Birmingham was any general attack on the Corn Laws as yet developing; the opposition was directed against the

---

[1] Wright, *op. cit.*, pp. 62-4.
[2] A. Prentice, *Historical Sketches . . . of Manchester* (2nd edition, 1851), pp. 69-70.

proposed *increases* of duty, rather than against the duties in themselves. Moreover, there was a tendency on the part of the manufacturers to emphasise the relationship between corn prices and wages, in a manner which was deprecated by the Anti-Corn-Law leaders of a later generation. It would be a mistake, also, to assume that opposition to the new Corn Laws was already enthusiastic ; the Manchester meeting received very meagre notices in the local newspapers, and Prentice, who was already a thorough-going apostle of free trade when he migrated from Glasgow to Manchester in 1815, reports that " I did not find many persons of my own class in Manchester, whose opinions on free trade in corn were in accordance with my own. . . . I found that opposition to the bill had been very faint." [1]

During the twenty years which followed the Napoleonic wars, the merchants of both Manchester and Birmingham tended to concentrate their efforts upon the modification and relaxation of the Corn Laws, regarding their total repeal as being outside the scope of practical politics : with this difference, that the Manchester merchants became more definite in their opposition as time went on, whereas the Birmingham Chamber maintained a rather equivocal attitude, and seemed inclined to accept the principle of moderate protection for both industry and agriculture. In Manchester, some progress towards clearer views on the question may be traced from the establishment of the Chamber of Commerce in 1820. One of the Chamber's earliest petitions, a protest against the official method of calculating average corn prices in the English market, illustrated the new trend of thought. In this petition the effect of the Corn Laws upon wages was not mentioned ; the main emphasis was placed on the fact that the Corn Laws violated the principle of free trade, and were " a serious injury to the foreign commerce of this country." The petitioners were " sensible of the impolicy, on general principles, of all restrictions on trade in corn," and pointed out that the cotton industry had been in just as bad a condition as agriculture, yet they had never attempted to seek relief in protective legislation, being " well aware that such would be of no avail." [2]

[1] A. Prentice, *Historical Sketches . . . of Manchester* (2nd edition, 1851), pp. 68-9, 71.
[2] *First Annual Report of the Manchester Chamber of Commerce*, 1822.

After 1824 an increased significance was given to the Corn Law question by Huskisson's schemes for the reduction of the protective import duties on foreign raw materials and manufactured goods. Relaxation of the Corn Laws now became a *quid pro quo* demanded by the manufacturers as compensation for the withdrawal of protection from industry.[1] Resolutions passed at a special general meeting of the Manchester Chamber of Commerce in 1826 gave a very full exposition of the manufacturers' objections to the existing Corn Laws, and marked a definite advance on the ideas of 1815. According to these resolutions, the recent economic distress had been aggravated, and recovery had been retarded, by the operation of the Corn Laws. " While the Corn Laws have been highly injurious to the cultivators of the soil, by causing great fluctuations in the value of agricultural produce, they have at the same time been silently and gradually undermining the commerce and manufactures of the country," both by increasing British labour costs and by depriving some other countries of their only means of purchasing British manufactured goods, thereby forcing them to manufacture their own sooner than they otherwise would have done. If only a moderate duty were imposed on grain, the amount of foreign corn imported would be so small, compared with the total consumption, that it " would not derange the interests of agriculture nor cause such a decline in the price of corn as would not be amply compensated by the greater steadiness in its value, by diminished poor rates, and by the increased prosperity of all the other great interests of the country." Above all, a moderate duty " would show that England sincerely wished to establish a more liberal commercial policy, and would therefore create or strengthen a mutually beneficial intercourse with every country in the world." [2]

Meanwhile the Birmingham Chamber of Commerce, in 1825, had passed Anti-Corn-Law resolutions of the traditional kind, and had petitioned both Houses of Parliament for such a modification of the system as in their wisdom might seem sufficient, " consistently with a due regard to the other important interests involved in such a measure." In November, 1826 (just a week after the drafting of the Manchester resolutions), the Birmingham Chamber prayed

[1] *Proceedings of the Manchester Chamber of Commerce*, 15th March, 1824, 14th February and 13th April, 1825.
[2] *Ibid.*, 8th November, 1826.

Parliament " so to modify the laws for regulating the importation of corn as to accord with . . . those free principles of trade, which have been so ably advocated by his Majesty's Ministers and sanctioned by both Houses of Parliament " ; but to this rather indefinite request there was added the significant resolution, " that this meeting, in urging the importance of such increased freedom in the foreign corn trade as shall be commensurate with the reduction of protecting duties upon imported manufactures, nevertheless unequivocally recognises the necessity of such degree of protection, both for the British agriculturist and the manufacturer, as shall cover so much of the cost of production as is referable to the burdens sustained for discharging the public engagements of the country." [1]

Huskisson and his colleagues in the Government were not unmindful of the fact that their reduction of the protective import duties on manufactured goods gave the industrialists a right to expect some corresponding relaxation of the Corn Laws. The Government's proposal was to set up a sliding scale for corn in place of the existing prohibitory system, with a view to preventing the excessive fluctuations in price which were said to have been aggravated by the Corn Laws of 1815. Huskisson's sliding scale was approved by the House of Commons in 1827, but was held up in the House of Lords by the Duke of Wellington, who carried a suspending amendment which (in Huskisson's opinion) directly contravened the purpose of the measure. In the ensuing controversy, the Manchester merchants supported the Government's sliding scale as being preferable to the existing prohibitory system, and as the best compromise which could be immediately hoped for. In June, 1827, the Manchester Chamber viewed " with regret and alarm " the probable failure of the Government's measure, and declared that " though the bill proposes a scale of protecting duties higher than sound policy suggests and the welfare of the general interests of the country requires, it is nevertheless founded on just and salutary principles, and tends to mitigate the evils of the existing Corn Laws." [2]

The question was evidently of some immediate importance to the Manchester merchants in 1827, for the Chamber

[1] Wright, *op. cit.*, pp. 93-4, 97-8.
[2] *Proceedings of the Manchester Chamber of Commerce*, 27th June, 1827 ; *Manchester Mercury*, 29th June, 1827.

of Commerce reported that "the prospect of a better system being adopted in the Corn Laws had caused an improvement in the trade of the town and neighbourhood. The disappointment of that expectation has already produced an opposite effect. Considerable orders for our manufactures have been countermanded in consequence." Sentiments of the same kind were expressed in a petition which the Board of the Chamber sent to Parliament in 1828,[1] when the new Wellington Ministry found itself compelled to sponsor sliding-scale proposals similar to the Canningite scheme which Wellington had defeated in the preceding year. With the successful passage of the new scale of duties, the Manchester merchants were for the time being forced to rest content ; Parliament, as then constituted, was not prepared to acquiesce in any more drastic modification of the Corn Laws, and many other fiscal problems were competing for attention.

[1] *Proceedings of the Manchester Chamber of Commerce,* 30th April, 1828.

CHAPTER XI.

THE STRUGGLE FOR FREE TRADE : (ii) SPECIAL QUESTIONS AND THE CORN LAWS, 1820-46.

TOWARDS the more general movement in favour of Free Trade the Manchester Chamber of Commerce had been actively favourable since its inception in 1820. The increase of commercial freedom had been laid down as one of the main objects of the new Chamber : " the duty of the Association should be . . . to promote at proper seasons and by proper means the removal of existing regulations injurious to the freedom of trade and not requisite for purposes of necessary revenue." [1] In their free-trade petition of May, 1820, the Manchester merchants declared that " to indulge an expectation that other countries will take the manufactures of this kingdom without our receiving in return such articles as they produce, is delusive and injurious to our best interests " ; they therefore asked, cautiously enough, for " the removal of all such restrictions on imports as can be relinquished without injury to the agriculture and manufactures of this country." [2]

The most urgent object of the Manchester merchants, at this time, was to secure the abolition of the import duties on raw materials, especially on raw cotton ; they considered that " the imposition of heavy duties on those raw materials which form the basis of our manufactures is in the highest degree impolitic, evidently tending to diminish the labour and reduce the wages of our industrious population, on the full employment and adequate remuneration of which the prosperity of the State essentially depends." The import duty on raw cotton had reached its highest point in 1809, when 16s. 11d. had been charged on every 100 lb. imported in a British-built ship, and 25s. 6d. on every 100 lb. otherwise

[1] *Report Book of the Manchester Chamber of Commerce*, 30th January, 1822 ; cf. *Manchester Mercury*, 19th December, 1820.
[2] *Manchester Chronicle*, 27th May, 1820.

139

imported. In 1815 and 1819 there had been successive reductions of the duties; but this was declared by the Chancellor of the Exchequer to have resulted in considerable loss to the revenue, and the Manchester manufacturers had therefore good reason to fear that the Government's policy might be reversed.[1] During the 'twenties and 'thirties the Manchester Chamber of Commerce sent one memorial after another to the Government, demanding the repeal of the cotton duties, but without getting more than partial satisfaction. In 1831, indeed, Lord Althorp actually increased the import duty on raw cotton as a compensation to the revenue for the withdrawal of the excise duty on printed calico. Despite further continuous agitation by the Manchester Chamber of Commerce, backed by Glasgow, Belfast, Nottingham and other textile centres, it was not until Peel's tariff reforms of 1845 that the duties were totally repealed and the importation of raw cotton freely permitted.

The excise on printed cotton goods (with a drawback on export) was even more vexatious than the import duties on raw cotton. This excise duty was unsatisfactory even from the point of view of the revenue, because in addition to the expense of collecting £2,000,000 from the calico printers there was the expense of returning to them £1,500,000 as drawback. It was very objectionable to the calico printers, for the delays and expenses to which it subjected them imposed a tax of approximately £200,000 a year on the trade, and increased the cost of prints by 30 or 40 per cent. Nor did the vexations of the tax end with its imposition. In 1823 the attention of the Manchester Chamber of Commerce was drawn to a new regulation of the Board of Excise, by which the traditional practice of taking a pattern from each piece of printed cotton, on packing for export, was forbidden, with the result that large quantities of goods were held up.[2] In the following year the Board of the Chamber felt called upon to express its sympathy with several merchants who had been forced to refund the drawback on certain printed calicoes, because the printer of the calicoes, over whom they had no control, had forged the excise stamps on the goods.[3] On more than one occasion during the 'twenties the Manchester merchants protested

---

[1] *Manchester Mercury*, 27th June, 1820.
[2] *Proceedings of the Manchester Chamber of Commerce*, 9th July, 1823.
[3] *Ibid.*, 21st January, 1824.

against " the impolicy and vexatious nature of the excise on printed calicoes." In 1826 the Chamber of Commerce announced its intention of co-operating with the calico printers in working for the repeal of the duty, and resolved to send a memorial to the Treasury ; [1] but, in spite of these strong expressions of local feeling, the obnoxious impost was not finally withdrawn until 1831, and even then the effect of its abolition was marred by Althorp's ungracious increase of the import duty on raw cotton.

The Manchester Chamber of Commerce had been intimately concerned, also, in the struggle against the overlong continuance of the Irish Union Duties. During the later eighteenth century a considerable cotton manufacture had grown up in Ireland, and had been able to compete with Lancashire on equal terms ; but by the end of the century the English industry had secured a decided technical superiority, and the Irish cotton manufacture could not hope to maintain its position if English manufactured goods were to be imported freely. The Act of Union of 1800 established free trade between England and Ireland in some classes of goods, and greatly reduced the duties on all others ; but the Irish cotton industry received special consideration. The general low duty of 10 per cent. on cotton goods was abandoned ; in both countries, calicoes and muslins were to pay the same duties as had formerly been charged on goods exported from Great Britain to Ireland, namely, 10 per cent. *ad valorem* and 12½d. a square yard in addition. This duty was to remain until 1808, after which it was to be annually reduced in equal proportions until 1816, when it was to remain at a flat rate until 1821. The same duties were to be charged on the importation of cotton yarn or twist, but in this case all duties were to cease after 1816. Under this scheme the Irish cotton industry made progress ; but it was generally agreed that the Irish manufacturers would not be able to maintain their competition if the protective duties were withdrawn in 1821.

In 1820 a " compromise " was arranged, in the interests of the Irish industry. The duties were to remain at 10 per cent. until the end of 1825 ; thereafter they were to be decreased by four equal quinquennial reductions, and were finally to cease in 1840. No sooner had this arrangement

[1] *Proceedings of the Manchester Chamber of Commerce*, 3rd February, 1824, 26th July and 16th August, 1826.

been reached than a petition was received from the Manchester Chamber of Commerce, which declared that " public opinion loudly proclaimed the urgent necessity for the removal of every possible restriction on the commerce of this country," and that " an unshackled trade between Great Britain and Ireland would be highly advantageous to both countries, by promoting an interchange of various cotton and other manufactures, which during the duties has been prevented." [1] Though the petitioners were aware that some branches of Irish industry might be injured by the withdrawal of the protective duties, yet they considered that " the benefit which would accrue to the general interests of both countries would more than compensate and ought to outweigh considerations for partial or individual interests ; and further, the removal of all restrictions would tend to direct the capital and industry of both countries to prosecuting those various manufactures for which each possessed the greatest natural qualifications." In 1821 the Manchester merchants exerted still more pressure on the Government, in a memorial which urged " that to levy duties on merchandise passing between parts of the same Empire is injurious to their common prosperity and contrary to the just principles of political economy." [2]

In the ensuing parliamentary inquiry, the Manchester Chamber of Commerce was particularly energetic in furnishing evidence, collecting statistics, and securing legal opinions ; it invited the co-operation of all the principal towns of Great Britain, and corresponded actively with Liverpool, Leeds, the Potteries and other districts.[3] A long petition presented in 1822 denied that the English cotton industry possessed any important or exclusive advantages of production as compared with the Irish, and considered that freer intercourse would actually assist the development of Irish industry, by encouraging the investment of British capital in Ireland. " The interests of the people of the two countries would be identified, and British capital would be used for the object so much desired by Parliament—the industrious occupation and comfortable support of the

---

[1] *Manchester Chronicle*, 10th March, 1821.
[2] *Ibid.*, 30th June, 1821.
[3] *First Annual Report of the Manchester Chamber of Commerce*, 1822 ; *Proceedings*, 27th October, 1821, 27th and 30th March, 1822, and 3rd April, 1822.

peasantry in Ireland."[1] A further attempt at compromise
was made in 1823, when provision was made for the reduction of the duties by annual stages until they should be
completely extinguished in 1829 ; but this failed to pacify
the English manufacturers, and their further agitation compelled the Government to agree, in 1824, to the immediate
and total abolition of the remaining duties.

Throughout the second quarter of the nineteenth century
the Manchester Chamber of Commerce was playing an active
part in the general Free Trade Movement by pressing for
the removal of the import duties on particular commodities,
some of which had no very obvious bearing on the prosperity of the cotton manufacture. In 1824 the salt manufacturers attempted to secure the continuance of the salt
duty beyond the date fixed for its expiration ; this proposal
was opposed and defeated by the Manchester merchants,
who pointed out that the abolition of the salt duty would
lower the price of muriatic acid, which would then become
available for use in some processes of the cotton industry.[2]
In the following year the calico printers and dyers of Manchester acted through the Chamber of Commerce to secure
concessions in the alteration of the sulphur duties ; in this
case the connection with the cotton industry arose from the
fact that sulphuric acid and chloride of lime were used
extensively in the finishing processes.[3] The Manchester
merchants' interest in the duty and drawback on soap may
be explained in a similar fashion, as soap was used in some
processes of the flax, cotton and silk manufactures. When
the drawback on soap used in manufacture was due to expire,
in 1835, the Manchester merchants took the opportunity to
petition for the total repeal of the duty ; the petition was
not directly successful, but indirectly it may have served
its purpose, as the drawback was retained.[4] Even the
Chamber of Commerce, however, could not find any direct
relationship between the cotton industry and the duty on
pepper ; the Manchester petition for the reduction of the
pepper duty, in 1836, could only plead that a diminished
rate of duty would increase the demand for pepper, stimulate

[1] *Proceedings of the Manchester Chamber of Commerce,* 24th April,
1822.
[2] *Ibid.,* 12th May, 1824 ; 4th Annual Report, 14th February, 1825.
[3] *Ibid.,* 18th May and 8th June, 1825.
[4] *Ibid.,* 1st April, 1835.

its cultivation in certain parts of India, and beneficially affect British commerce with Malabar ![1]

The long struggle concerning the sugar and coffee duties, which went on all through the second quarter of the nineteenth century, turned partly on a question of colonial preferences, partly also on a differentiation between slave-grown and free-grown produce ; the main conflict was between the West Indian and East Indian interests, and in this conflict the Lancashire merchants were active on the East Indian side. During the eighteenth century India had sent large quantities of fine textile goods to England, and had been a dangerous competitor of the growing Lancashire cotton industry ; by the end of the Napoleonic wars, however, the position had been reversed, and the Manchester merchants now hoped to develop a large market in India for Lancashire goods. If this was to happen, India must develop the large-scale cultivation of produce for export, in order to pay for the manufactured goods she was to import ; and among the export crops which the Indian peasant was to be encouraged to cultivate, prominence was given to such commodities as cotton, indigo, coffee and sugar. To the large-scale cultivation of sugar in India there was, however, a serious barrier in the heavier duties imposed on East Indian as compared with West Indian sugar. During the post-war period the import duty on West Indian sugar was 28s. per cwt., while the duty on East Indian sugar was 38s.[2]

The Manchester Chamber of Commerce, in association with the merchants of London and Liverpool,[3] made strenuous efforts to get rid of this discrimination, and several parliamentary petitions were presented, at first against the proposal to impose another 10s. extra duty on East Indian sugar, later against the whole principle of fostering the trade of one part of the Empire at the expense of another. Even with this preferential treatment, the West Indian sugar trade was in a very depressed condition ; the depression was attributed, however, not to the competition of East Indian sugar, but to the fact that the natural advantages enjoyed by the West Indies (shorter voyages to

---

[1] *Proceedings of the Manchester Chamber of Commerce*, 23rd July, 1836.
[2] Manchester Chamber of Commerce's Petition on the Sugar Duties, printed in the *Manchester Chronicle*, 30th June, 1821.
[3] *Ibid.*, 12th May, 1821.

England, cheaper freights and insurance, etc.) had been temporarily reduced by the return of peace and the consequent glut of shipping. The Manchester merchants did not deny that their anxiety for a reform of the sugar duties arose from their desire to extend the Indian market for Lancashire cotton goods ; in 1823 they declared definitely that this market had been restricted by the tariff discrimination against East Indian sugar.[1] The assertion was made even more forcibly in 1827, when a special committee of the Manchester Chamber reported that " the use of sugar and cotton as dead weight to ships returning from India is essential to the existence of the trade with that country . . . but while the protecting duties granted to West Indian planters, securing to them a preference in the home market (in fact a monopoly of it) are continued, our trade in sugar cannot be prosecuted successfully, and the demand is thus limited by the difficulty of procuring returns." [2] The whole question came up for discussion in the House of Commons during the summer of 1827, but the Government at that time was not disposed to add to the grievances of the West Indian planters, and no action was taken, either in the sugar dispute or in the related controversy concerning the tariff discrimination between East Indian and West Indian coffee.

After 1833, partly as a result of the abolition of slavery in the British Empire, the supplies of West Indian sugar and coffee began to fall off, and became inadequate to the English demand ; the agitation for the removal of the discrimination against East Indian produce therefore gathered strength, and the Manchester Chamber of Commerce was soon acting in co-operation with the commercial organisations of London, Liverpool, Glasgow and Bengal, in petitioning Parliament ; [3] by 1836 the campaign had gained its immediate objectives, and the duties on East Indian and West Indian produce had been equalised. At the annual meeting of the Manchester Chamber, early in 1837, the Board was able to report that " the sugar of the two hemispheres has now been brought into fair and advantageous competition in the British market." The struggle thenceforth developed into an attack on the tariff discrimination between foreign and colonial produce, which was defended

---

[1] *Proceedings of the Manchester Chamber of Commerce*, 9th April, 1823.
[2] *Ibid.*, 14th March, 1827.
[3] *Ibid.*, 27th March and 22nd July, 1835.

as a differentiation between slave-grown and free-grown produce. From agitating against the colonial preferences it was a short step to demanding the total abolition of the duties ; in this fashion the disputes concerning sugar and coffee gradually merged into the wider free-trade movement of the 'forties.

Early in 1838 the commercial organisations of Manchester and other towns co-operated in an unsuccessful attempt to secure permission to refine foreign sugars for export, and to effect a *reduction* of the duties on foreign sugar and coffee ; within a year, however, the merchants had ceased to advocate the reduction of the duties, and were demanding their total abolition. In 1839 the Liverpool Brazil Association sought the co-operation of the Manchester merchants in procuring the revision of the duties on Brazilian coffee and sugar, and asked the Manchester Chamber of Commerce to memorialise the President of the Board of Trade for permission to distil molasses into spirits for export. The Manchester merchants replied that they intended asking for the total abolition of all duties on foreign sugar and coffee, and did not consider that a merely partial relaxation should be demanded. It is only fair to state, however, that the Manchester petition of that year, for the total abolition of the duties, was largely concerned with the development of the trade with Brazil ; it was considered unjust that Brazilian produce should be excluded from British markets by exorbitant duties while Brazil admitted British goods on favourable terms.[1] The claims of Brazilian sugar and coffee were given a prominent place also in the Manchester petition of 1840, which stressed the urgency of the question. Lancashire cotton goods found a better market in Brazil than in the West Indian colonies ; the commercial treaty between England and Brazil would come up for revision in 1842, and it was feared that, if the English duties on Brazilian produce remained unrectified, Lancashire cottons would be penalised by tariff retaliation.[2]

Reductions in the coffee duties were made by Peel in 1842, and again in 1844 ; thenceforward the merchants' attack tended to become concentrated against the sugar duties, and especially against the discrimination between slave-grown and free-grown produce. Here commercial interests

---

[1] *Proceedings of the Manchester Chamber of Commerce*, 11th February, 25th April and 9th May, 1839.   [2] *Ibid.*, 24th June, 1840.

came into direct conflict with humanitarian conviction, which held that, since sacrifices had been made for the purpose of abolishing slavery, it was justifiable to penalise the trade of countries where slave labour was still employed. To this the Manchester merchants replied that it was no more wrong to buy slave-grown sugar than to buy slave-grown cotton ; moreover, the West Indian planters had done well out of the compensation paid to them for the emancipation of their slaves, and had already enjoyed the preferential duties long enough to adjust their position to the changed circumstances.[1] Similar arguments were brought forward in 1843 and 1844, but failed to carry conviction, and in this instance the Manchester Chamber had to acknowledge that its efforts had been futile.

The further reduction of the coffee duties in 1844, and the simultaneous reduction in the duties on foreign free-grown sugar, roused the Manchester merchants to strenuous activity in 1845 ; but it was not until after the fall of Peel's Ministry that the sugar question was settled. The new Whig Government reduced the duty on foreign slave-grown sugar to that on foreign free-grown sugar, and made provision for the gradual reduction of all the duties to the rate levied on the colonial product, which was to fall to 10s. per cwt. on the standard qualities. The final equalisation of the duties did not actually take place until 1854 ; but the Manchester merchants, though they grumbled at the tardiness of the changes, were well content with a final victory which they had not really expected. In the meantime they had also carried their point concerning the coffee duties. In 1850 the Manchester Chamber of Commerce petitioned against the tariff preference still given to colonial coffee, demanding " the admission of foreign coffee at an equalised duty, and a reduction in the present rate " ;[2] within a year the duties were equalised, and reduced to a rate of 3d. per lb. on coffee of whatever growth and whencesoever imported.

It is to be remembered that the Manchester merchants, when in 1842 they stressed the analogy between slave-grown sugar and slave-grown cotton, were still carrying on a strenuous campaign against the import duties on raw cotton ;

[1] *Proceedings of the Manchester Chamber of Commerce*, 1st June, 1842.
[2] *Ibid.*, 30th May, 1850 ; *cf. Proceedings of the Manchester Commercial Association*, 13th June, 1850.

in this case, also, there had been a question of colonial preferences, as well as a struggle for the total repeal of the duties. West Indian cotton had been exempted from duty in 1821 ; the duties on other kinds were reduced in 1828, after which 6 per cent. *ad valorem* was paid on foreign-grown cotton, and 4*d.* per cwt. on cotton grown in British possessions. Althorp's proposal to increase the cotton duty in 1831 was naturally denounced as a retrograde measure by the Manchester Chamber of Commerce, which invited more than a dozen textile towns to co-operate in sending a lengthy protest to the Chancellor of the Exchequer.[1] In this memorial, the English cotton industry's concern for India was once more evident ; for it was pointed out that " the increased duty of 1*d.* per lb. would be an addition to the cost of about 25 per cent. on the product of British India, 15 per cent. to 20 per cent. on that of other countries (which comprise the bulk of the supply), and 5 per cent. to 10 per cent. on the finer qualities grown in U.S.A. and Egypt, thus discouraging the growth in our own possessions and encouraging that of our rivals." The memorial, and the deputation which presented it, might claim to have achieved some measure of success, for the Government agreed to reduce the amount by which the duty was to be increased ; even this smaller increase of the duty was decidedly unpalatable to the Manchester merchants, but further protests produced no immediate results.

Perseverance in the sending of petitions and memorials brought a further instalment of relief in 1833, when the duty was halved ; thereafter the merchants' demand was for the total repeal of the remaining duty, and each succeeding year produced its crop of petitions on the subject, until the movement was temporarily checked by the commercial collapse of 1837, which increased the financial difficulties of the Government, as well as of the merchants. The attack was renewed in 1839, and during the following five years Manchester alone presented to the Government four petitions and one memorial on the subject, not to mention the holding of special protest meetings and the sending of deputations ; meanwhile such other cotton-manufacturing towns as Glasgow, Nottingham and Belfast were taking similar and co-ordinated action. Considering the obviously desirable character of the

[1] *Proceedings of the Manchester Chamber of Commerce,* 3rd, 9th and 14th February, 1831.

reform demanded, and the persistence of the agitation, it is rather surprising that the Government (which had already freed hemp, flax and silk from duty, and had reduced the duty on foreign wool) should have delayed the abolition of the cotton duty until 1845 ; the tardiness and reluctance with which the Government agreed to this reform may well have increased the pressure of free-trade enthusiasm in all the cotton-manufacturing districts of the kingdom.

The question of tariff discrimination came up for discussion in the case of the tea duties, as it had done in the struggles concerning sugar, coffee and cotton ; in each case, campaigns for the equalisation of the duties proved a convenient starting-point for further attacks, aiming at the general reduction of the duties and ultimately at their total abolition. After the cancellation of the East India Company's commercial privileges, the administration of the tea duties was transferred in 1834 from the Excise to the Customs, and Althorp made the tax differential according to the various kinds and qualities of tea, in order to increase the yield of revenue. The change led at once to considerable opposition, and the Manchester Chamber of Commerce was asked to assist in obtaining the imposition of a uniform and fixed duty in place of the differential duties proposed.[1] The differential duties were attacked on the ground that they would expose the importer to considerable loss if any dispute should arise about the exact specification of the tea he was importing. Moreover, the duty would unfairly penalise the importation of the better kinds of tea. At the same time, the customs inspector's discretion in deciding which rate of duty should be charged would lay him open to bribery by the importer. To prevent evasions of duty, every chest of tea would have to be examined separately, which would result in great inconvenience and loss of time, whereas a uniform poundage duty would protect the trader from loss, and the inspector from corruption, as well as encourage the importation of superior types of tea. Arguments of this nature led to the appointment of a parliamentary committee of inquiry, which reported in favour of giving the differential duties a longer trial ; nevertheless, the discrimination was removed in the course of the same session, and a uniform duty of 2s. 1d. per lb. was substituted.

[1] *Proceedings of the Manchester Chamber of Commerce*, 18th April, 1834.

Thereafter, the initiative in agitating for the reduction or abolition of the tea duty lay with Liverpool rather than Manchester ; the Manchester merchants were, indeed, inclined to be apathetic on the subject for many years. In 1844 the Manchester Chamber of Commerce promised the East India Association of Liverpool that it would do its best to obtain the repeal or reduction of the duties ; nevertheless, no serious campaign was set on foot until after the repeal of the Corn Laws. In November, 1846, the Manchester Chamber appointed a deputation to meet the newly-formed Liverpool Association for the Reduction of the Tea Duty ; but the deputation was ordered not to commit itself in any way.[1] Eventually, it is true, the Manchester merchants presented a memorial to the Chancellor of the Exchequer in favour of a reduction of the duty, and joined with the Liverpool association in appointing a deputation to interview Lord John Russell ; [2] but the commercial fluctuation and financial stringency which developed during the year 1847 did not encourage further remissions of taxation. It is possible that, even in Liverpool, the agitation against the tea duties was no more than lukewarm; for in December, 1847, the Liverpool association asked the Manchester Chamber whether the movement for the repeal of the tea duty could not be transferred to Manchester. This the Directors of the Manchester Chamber were unwilling to countenance ; but they arranged to hold a public meeting under the auspices of the Mayor, and printed a pamphlet on the tea duties, which were denounced as EXORBITANT, DISPROPORTIONATE, UNJUST, IMPOLITIC and INJURIOUS.

Throughout the early 'fifties the Liverpool Association for the Reduction of the Tea Duties continued to co-operate with the Manchester Chamber of Commerce (and also with the Manchester Commercial Association) in putting pressure upon the Government,[3] and it is possible that their memorials had some influence upon policy. Disraeli, in 1852, planned to reduce the duty to 1s. per lb. by successive stages spread over six years, and Gladstone's Budget of 1853 provided for the quickening of the process ; the outbreak of the Crimean

---

[1] *Proceedings of the Manchester Chamber of Commerce*, 16th November, 1846.   [2] *Ibid.*, 2nd December, 1846.
[3] See *ibid.*, 10th January, 1850, 16th January, 1851, 9th December, 1852 ; *cf. Proceedings of the Manchester Commercial Association*, 20th December, 1849, 20th January, 1850, 7th October, 1852.

War upset all financial calculations, however, and put a temporary check on further fiscal reform.

The special campaigns for the abolition or reduction of the taxes on particular commodities (such as cotton, copper, salt, soap, timber, sugar, coffee and tea) were all aspects of the general free-trade movement which was gathering strength during the second quarter of the nineteenth century. The preoccupation of the different manufacturing districts with those campaigns which promised most direct benefit to their local industries tended for a long time to weaken the more general movement, and to obscure its principles. Towards the end of the 'thirties, however, a greater unity and clarity was given to the free-trade progamme by Cobden and his friends in the Manchester Chamber of Commerce and the Anti-Corn-Law League ; the attack upon the Corn Laws, though in origin and form it was a special campaign against the taxation of particular commodities, proved to be an admirable device for rousing all the industrial interests to united action in defence of their common interests. The guiding principles of the free-trade movement had been clearly laid down by Thomas Tooke in 1820, when he asserted that " Freedom from Restraint is calculated to give the utmost extension to Foreign Trade, and the best direction to the Capital and Industry of the Country," and that " the maxim of buying in the Cheapest Market, and selling in the Dearest, which regulates every merchant in his individual dealings, is strictly applicable as the best rule for the trade of the whole Nation." His declaration in favour of complete freedom of trade did not immediately find general acceptance ; but its cogency became increasingly recognised during the period of financial stringency and commercial stagnation which followed the economic crisis of 1836.

The relationship between the revival of the general free-trade movement and the growth of the Anti-Corn-Law agitation, in the later 'thirties, may be clearly traced in the records of the Manchester Chamber of Commerce. The concluding paragraph of the petition, proposed by Cobden at an adjourned special meeting of the Chamber in December, 1838, implored Parliament " to repeal all laws relating to the importation of foreign corn and other foreign articles of subsistence, and to carry out to the fullest extent, both as affects agriculture and manufactures, the true and peaceful principles of free trade, by removing all obstacles to the unrestricted employment of industry and capital."[1] Towards the end of 1839 the Board of the Chamber, again on the motion of Richard Cobden, resolved that " the welfare of both capitalists and labourers composing the manufacturing community imperatively calls for the removal of all legislative restraints upon the trade of the country " ; at the same meeting it was also declared that " the prosperity, peace and happiness of the people of this and other nations can alone be promoted by the adoption of just principles of trade, which shall secure to all the right of a free interchange of their respective productions."[2]

This growing movement in favour of complete freedom of trade received a powerful stimulus from the publication of the parliamentary *Report on Import Duties* (1840), which declared that the customs tariff of the United Kingdom presented neither congruity nor unity of purpose, and that its sole definitely ascertainable effect was to hinder the development of foreign trade of every kind. The Manchester merchants applauded the general tone of this report, but felt that its recommendations did not go far enough ; they therefore published their own *Report on the Injurious Effects of Restrictions on Trade*, which was widely distributed throughout the country in 1841.[3] The Manchester *Report* dealt in detail with the iniquity of the various taxes on particular classes of commodities, and laid great stress on the question of the Corn Laws ; but the culmination of the report was a plea for complete freedom of trade, and a declaration that " Monopolies can no longer be tolerated." Thenceforward the Chamber's enthusiasm for complete freedom increased rather than abated, and even Peel's daring tariff reforms of the next few years seemed curiously dilatory to the Manchester merchants, one of whom (Mr. Stocks) declared that Sir Robert Peel was " the most dangerous man in England."[4] Several free-trade petitions were sent to Parliament from Manchester in 1841, and the principles of the movement were reaffirmed in one special meeting after another. At one of these meetings Richard Cobden secured general agreement for his assertion that to sell everything and buy

---

[1] *Proceedings of the Manchester Chamber of Commerce*, 20th December, 1838. [2] *Ibid.*, 14th November, 1839.
[3] *Ibid.*, 23rd December, 1840, 8th February and 11th March, 1841.
[4] *Ibid.*, 20th May, 1841.

nothing was to destroy all foreign commerce ; this (he said) was what British statesmen were trying to do, and it was for bodies like the Manchester Chamber of Commerce to prevent them.

By that time Cobden and many other members of the Manchester Chamber were devoting their main energies to the work of the Anti-Corn-Law League, which was becoming "a great fact," and a new power in the State.[1] For the next few years the political activities of the Manchester merchants centred round the task of securing a decisive victory over the landowners, and the business qualities which had pushed Lancashire goods into new markets throughout the world were triumphantly used in the organisation of popular propaganda on an unprecedented scale. The story of the campaign against the Corn Laws is too generally known to need recapitulation ; [2] it may not be out of place, however, to notice that even in Manchester the advocates of "total and immediate repeal" had to fight hard against both apathy and active opposition throughout the early stages of the agitation. During the earlier 'thirties the Chamber of Commerce was decidedly apathetic about the Corn Laws. In 1834 the Board of the Chamber cautiously declared that it would not fail "to avail itself of the first opportunity to advocate such a change in the Corn Laws as reason, the wants of the community and true policy require " ; [3] but no decided action was taken. At that time the Chamber was in favour of a low fixed duty on corn, in place of the vexatious sliding scale set up in 1828 ; [4] the immediate and total repeal of the Corn Laws was not yet considered to be within the sphere of practical politics.

It was apparently the coincidence of a bad harvest with renewed depression of trade in 1837 which led to the quickening of interest in the movement. In the annual report presented in February, 1837, the retiring Directors of the Manchester Chamber of Commerce referred to the recent ominous rise in the price of wheat, and recommended their successors " to solicit the attention of Parliament to an early consideration of the question with a view to the thorough revision of the existing system, the pernicious character

[1] *The Times*, 18th November, 1843.
[2] For an elaborate (but uncritical) account of the movement see Archibald Prentice's *History of the Anti-Corn-Law League*, 1853.
[3] *Proceedings of the Manchester Chamber of Commerce*, 10th February, 1834.   [4] *Ibid.*, 25th November and 9th December, 1835.

of which admits of such easy proof." Before the end of
the year, their successors had bettered the instructions.
In December, 1837, Mr. J. B. Smith had drafted a petition
(subsequently approved by the Board of the Chamber) which
contained a full statement of the case against the Corn Laws,
and prayed that the principles of free trade might be " fully
established both in manufactures and in agriculture." [1] At
the annual meeting held in February, 1838, Cobden attempted
to intensify the influence of this growing enthusiasm for
free trade, by proposing that the Chamber should hold
quarterly, instead of annual, general meetings ; but the
Chamber was not to be suddenly persuaded and the motion
was withdrawn. [2]

The public campaign against the taxation of grain entered
upon a new phase in October, 1838, with the foundation of
the Manchester Anti-Corn-Law Association, which was later
to develop into the Anti-Corn-Law League. It was generally
recognised that the new Association was, in effect, an off-
shoot from the Manchester Chamber of Commerce ; the
hurriedly-formed Committee of the Association included
about forty prominent members of the Chamber of Commerce (such as Elkanah Armitage, John Bright, Thomas
Potter, Richard Cobden, John Edward Taylor), and the
indefatigable J. B. Smith was Treasurer. It must not be
assumed, however, that the Chamber of Commerce had been
completely converted to the new gospel ; a great many
members were still in favour of a moderate fixed duty or
a modified sliding scale, and were not prepared to ask for
the repeal of *all* duties on grain. The draft petition on the
Corn Laws, which the President of the Chamber presented
for approval at a special general meeting on the 13th
December, 1838, was almost ludicrously vague and mild ;
yet it was stated to have been unanimously adopted by
the Board of Directors as suitable for presentation to Parliament. After enumerating the evils of the Corn Laws in
traditional fashion, the draft petition concluded with remarkable restraint :

" Your Petitioners address your Honourable House
on this subject in no spirit of partisanship. They do
not desire the exclusive advantage of a class, but the

---

[1] *Proceedings of the Chamber of Commerce,* 13th and 27th December,
1837.   [2] *Ibid.,* 14th February, 1838.

equal good of all ; they wish to see the trade in corn
conducted as far as possible on the principle of other
trades, in a sober, regular course . . . supplying the
real wants of the country without overwhelming it.
Your Petitioners hope that your Honourable House will
take measures in accordance with these sentiments, and
with the opinions they have ventured to offer to your
notice."

Mr. J. B. Smith at once made it clear that he and his
friends would not willingly acquiesce in the presentation of
such a lukewarm petition ; and after a very heated discussion,
Mr. Richard Cobden secured the adjournment of the meeting
for a week, within which time a petition was to be drafted
for the total repeal of *all* protective duties. At the adjourned meeting [1] the Directors again submitted their original
draft petition, but with a stronger conclusion : " your
Petitioners earnestly conjure your Honourable House that the
existing corn laws may be repealed." Repeal of the *existing*
Corn Laws was far from satisfying the demands of the Anti-
Corn-Law League ; after some preliminary skirmishing by
J. C. Dyer and J. B. Smith, the main attack upon the Directors'
position was opened by Mr. Alderman Cobden [2] himself, who
considered that the petition, as drafted by the Directors,
"would have no more weight, however ingeniously urged, than
a thesis drawn up by some tyro in political economy at a University." He went at some length into the questions of foreign
competition and the effects of the German Commercial Union
upon British industry, and ended by submitting to the
meeting his own draft petition, which was eventually adopted.
The petition presented much the same arguments as had been
outlined in his speech, and concluded by imploring Parliament " to repeal all laws relating to the importation of
foreign corn and other foreign articles of subsistence, and
to carry out to the fullest extent, both as affects agriculture
and manufactures, the true and peaceful principles of *free
trade*, by removing all existing obstacles to the unrestricted
employment of industry and capital."

After the adoption of this petition the Manchester
Chamber of Commerce ceased to take any prominent part

[1] *Proceedings of the Manchester Chamber of Commerce*, 20th December,
1838.
[2] In the interval between the two meetings the municipal elections
for the newly incorporated borough of Manchester had taken place.

in the Anti-Corn-Law agitation. The excited meetings and heated discussions of December, 1838, had shown that the question might lead to disruption within the Chamber; and this danger was emphasised at the annual meeting held early in 1839, when the official list of nominations to the Board of Directors was rejected, in favour of a list of sixteen thorough-going Cobdenites. Thenceforward it was considered safer for the reformers to work mainly through the Anti-Corn-Law League, the Chamber of Commerce intervening in its own name only at critical moments in the controversy. Thus, Peel's retention of the sliding scale in a modified form, in 1842, called forth a petition of protest from the Manchester Chamber; the petition pronounced the Government's proposal as inadequate, exposed the evils of a sliding scale which increased speculation in a changing market, and declared that the real interests of England were being sacrificed for a class whose sole aim was to prevent the free interchange of British manufactured goods for the foodstuffs which other countries could supply.[1] Similar action was taken in the following year, in consequence of the Government's reduction of the duty on Canadian wheat. Again, at the very crisis of the Anti-Corn-Law movement in the autumn of 1845, the Chamber of Commerce was moved to action by the partial failure of harvests throughout Europe, and the anticipation of a potato famine in Ireland. The memorial presented by the Chamber urged Sir Robert Peel to consider the report of scarcity to be sufficient warrant for removing the restrictions on the corn trade, and not to wait until actual famine forced the laws aside.[2]

By this time the whole country had awakened to the necessity of suspending the Corn Laws, and the Manchester Chamber of Commerce was doing no more than its formal duty in multiplying its applications to the Government. In January, 1846, the Chamber sent a memorial to the Queen and petitions to both Houses of Parliament, just before the opening of the new session, in which Peel was to bring his tariff reforms to a climax and sweep away the Corn Laws. While the momentous Bill was passing through Parliament, the House of Lords received another petition from the Chamber, praying that the Government's proposals might pass without mutilation, and that the change of system

---

[1] *Proceedings of the Manchester Chamber of Commerce*, 17th February, 1842.   [2] *Ibid.*, 22nd October, 1845.

might take place with as little delay as possible, in order that commercial instability might be reduced to a minimum.[1] When the victory had been finally achieved, the Directors presented their formal congratulations to Sir Robert Peel, in an address which applauded his unselfish courage and affirmed that he would have his reward in the knowledge that he had conferred great benefits upon humanity.[2] On the very next day, the Anti-Corn-Law League was condition ally dissolved ; but the Manchester Chamber of Commerce still remained on guard, ready to protest by petition or memorial against any resumption of the sliding scale, any threatened return to a general policy of tariff protectionism in England, or any increase of protective tariffs abroad.[3]

[1] *Proceedings of the Manchester Chamber of Commerce,* 21st May, 1846.
[2] *Ibid.,* 1st July, 1846.
[3] *Ibid.,* 20th January, 1848 (petition against the resumption of the sliding scale) : 9th March, 1852 (memorials against the protectionist proposals of the Derby Ministry), etc.

CHAPTER XII.

CURRENCY AND BANKING QUESTIONS.

THROUGHOUT the first half of the nineteenth century there was fairly general agreement that the instability of trade was partly the result of weaknesses inherent in the currency and banking system of the country : though there was not equal agreement as to the remedies which should be adopted. During the Napoleonic wars, while cash payments were suspended at the Bank of England, the financial instability of the country seemed evident ; Napoleon, indeed, considered that England was on the verge of financial collapse, and hoped that her economic ruin would give him the victory even if military measures failed.[1] After the wars the British Government decided in favour of adopting the gold standard, and cash payments were eventually resumed by the Bank of England in 1821. Commercial opinion, however, was by no means unanimous in favour of this policy of currency deflation. In 1821 the Birmingham merchants sent to Parliament a petition for the repeal of the Act authorising cash payments ;[2] and Thomas Attwood found many supporters for his assertion that all the economic instability of the post-war generation arose from the error of restricting the expanding trade of a growing population within the inelastic bonds of a gold currency. The country gentry attributed the agricultural distress of the period to the currency policy of the Government, and Cobbett complained that Peel's Act had almost doubled the burden of mortgages on landed estates.[3]

From this attack upon the gold standard the Manchester merchants held steadily aloof. Mr. G. W. Wood, the Treasurer of the Manchester Chamber of Commerce, reflected the public opinion of the town when he declared

[1] See E. F. Heckscher, *The Continental System*, 1922, pp. 71, 354, etc.
[2] *Manchester Chronicle*, 17th February, 1821.
[3] See the *Manchester Mercury*, 13th June, 1820.

that " we want a regulating medium ; and there is nothing like gold for that purpose. No circumstance can depreciate its value. Nothing can impair our confidence in it." [1] That Manchester traders welcomed rather than feared the return to a metallic currency is reflected in their hostility to any issue of local banknotes. During the wartime restriction of cash payments the Manchester banking houses had refrained from issuing their own notes, and had relied on the issues of the Bank of England, with satisfactory results. In 1821, however, several Manchester banks (Jones Loyd & Co., Heywood Bros. & Co., and Daintry, Ryle & Co.) announced their intention of issuing local notes, " from the impossibility of providing a sufficient quantity of cash to meet the weekly payments required by the manufacturing interests in this district." [2] Immediate alarm was felt by the merchants and manufacturers at this threat to financial stability, and a great public meeting was summoned, at which the bankers' proposal was emphatically denounced.

It was maintained that the wartime conservatism of the Manchester banks had exerted a steadying influence upon Lancashire trade, whereas " in every district of the United Kingdom, agricultural as well as commercial, when an issue of local notes has driven national currency from circulation, the most extensive and aggravated suffering has frequently been produced by the simultaneous failure of many private banks and the consequent sudden annihilation of a currency dependent solely on their individual responsibility." It was admitted that notes issued by the old-established banks of Manchester could be accepted with confidence, but it seemed inevitable that the practice of issuing local notes would rapidly spread to less responsible banking firms ; and the risk of loss in notes of inferior character would affect not only the person who first circulated them but also all the people who were compelled to accept them in payment for goods or services. The merchants present at the meeting pledged themselves not to accept any currency except gold or Bank of England notes, except in cases of extreme necessity, in which cases they promised not to circulate such notes. Ten days later a similar meeting of protest was held at Stockport. [3]

---

[1] *Manchester Chronicle*, 25th August, 1821.
[2] *Ibid.*, 14th July, 1821.
[3] *Ibid.*, 25th August and 8th September, 1821.

The financial crisis of 1825 confirmed the Manchester merchants in their hostility to the unregulated issue of private banknotes, and in their loyalty to the gold standard. The Manchester Chamber of Commerce, in a petition on the crisis, pointed out that the local losses would have been much greater if the town had not been so firm in its financial conservatism ; " the comparative confidence and quiet of Manchester " was contrasted with the " fear and suffering elsewhere," and a demand was made for the introduction of a metallic currency throughout the country.[1] Nevertheless, although they were opposed to the extension of irresponsible private banking, it must not be imagined that the Manchester merchants were by any means content with the existing organisation of the credit system. Even before the crisis of 1825 they protested against the monopolistic position of the Bank of England, and demanded the right to establish joint-stock banks, which might be expected to pursue a more responsible policy than that of the private bankers. At the Annual General Meeting of the Manchester Chamber of Commerce, held in February, 1825, it was resolved " that the repeal of so much of the Charter as prevents the establishment of banks having a number exceeding six partners, is a measure of decided importance with a view to the protection of the public against loss by the insolvency of banking establishments," [2] and a petition to this effect was presented to Parliament. The Bank Act of 1826 partly satisfied this demand by permitting the establishment of joint-stock banks, provided that they were not less than sixty-five miles from London ; the same Act also gave the Bank of England power to establish branches in any part of England. Manchester was one of the first places to benefit from this reform ; before the end of 1826 there was a branch of the Bank of England in the town, and in 1829 two joint-stock banks were established.

The mixture of financial conservatism and reforming zeal, which was a notable feature of Manchester opinion during the earlier nineteenth century, may be traced in the attitude of the Manchester merchants towards the Usury Laws, under which (since the reign of Queen Anne) 5 per cent. had been fixed as the maximum rate of interest. Financial conservatism predominated in the protest of the

[1] *Proceedings of the Manchester Chamber of Commerce*, 18th February, 1826.   [2] *Ibid.*, 13th February, 1825.

Manchester Chamber of Commerce against the proposed establishment of a Manchester Equitable Loan Society in 1824. The object of the proposal was (according to the Chamber of Commerce) " to create a joint-stock company with an alleged capital of half a million pounds, to be lent out on deposit of pledges, in Manchester and Salford, at an exorbitant rate of interest." This was opposed, on the ground that it would be unfair " to grant to certain individuals a monopoly of exemption from the Usury Laws " : that " advances of money would be systematically forced on unprincipled tradesmen at a rate of interest ruinous to the individuals themselves, whilst the operation of such a system must prove pernicious to the fair trader " : and that such a measure was wholly uncalled for by the traders or inhabitants of Manchester, who had never been consulted about it or subscribed for any shares in it.[1] The Bill did not pass ; and when the scheme was revived, in the following year, under the new name of the London and Manchester Equitable Loan Company, the Chamber of Commerce was as decided as before in its opposition.[2]

Although the Manchester merchants were determined to prevent any special exemptions from the Usury Laws, it must not be supposed that they were favourable to such restrictions upon financial freedom. On the contrary, the Chamber of Commerce was actively concerned in the agitation for the abolition of the Usury Laws, believing that there was no " good reason why money should not be left at all times to find its value in the public market like any other commodity." [3] In February, 1826, the Chamber sent its deputation to London to present a memorial on the issue of exchequer bills. The deputation was instructed to interview (if possible) the First Lord of the Treasury, the Chancellor of the Exchequer, and the President of the Board of Trade, " to urge upon them the advantage of an immediate repeal of the Usury Laws, and to point out the relief which this measure would afford in seasons of distress like the present, when loans of money cannot be obtained on the pledge of goods and produce, within the prescribed rate of interest, and parties are consequently compelled to have recourse to troublesome and expensive modes of obtaining assistance,

---

[1] *Proceedings of the Manchester Chamber of Commerce*, 9th June, 1824.
[2] *Ibid.*, 4th May, 1825.   [3] *Ibid.*, 25th February, 1826.

which, but for these laws, might be had on much more favourable terms." [1] A fortnight later, the deputation's efforts were backed up by the despatch of a special petition against the continuance of the Usury Laws, on the grounds that they were injurious to commerce and that they aggravated the financial embarrassment and consequent distress from which the industrial districts were suffering. It was felt that " considerable funds would be brought into circulation if it were permitted to lend money at a rate of interest commensurate with its actual value." [2]

Early in 1827 the Board of the Chamber of Commerce reported that " Ministers appeared to be well assured of the propriety of some change in those laws." [3] In spite of this favourable atmosphere, however, and in spite of a parliamentary committee's report in favour of abolishing the Usury Laws, the laws were not actually repealed until 1854 : [4] though some of the most vexatious restrictions had been removed before that time. In 1839 a statute had been passed which exempted from the operation of the Usury Laws all bills of exchange and all contracts for sums greater than £10 ; and by its new charter of 1833 the Bank of England had been exempted from the Usury Laws so far as concerned bills of exchange with not more than three months to run. [5] Strangely enough, the Manchester Chamber of Commerce does not appear to have objected to this special exemption granted to the Bank of England in 1833, though the Directors of the Chamber scrutinised the clauses of the new Bank Charter very closely.

In general the Manchester merchants were anxious that the new Bank Charter should not upset the existing monetary arrangements, which were considered to be working very satisfactorily ; they were especially anxious that no restrictions should be placed upon the local circulation of gold. The usual method of payment in the Manchester district had been either by cash or by Bank of England notes, which were issued (after 1826) by the local branch of the Bank and were easily convertible into gold, thus

---

[1] *Proceedings of the Manchester Chamber of Commerce*, 10th February, 1826.

[2] *Ibid.*, 25th February, 1826.

[3] *Ibid.*, 6th Annual Report, 12th February, 1827.

[4] 17 & 18 Vict. cap. 90 : see Gregory's *British Banking Statutes*, 1929, Vol. II, pp. 46-9.

[5] 3 & 4 Will. IV. cap. 98 ; Gregory, *op. cit.*, Vol. I, p. 23.

facilitating the payment of large wages bills weekly in cash
If there should be any difficulty in obtaining gold, however,
employers would pay several workmen jointly with one
large note, publicans and shopkeepers would then become
sub-bankers, by changing these notes into coin, and in times
of crisis this practice would add to the panic.

The fear of a local scarcity of gold arose from the proposal
to make the Bank of England notes legal tender, except at
the Bank itself. If this were done, would the Bank force on
the provinces notes issued by the central bank, and convertible into gold only in London, instead of notes issued by its
branches and convertible locally ? It was even possible that
the Bank would withdraw its provincial branches altogether
In that event, private bankers, who could only with difficulty obtain the large supplies of gold necessary for wages
would be compelled to demand the payment of a banker's
commission and agio (formerly 3 per cent.), which were not
necessary under the existing arrangements. Such matters
were considered too important to be left to the discretion
of a Board of Bank Directors elected annually ; the Manchester Chamber of Commerce therefore proposed that the
Bank of England should be compelled to maintain its existing
provincial branches, and that such branches should be
allowed to circulate only their own notes.[1] On these points
the Governor and Directors of the Bank of England gave
reassuring replies ; they consented to the introduction into
the charter of a provision that the provincial branches of
the Bank should only issue their own notes, and they explained that the Bank had no intention of withdrawing its
existing country branches, but rather of extending them.

The financial crises of 1836 and 1839 did not shake
the Manchester merchants' loyalty to the gold standard,
but strengthened their conviction that the note issue of
the country needed a more authoritative regulation than
had been exercised in the past, and that this task could
not safely be entrusted to the Directors of the Bank of
England. So strongly did the Directors of the Manchester
Chamber feel on this point that in December, 1839, they published an elaborate report on *The Effects of the Administration
of the Bank of England upon the Commercial and Manufacturing
Interests of the Country.* From this report it is possible to

---

[1] *Proceedings of the Manchester Chamber of Commerce*, 12th July, 1833.

see not only the ways in which Manchester trade had been affected by the crises, but also the ideas of the Manchester merchants about the currency and banking problems of the time. Briefly, the Manchester report asserted that throughout the years 1833-39 the Bank of England's note issues had been manipulated "for the exclusive benefit of a body of bank proprietors," without any close regard for the financial stability of the country or for the steady prosperity of trade. This irresponsible policy of the bank had caused an alternation of over-speculation and commercial stagnation, with consequent irregularity of industrial employment and widespread social distress. There had been almost seven hundred more fiats of bankruptcy issued in 1837 than in the preceding four years, and it was estimated that about £40,000,000 had been lost through the collapse of prices in that year, by merchants whose trade was principally with foreign countries. Then had come the renewed expansion of credit currency in 1838, with a consequent rise in the price of raw materials, followed in 1839 by a further restriction of credit and a fall of from 20 to 30 per cent. in prices. The manufacturing interest could not withstand such stupendous fluctuations, which had brought to " some of the most prudent and wealthy of our merchants and manufacturers . . . that ruin which, in a more wholesome and natural state of the circulating medium, could befall only the reckless adventurer or gambler." To the Manchester merchants it seemed singularly anomalous "that such a power over the property . . . the health, morals, and very lives of the community should be vested in the hands of twenty-six irresponsible individuals ; " the Chamber of Commerce therefore demanded that the regulation of the Bank's note issues should be subjected to public control, for the prevention of commercial fluctuations in the future.

The Birmingham currency reformers thought this a favourable opportunity to wean Manchester from its adherence to the gold standard. In 1840, representatives of the Birmingham Currency Committee interviewed the Directors of the Manchester Chamber of Commerce, and Mr. Samuel Goddard [1] advocated the adoption of a permanently inconvertible paper currency, of which the amount was to be

---

[1] Author of a pamphlet, *Free Trade and the Present Monetary Difficulties*, received by the Manchester Chamber of Commerce on the 6th May, 1847.

governed by the rise or fall of prices round the existing level. His colleague, Mr. Clutton Salt, supported him in his denunciation of the gold standard, and urged that it was wrong to use as a medium of exchange a commodity whose fluctuations had caused such severe distress.[1] Once more the Manchester Chamber turned a deaf ear to the currency heretics, and gave its full support to the Bank Charter Act of 1844, which maintained the gold standard but severely restricted the Bank of England's note issues.

Even after the financial crisis of 1847, the Manchester merchants still upheld the currency system established in 1844, though there was a fairly general feeling throughout the country that the Bank Charter Act had proved insufficiently elastic to cope with the emergency. When the Newcastle Chamber of Commerce wrote in 1847 to secure co-operation in an agitation for further banking reforms, the Manchester Chamber replied that it could give no assistance to such a project, as it was not satisfied that banking policy had been by any means the chief cause of the recent commercial dislocation.[2] To the renewed solicitation of the Birmingham enthusiasts the Manchester merchants replied that they " could not consent to advocate any temporary interference with the Act of 1844, believing that expedients to correct monetary pressure generally eventuate in more harm than benefit ; and they could still less sympathise with those who, without any tangible scheme, would advocate loose, unsound and impracticable changes in the basis of our currency." [3]

During the next few years the monetary tension was unexpectedly relaxed as the result of gold-mining developments in California and Australia. The consequent influx of bullion was described as " The Currency Extension Act of Nature," and the currency reformers who had demanded the expansion of the credit currency saw their dreams come true without any abandonment of the gold standard. The new supplies of gold arriving in England were reported to have " operated at once as the solvents of actual or prospective financial difficulties and straits which could not have been cured so effectually, or so speedily, by any other means." [4] Never-

[1] *Proceedings of the Manchester Chamber of Commerce*, 18th November, 1840.
[2] *Ibid.*, 7th October, 1847.   [3] *Ibid.*, 14th February, 1848.
[4] Tooke and Newmarch, *op. cit.*, Vol. VI, p. 203.

theless, the decennial trade crisis arrived punctually in 1857, and the Bank Charter Act of 1844 had again to be suspended, as it had been during the crisis of 1847. This inevitably reopened the question of the gold standard, and cast sus-picion upon " the wisdom of legislation which appeared to break down at the moment of greatest strain." [1]

By this time even the Manchester merchants were ready to admit that the legislation of 1844 had not completely and permanently solved the problem of banking organisation, though they were still loyal to the gold standard. In their view, the main cause of financial instability was now the policy pursued by the joint-stock banks, and they were especially suspicious of the Scottish banks. The Manchester Chamber of Commerce asked the Government to institute an inquiry into the existing monetary system, and especially into the course adopted by certain joint-stock banks ; the Manchester Commercial Association suggested that there should be an inquiry into the reasons for the suspension of the Bank Charter Act, and stated that some joint-stock banks had been forced to suspend payments because they had not confined themselves to purely banking business.[2]

Among other banking questions which presented them-selves to the Manchester merchants, as needing discussion in the light of this crisis, were (a) the abolition of Scottish bank notes, (b) the discounting of " accommodation paper " by the Scottish banks, and (c) the expansion of the issue of Bank of England notes beyond the fiduciary maximum of £14,000,000 allowed by the Bank Charter Act of 1844. The condemnation of the Scottish banking system, apparent in the first two of these points, may be accounted for by the fact that the crisis had been precipitated by the collapse of several Scottish banks ; the Western Bank of Scotland and the City of Glasgow Bank both suspended payment in November, 1857. That the abuse of " accommodation paper " was an important factor in the crisis seems clear from the Report of the Select Committee on the Bank Failures of 1857 : " We have traced a system under which extensive fictitious credits have been created by the means of Accommodation Bills and open credits, great facilities for which have been

---

[1] Gregory, op. cit., Introduction, p. xxv.
[2] Proceedings of the Manchester Chamber of Commerce, 2nd December, 1857 ; Proceedings of the Manchester Commercial Association, 27th November, 1857.

offered by the practice of the Joint-Stock Banks discounting such Bills and re-discounting them with the Bill Brokers in the London market upon the credit of the Bank alone, without reference to the quality of the bills otherwise." The third point presenting itself for further discussion in 1857, namely, the expansion of the fiduciary issue of the Bank of England, called into question the central principle of the Bank Charter Act ; but there is no evidence that the Manchester merchants wished to make any radical alteration in the settlement of 1844.

Even in Birmingham the currency " expansionists " were now apparently losing ground. The Birmingham Chamber of Commerce, after a very fitful and discontinuous existence during the 'thirties and 'forties, was re-established once more in 1855 ; and almost at once Mr. T. C. Salt moved that a sub-committee be appointed to draw up a memorial on the " present defective state of the currency." This motion was not even seconded, and a subsequent motion on the same subject was rejected by a general meeting of the Chamber ; in the end, however, Mr. Salt's pertinacity secured the appointment of a committee, under the chairmanship of Mr. R. Spooner, to report on the " present state of the monetary laws." Within a month the committee made a long report, containing no less than eighteen resolutions, which they submitted for the consideration of the Council of the Chamber. The resolutions differed from the earlier Attwoodite proposals in that they had to take account of the influx of new gold and the financial effects of the Crimean War, which was then going on ; but they reached the traditional conclusion, that " as long as gold is the only foundation of the circulation it is impossible to keep a steady and sufficient circulation." The Council, however, rejected all the main conclusions of the committee, and declared that " it is inexpedient for the Council, notwithstanding the recent exportations of gold, to recommend any immediate alteration of the existing law." Further agitation resulted in the formation of a new committee, and the rejection of its report ; but the Council was eventually persuaded to agree that " it is the incumbent duty of Parliament to take into immediate consideration the effect produced by the Acts of 1819 and 1844, with a view to calling out the energy and power of the nation." Mr. Salt attempted to re-open the question at a subsequent general meeting (31st January, 1856), " with a view to come to some practical results " ; but the Chamber decided by an overwhelming majority not to proceed further with the discussion until the subject had been brought before Parliament.

All this agitation in Birmingham took place before the crisis of 1857 developed ; after the crisis the Bank Charter Act came under fire once more, and a Birmingham deputation was appointed to confer with the Wolverhampton Chamber of Commerce ; but the Wolverhampton representatives showed a marked disinclination to support any movement savouring (however remotely) of the " Birmingham Currency School," and the idea of joint action was abandoned. The Council of the Birmingham Chamber now framed a new petition, recommending that the fiduciary issue of the Bank of England should be withdrawn, and that the Government should be authorised to create " national paper " to such an amount as it considered necessary, subject to the amount not exceeding one-fourth of the annual revenue. Round this very drastic proposal discussion raged hotly for a long time, and with a somewhat ironical result. Various amendments were moved, and were all rejected ; but when the adoption of the petition was moved, as the substantive motion, this also was rejected.[1] The Gold Standard and the Bank Charter Act, in spite of their obvious defects, had evidently been accepted by the provincial merchants as preferable to a " managed currency " dependent on the discretion of Government officials.

[1] Wright, *op. cit.*, pp. 126-31, 134-5, 144-7.

CHAPTER XIII.

INLAND TRANSPORT AND COMMUNICATIONS.

Improved facilities for transport and communications were as important in promoting the circulation of goods as the improvements in financial organisation were in assisting the circulation of capital. Developments in finance and transport underlay all the industrial and commercial progress of the eighteenth and nineteenth centuries ; and the changes in transport were certainly not less rapid or far-reaching than the changes in currency and banking. When the Manchester Chamber of Commerce was founded, in 1820, the transport system of England was still dependent on the carrier's waggon, the stage-coach, the canal barge, and the wooden sailing ship ; the railroad was still in an embryonic state, and had not yet abandoned horse-traction. By the middle of the century, the steam railway had defeated the waggon, the coach, and the canal barge in almost every department of inland traffic, while the iron steamer was steadily overhauling the wooden sailing ship in ocean transport.

During the closing decade of the eighteenth century the Manchester Commercial Society had to face a difficult problem concerning the carriage of Manchester goods to Hull ; this question became increasingly important after the French conquest of Italy, since the closing of the Mediterranean ports to English ships diverted much Manchester trade to the Baltic countries, for which Hull was the most convenient port. At that time Manchester goods were usually sent to Hull by one of two routes. One alternative was to take the goods in waggons by land to Huddersfield, put them into boats there and take them down Sir John Ramsden's canal as far as Cooper Bridge, where it joined the Calder and Hebble Navigation. The other alternative was to take the goods by land to the Sowerby or Salterhebble wharves, and there put them direct on to the Calder and Hebble Navigation. By whichever route the goods were sent to Hull, the Manchester merchants were dependent on a branch of the Aire and Calder Navigation Company; and their disputes with that Company occupy a prominent place in the minute books of the Manchester Commercial Society between 1796 and 1801.

The disputes, as was natural during that period of abnormal wartime risks, usually concerned the responsibility for damage suffered by goods whilst in transit to the ports of Hull or London. The Navigation Company contended that the merchants should either bear this responsibility themselves or allow the Company to raise the rates of freight; a test case concerning the ordinary responsibility for damage had gone against the Navigation, and the Company therefore determined to exact higher charges, by way of insurance. Early in 1796 the proprietors of the Aire and Calder Navigation gave notice that in future all merchants and shippers of goods on their vessels going from Sowerby or Salterhebble wharves were to pay 2s. 6d. per £100 *ad valorem*, in addition to the common rate of freight, unless they were willing to bear their own risks.[1] This declaration caused the Manchester Commercial Society to seek the co-operation of " the merchants of Leeds, Halifax and other places on the best mode to insure safety to the shippers "; a conference was arranged, to meet at Halifax on the 6th May, and invitations were sent to the merchants of Leeds, Halifax, Bradford, Huddersfield and Rochdale. At this conference, to which delegates were sent from Manchester, Halifax and Rochdale, a certain Richard Milnes of Dewsbury offered to undertake the carriage of goods from Sowerby, Salterhebble and Huddersfield wharves, to and from Hull, under the following conditions :

(*a*) A total subscription of £5000 was to be raised by not less than a hundred subscribers, to enable him to fit out a sufficient number of vessels to allow one vessel to depart daily from the wharves mentioned.

(*b*) Milnes was to pay 5 per cent. interest to the subscribers; out of this they were to bear one-half of the losses or damages " that might not proceed from mismanagement, misconduct, or negligence on the part of Mr. Milnes' servants or agents."

[1] *Proceedings of the Manchester Commercial Society*, 7th April, 1796.

(c) The rates of freight were to be determined at an annual meeting composed of representatives of the subscribers.

The delegates present at the Halifax conference resolved that the scheme should be accepted, provided the £5000 could be raised, and a scale of freights was agreed upon, appreciably lower than that of the Aire and Calder Navigation.

It may not be out of place to mention that Milnes was already an old enemy of the Navigation Company. As early as 1788, Richard Milnes, Humphrey Davenport and Company were advertising " a regular, expeditious and cheap convey-ance of goods, to and from Manchester and Hull, and all other places in that line, by way of Huddersfield "; [1] and the rates then quoted were the same as those proposed in 1796. This venture seems to have met with " a degree of encouragement exceeding their most sanguine expectations," and Milnes extended his ambitions to the alternative route by way of Sowerby or Salterhebble ; but in 1792 his schemes were blocked by the opposition of the Aire and Calder Navi-gation who claimed that they had " established these vessels purposely for this trade, and prior to Mr. Milnes ever keeping any himself." It is fairly clear, then, that in 1796 Milnes was using the associated bodies of merchants as reinforcements in his private battle with the Aire and Calder Navigation ; but from subsequent events it becomes equally clear that the mer-chants were using Milnes as a stalking horse in *their* resistance to the increased charges of the Company. For some time the scheme adopted at the Halifax conference in 1796 seemed to be progressing, though difficulty was encountered in raising the required capital ; but the Undertakers of the Aire and Calder Navigation had already begun to repent. Within a month, they had decided " not only to continue the carriage of goods as heretofore, but absolutely to rescind all their former resolutions respecting an indemnification for losses " : also that they would make good damages " from any cause whatever," and that their charges would be lower than those proposed by Mr. Milnes.[2]

The victory had been won too easily to be accepted immediately, and the Manchester Commercial Society decided

[1] *Manchester Mercury*, 22nd January, 1788.
[2] *Proceedings of the Manchester Commercial Society*, 21st and 25th May, 1796.

to continue its assistance to Mr. Milnes, because he had "evinced such a spirit of enterprise to serve the trade, and was solicitous to open a competition." Thereupon the Aire and Calder Navigation came promptly to heel. The representative of the Undertakers apologised for the offence given to the Manchester merchants by the proposal to increase the rates of freight ; the proposal had been made (he said) merely to appease the wealthy proprietors, who were either members of Parliament or permanently resident in London. The merchants of Leeds and Wakefield had voluntarily agreed to pay increased rates if the proprietors of the Navigation would bear all risks, and the proprietors had therefore felt justified in proposing similar terms to the merchants of Manchester, Rochdale and Halifax. Twelve years earlier, the Undertakers had "built new stout sloops for the better conveyance of goods from Selby to Hull, and the days of loading at Leeds, Sowerby and Salterhebble were so contrived that the boats generally met at the same point at Selby, where they were sure of meeting one or more of the sloops," which then carried the goods on to Hull. This "perfect arrangement," however, had been upset when part of the Manchester goods began to go by way of Huddersfield ; the Sowerby boats were thus deprived of part of their expected loads, and had to make up the cargo with paving-stone from various quarries, which caused delay and confusion. Since it had been suggested that goods would go through to Hull more quickly in vessels which did not stop at Selby, the proprietors had built twelve new boats for that purpose ; these were for the use of the merchants of Leeds, but the Undertakers were willing, if necessary, to have some more built for the trade of Manchester.

The victory now seemed as complete as could be expected ; the Manchester Commercial Society therefore replied that the terms offered by the Undertakers would be acceded to, and that the Society recommended "the quickest despatch in the conveyance of goods as being the certain means of insuring a preference." Mr. Richard Milnes, it is true, still troubled the Undertakers by circulating handbills concerning his agreement with the merchants of Manchester, Rochdale and Halifax ; but there can be little doubt that the merchants, having achieved their purpose, had now thrown him and his schemes overboard.

The battle, however, was not yet over. In September,

1796, the owners of all ships employed in coasting and inland navigation met at Hull and announced their intention of petitioning Parliament that they might not have to make good any damages incurred by merchandise in process of conveyance ; in this application they were supported by the proprietors of canals and the carriers on land.[1] The petition was followed up in a Ship Owners' Relief Bill, which was successfully opposed by a combination of the merchants of Manchester, Leeds, Birmingham, Halifax, Huddersfield, Wakefield, Nottingham, Norwich, and even Grantham ; but in the following year (1797) a second Ship Owners' Relief Bill was promoted, which contained proposals " inconsistent with the safety of trade, exorbitant in their demands, and impracticable in their execution." To meet this new attack the associated merchants of the Lancashire and Yorkshire industrial towns proposed to form themselves into a company for the conveyance of their own goods to Hull, along the lines laid down by Mr. Milnes in 1796 ; but the same difficulty was encountered in raising the necessary capital by voluntary subscriptions, and the scheme had to be abandoned, though Mr. Milnes was told that this need not deter him from going forward with his plan on his own account. [2]

Eventually the Ship Owners' Relief Bill passed into law, with some modifications. In July, 1798, the proprietors of the Aire and Calder Navigation decided that the merchants of Manchester, Leeds, Wakefield, Halifax, Huddersfield, Bradford and Rochdale should be invited to send delegates to a joint conference on the question of responsibility for damages to goods. " Since, at the present time, the Undertakers were responsible for damages occasioned by one cause, and the owners of goods for damages by another cause, there would be frequent need for litigation. It would be better, therefore, if the shipowners were made wholly responsible (and receive an additional premium in consequence) or the owners of goods be wholly responsible (in which case the Undertakers should receive a reasonable reward for carriage only). The owners of goods would probably prefer the former alternative." [3] Thus the shipowners, after all, had put the merchants into an untenable position, and were

[1] *Proceedings of the Manchester Commercial Society*, 13th October, 1796.
[2] *Ibid.*, 2nd and 30th November, 1797, and 5th January, 1798.
[3] *Ibid.*, 25th July, 1798.

able to enforce their demands for increased rates of freight. Considering the upward course of prices and wages in general, between 1793 and 1798, the merchants might think themselves lucky to have staved off the increase of freight charges for so long.

Soon other causes of friction arose between the Manchester merchants and the Undertakers of the Aire and Calder Navigation. At the beginning of the French wars there was no water transport between Manchester and Sowerby, and the land carriage between the two places cost nearly as much as the water carriage over the much longer distance from Sowerby to Hull. To remedy this defect, the Rochdale Canal from Sowerby Bridge to Manchester was projected, and the scheme received parliamentary sanction in 1794. During the next few years the cutting of the canal went on slowly, and in the spring of 1798 it cannot yet have been in operation even as far as Rochdale ; for in April of that year the persistent Mr. Milnes was propounding to the Manchester Commercial Society a scheme for carrying goods to and from Sowerby Wharf and Rochdale, " as soon as that canal shall be opened." [1] In 1800 the canal was still uncompleted,[2] but it was by that time in operation as far as Rochdale, using the vessels of the Aire and Calder Navigation. From this situation arose complaints of partiality and unfair preference. The Rochdale Canal Committee depended chiefly on the patronage of the Manchester merchants ; the Aire and Calder Navigation, on the other hand, was more closely dependent on the Yorkshire merchants, and therefore tended to give Yorkshire goods preferential treatment.

In December, 1800, the Manchester Commercial Society called a meeting of all persons concerned in forwarding goods to Hull, to consider " the delays and inconveniences that have lately arisen in that trade." It was alleged that " an extraordinary preference had been given, and great partiality exercised in this mode of conveyance, which calls aloud for immediate correction and redress." Complaint was made to Dr. Drake, the Chairman of the Rochdale Canal Committee, who replied in due course that he had recently written to those in charge of the Aire and Calder Navigation, asking for more vessels, and also requesting that they should start from Rochdale at stated times. The

---

[1] *Proceedings of the Manchester Commercial Society,* 5th April, 1798.
[2] It was not completed and formally opened until 1804.

proprietors of the Navigation, however, refused both requests, and openly stated that they would not discontinue the granting of preferential treatment to the goods of their own friends. Thereupon the Rochdale Canal Committee obtained vessels of their own, and announced that these would leave Rochdale regularly every Tuesday and Friday; the Manchester merchants were thus left with the comparatively simple task of arranging for the conveyance of their goods by land from Manchester to Rochdale. To this solution of the problem the Manchester Commercial Society gave its friendly support, and went further by appointing its own agents at Hull.[1]

Such squabbles about the provision of an adequate service of canal boats may seem curiously remote from the transport problems, not merely of the twentieth century, but even of Victorian times; yet, in fact, disputes between the Manchester merchants and the proprietors of the Aire and Calder Navigation still went on during the earlier nineteenth century. The project for a new canal between Wakefield and Ferrybridge, which received the support of the Manchester Chamber of Commerce in 1827, was intended to cheapen and quicken the carriage of goods between Manchester and Hull by cutting across part of the Aire and Calder Navigation. According to the draft petition of the Manchester Chamber, " by this intended Canal the distance will be reduced seven miles in a space of nineteen miles, which is the length of the present navigation of the rivers Aire and Calder. In addition to this, the navigation will not be subject to those impediments and hindrances which are always experienced on river navigation, liable to floods and shoals. Besides this, it is contemplated that the rate of tonnage will be reduced 2s. 3d. per ton." [2] The advantages of the project were further explained in a letter to the *Manchester Mercury* a few weeks later. Manchester already had two lines of water communication with Wakefield, one by Ashton-under-Lyne and the other by Rochdale. " Both these will equally communicate with the intended canal, and form by much the shortest and most convenient route for all goods to and from Germany, the Netherlands and the Baltic. The proposed

---

[1] *Manchester Mercury*, 20th January, 1801 ; *Proceedings of the Manchester Commercial Society*, 24th January, 1801.

[2] *Proceedings of the Manchester Chamber of Commerce*, 31st January, 1827.

canal will not only shorten the absolute distance but also take away some considerable inconvenience in the present river navigation, the causes of frequent and often of serious delays. It will also diminish the direct as well as the indirect expense, as the projectors of this canal propose to take a less toll by nearly one-half on bale goods than is paid on the present navigation. Besides, as vessels capable of going to any European port will be enabled to come up to Wakefield, the goods may be laid on there for their destined port and proceed thither without any change of bottom." [1]

Lord Milton, in moving the second reading of the Wakefield and Ferrybridge Canal Bill in the House of Commons, declared that "the only objection made against the bill was on the part of those ladies and gentlemen who held shares in the Aire and Calder Canal, and who thought that this rival establishment would be injurious to their interests." [2] To this it was replied that the undertaking was unnecessary, as the proprietors of the Aire and Calder were preparing to effect improvements by which all the objects proposed by the new canal would be obtained ; on this understanding, the bill was rejected by a narrow margin on the second reading. In defence of the Aire and Calder Navigation, it may be pointed out that the Undertakers had just completed (in 1826) the making of a new " cut " from Knottingley, to communicate with the river Ouse near Goole, with two collateral branches. On the defeat of the Wakefield and Ferrybridge project, the Undertakers of the Aire and Calder called in Mr. Telford, who made a survey and estimate for shortening the navigation between Wakefield and Ferrybridge, and also between Leeds and Castleford. It was estimated that when the proposed improvements had been made, " the depth of the water will be sufficient to admit vessels of one hundred tons burthen up to the towns of Leeds and Wakefield, and will enable vessels from Leeds and Wakefield to reach Goole in eight hours, and from Manchester within forty-five hours." [3] No strong parliamentary opposition to the projected improvements was encountered, and Baring probably reflected a general opinion when he declared in favour of the Aire and Calder Navigation as

---

[1] *Manchester Mercury*, 21st February, 1827.
[2] *Ibid.*, 20th March, 1827.
[3] Priestley, *Historical Account of the Navigable Rivers, Canals, and Railways of Great Britain*, 1831, pp. 17-18.

being the most important piece of inland navigation in the country and at the same time the worst. If the Company would make a good navigation (he said) they had a right to the preference in consideration of their long standing.

By that time (1828), the shadow of the steam railway was beginning to loom over the canal companies ; it is, indeed, a little surprising that the Manchester merchants should have attached so much importance to the improvement of their water communication eastwards, since they were already pinning their hopes of improved communication westwards, to Liverpool, upon the iron rail and the steam locomotive. It was not yet generally realised, however, that the steam railway would transform the inland transport of the country during the next generation ; in the post-war period, extensions of the canal system were still being made or projected, even on the Liverpool-Manchester line. In 1820 the opening of the Wigan and Leigh branch canal established a new link between the Duke of Bridgewater's Canal and the Leeds and Liverpool system.[1] The utility of the Bridgewater Canal was increased in 1821 by a reduction in the charge for the carriage of cotton to 3s. 4d. per ton, a fall of nearly 20 per cent. ; this concession applied to the carriage of all cotton on the Duke's canal and on the river Mersey to or from Liverpool.[2]

The times were almost ripe, however, for much more radical changes than these, in the inland transport system of the country. Just as Telford and his employers were conceiving that Wakefield might be made the starting-point for ships taking the trade of the West Riding to continental ports, so on the other side of the Pennines a scheme was already on foot for giving Manchester direct access to the sea by means of a ship canal. In 1825 it was proposed to cut a ship canal from Manchester to the mouth of the Dee, " thus obviating the necessity for canals and narrow rivers to convey our manufactures to Liverpool, by bringing our own ships and those of the foreigner at once to the centre of Manchester " ;[3] but the project failed to obtain parliamentary sanction, and Manchester had to wait over another half-century for her Ship Canal.

[1] See the *Manchester Observer*, 30th December, 1820.
[2] *Manchester Chronicle*, 24th October, 1821.
[3] Wheeler, *Manchester*, 1836, p. 279.

One reason why the ship canal project was not pressed further, in 1825, was that " the rival scheme of a railway superseded the desire and the necessity for this artificial inland ocean." In October, 1824, a prospectus had been published for the construction of a double railway between Liverpool and Manchester, and in February of the following year the subscribers secured leave to bring in a parliamentary Bill. The hundred and fifty merchants of Liverpool who promoted the scheme complained that they had " for a long time past experienced great difficulty in obtaining vessels to convey goods from this place to Manchester, and that . . . a new line of conveyance had become absolutely necessary to conduct the increasing trade of the country with speed, certainty, and economy." [1] A supporting petition sent to Parliament by the Manchester Chamber of Commerce in February, 1825, declared

> " That the merchandise requiring to be conveyed between Manchester and Liverpool has for a long series of years increased, and is still increasing.
> " That the delays and inconveniences of the present modes of conveyance have been seriously felt for some time past.
> " That the projected railroad will be a great benefit to Manchester and district because it will be shorter, more certain, quicker.
> " That the undertaking has long been under consideration, is totally unconnected with any of the recent schemes of a similar nature, and is under the management of gentlemen deserving the fullest confidence." [2]

It is hardly necessary to recount the struggles and tribulations of the " Liverpool and Manchester Railroad Company," from its first (and unsuccessful) Bill in 1825 to the triumphal (but tragic) opening of the Liverpool and Manchester Railway in 1830. [3] It may not be out of place, however, to notice that the first committee formed to promote the railway included H. H. Birley, Thomas Sharp, William Garnett, and Peter Ewart, who were all Directors

[1] Wheeler, *Manchester*, 1836, p. 280.
[2] *Proceedings of the Manchester Chamber of Commerce*, 23rd February, 1825.
[3] For a recent account see G. S. Veitch, *The Struggle for the Liverpool and Manchester Railway*, 1930.

of the Manchester Chamber of Commerce ; and the Manchester merchants were equally represented on the later committees by " gentlemen deserving the fullest confidence."

After 1830 the Manchester Chamber paid little attention to the canal system, except as an alternative means of communication which might prove useful in case the new railways broke down or became extortionate ; questions concerning railway amalgamations soon replaced disputes about canal charges, and the old fear of monopolistic practices gradually reappeared in a new form. At first the Manchester merchants were too grateful to the railways, for having delivered them from the clutches of the canal companies, to be actively hostile to the amalgamation schemes. Later on they began to realise that the railways (if they got the chance) might become as monopolistic in policy as the old canal companies had been ; but even in the 'forties and 'fifties, the Manchester Chamber of Commerce tended on railway questions to reflect the veering currents of popular opinion (or perhaps the particular interests of its members) rather than to make a bold stand on general economic principles. In 1837, when a critical stage had been reached in the negotiations for the amalgamation of the Manchester, Staffordshire and Cheshire Railway with the South Union line, the Manchester Chamber of Commerce intervened in order to facilitate the amalgamation ; [1] though the effect of the amalgamation was to reduce competition. By 1845, however, the Board of the Chamber had become definitely hostile to the larger amalgamations which were being carried through under the guidance of such men as Mr. George Hudson, the " Railway King " who had brought about the formation of the Midland Railway in 1844. In a petition presented to Parliament in June, 1845, the Chamber of Commerce expressed the view that the North Union Railway (from Warrington to Preston) must remain independent, in order to safeguard the development of Fleetwood, a rapidly growing port which must not be injured by being delivered into the power of hostile railway interests. In support of this view the petitioners asked why two companies, each paying dividends of 10 per cent., should wish to amalgamate with one paying only $6\frac{3}{4}$ per cent., and suggested that the

[1] *Proceedings of the Manchester Chamber of Commerce,* 13th February, 1837 ; 1st and 8th March, 1837 ; and 12th February, 1838.

motive underlying the amalgamation might well be monopolistic.[1]

In its ensuing Annual Report, the Board of the Chamber
had to confess that its protests had been disregarded, and
that its fears had been groundless ; the amalgamation had
been carried through, and no evil consequences had followed.[2]
Nevertheless, the Manchester merchants still felt that railway
speculation was assuming an unhealthy character, and called
for authoritative control. A petition presented by the
Chamber of Commerce in April, 1846, suggested that some
limitation should be placed on the number of bills for new
railway projects. The petitioners agreed that the railways
were conferring great benefits on the country, but contended
that they should not be allowed to cause an orgy of
wild speculation. A continued drain of capital into railroad construction would mean dearer money for industry,
which would suffer from lack of credit ; moreover, the unprecedented increase in the number of railway projects would
raise constructional costs.[3]

The forebodings of the Manchester merchants were very
quickly justified ; the railway mania came to a head in
1846 and then collapsed, leaving many thousands of shareholders to pay successive calls of capital to companies which
were never likely to pay dividends. After the crisis the
Manchester Chamber of Commerce once more attempted to
ease the situation by asking the Railway Commissioners to
extend the limits within which the calls had to be paid up,
and to give wider facilities to companies wishing to go into
voluntary liquidation.[4] It was now no longer necessary to
place restrictions on the number of new railway projects ;
the financial crisis had killed the public's desire for further
investment.[5]

Thereafter, the railway questions discussed by the Manchester merchants tended for some years to be of a minor
(not to say niggling) character. A typical case of this kind
concerned the curious fact, noticed in 1853, that the first-
class fares between Manchester and Littleborough had been
altered four times within a few months ; it is possible to
feel some sympathy with the harassed railway representative
who, when his attention was drawn to the matter, replied,

[1] *Proceedings of the Manchester Chamber of Commerce*, 18th July, 1845.
[2] *Ibid.*, 9th February, 1846.   [3] *Ibid.*, 18th April, 1846.
[4] *Ibid.*, 21st October, 1847.   [5] *Ibid.*, 14th February, 1848.

" I suppose you want me to alter them a fifth time." [1]   One more railway question of the 'fifties may be noticed, because it aroused echoes of the old canal disputes of the eighteenth century, and showed the realignment of interests brought about by the development of railways.   In 1856 the Rochdale Canal Company leased its line of navigation for twenty-one years to four associated railway companies.   The scheme was denounced as monopolistic by the Duke of Bridgewater's Trustees and the Aire and Calder Navigation Company, and its legality was disputed.   The Manchester Chamber of Commerce did not at first feel justified in taking action, but eventually decided to support its ancient enemies in their opposition to the scheme of its former ally.   In a memorial presented to the Board of Trade, the Chamber declared that the leasing of the Rochdale Canal Company's tolls would " place the bulk of the enormous traffic between this city and the Humber and the contiguous Eastern counties under great disadvantages," for the following reasons : (i) the Rochdale Canal was the most important link in the system of waterways connecting Manchester with the East Coast ; (ii) competition between the waterways and the railways had hitherto secured moderate rates of carriage ; (iii) " besides the import of raw materials and the export of manufactures over the German Ocean, Manchester has to import the food of its people, and in the cost of wheat, cattle and potatoes from Yorkshire and Lincolnshire carriage forms an important item " ; (iv) whilst recent parliamentary tariffs had generally fixed carriage by rail or water at 1d. per ton per mile, the Rochdale Canal had statutory authority to charge a toll of 4d. per ton per mile, " a power which the railways will acquire under the Lease " ; (v) the only other means of conveyance by waterways, from Manchester to the East Coast, was by canals too narrow for heavy traffic. [2]   The Chamber of Commerce therefore urged that a limitation should be placed upon the tolls to be levied by the railway companies ; the modesty of the request suggests that the railway companies had already gained an almost monopolistic control over the inland transport of the country.

In questions affecting inland water transport, Manchester had during the preceding generation been more deeply interested in the navigation of the Mersey than in the

---

[1] *Proceedings of the Manchester Chamber of Commerce*, 14th February, 1853.   [2] *Ibid.*, 6th and 13th March, 1856.

maintenance of the canal system. Even in disputes concerning the Mersey, railway developments affected the questions at issue, though the main struggle formed part of the protracted conflict between Manchester and Liverpool concerning the just apportionment of control over the Mersey navigation and docks. The railways threatened to hinder the navigation of the river by building bridges over it. This may strike the modern mind as a frivolous ground of complaint, and it is possible that the ostensible objection was in some cases not the real motive underlying the opposition ; but it must be remembered that in those days the steamer had not yet completely ousted the sailing vessel, even in river navigation.

An early instance of difficulties arising from the building of railway bridges occurred in 1838, when the Manchester Chamber of Commerce petitioned against the proposed con-struction of a railway over the Mersey at Fidler's Ferry (below Warrington). It was argued that a railway bridge there would greatly hinder the passage of many vessels trading to Bank Quay, whilst such a bridge would also prevent the improvement of the river navigation to give vessels of two hundred tons direct access to Manchester.[1] Substantially the same question was raised again in 1845, when the Chamber of Commerce protested against the con-struction of a bridge over the Mersey at Warrington, to make a deviation in the Grand Junction Railway.[2] Such a bridge (it was asserted) would prevent ships with sails from coming up the river, and would thus strengthen the monopolistic position of the railway ; it was possible, also, that the piers of the bridge would cause the formation of sandbanks in the river bed. Once more the appeal was successful ; but in the succeeding year the Grand Junction Railway circum-vented the opposition by securing powers to build its bridge lower down the river at Runcorn. The Manchester merchants petitioned the House of Commons against the new proposals, and memorialised the Mersey Conservators ; but in 1846 Parliament was not disposed to scrutinise new railway bills very closely, and the protests were disregarded.

If the importance of the Mersey was to be thus threatened, there was all the more reason why Manchester should have an adequate share in the control and protection of the river navigation. That this was not an entirely new issue may

---

[1] *Proceedings of the Manchester Chamber of Commerce*, 21st and 28th February, 1838.   [2] *Ibid.*, 30th January, 1845.

be seen from the objections raised by the Manchester Chamber of Commerce to the Mersey Conservancy Bill of 1837. In general terms, the Manchester merchants considered that the Bill contained provisions which would be prejudicial to all the trade of the river, but especially to the trade of Manchester, that many of the Bill's clauses were unjust in principle, and that they would prevent the free use of the Mersey tidal waters.   A more particular grievance was expressed in petitions presented by the Manchester Chamber of Commerce while the Bill was before the House of Commons. The petitioners strongly opposed the placing of the conservancy of the Mersey in the hands of twenty Commissioners, twelve of whom were to be chosen by the Liverpool Corporation. The Mersey was so important to the well-being of Manchester and district that the controlling authority should be chosen more equitably ; in particular, Manchester should be better represented, since its raw materials and food supplies from Ireland and Scotland entered by the tidal waters of the Mersey, whilst its manufactured goods left the country by the same channel.[1]

The form of this complaint changed within the next few months, but its substance remained the same. It was now proposed that control should be vested in ten Commissioners, of whom Liverpool should choose eight, whilst the Borough-reeves of Manchester and Salford should choose one each ; to this the Manchester merchants replied that Liverpool should choose five, whilst Manchester and Salford chose the other five, conjointly. The choice of Commissioners to be made by the Liverpool Corporation and Dock Company should not be confined to members of those bodies ; whilst the Manchester and Salford Commissioners were to be chosen by the Borough Magistrates, or by the Town Council of Manchester whenever the town should become incorporated, and in the meantime by the local Police Commissioners. The expenses of the conservancy should be paid from a separate fund levied on the general trade of the Mersey ; the conservancy, moreover, should not cease at Warrington Bridge, but should extend as far as the Mersey was navigable.[2] Objections of this scope and character amounted to a general denunciation of the Bill, and in due course the measure

---

[1] *Proceedings of the Manchester Chamber of Commerce*, 15th, 22nd and 29th March, 1837.   [2] *Ibid.*, 10th May, 1837.

was withdrawn; but the battle between Liverpool and Manchester was thereby merely adjourned, not terminated.

There were doubtless very definite financial reasons why Manchester found it necessary to claim a larger share in the control of the Mersey navigation. The Board of the Manchester Chamber declared (22nd March, 1837) that the dock and town dues levied at Liverpool were excessive and ought to be reduced; while one of the Chamber's objections to the Mersey Bill was that it would legalise the exaction of dock and town dues upon all vessels passing Liverpool and sailing up the Mersey, even though they had not entered the Liverpool docks. Further action against excessive charges at Liverpool was taken in 1840, when the Manchester Chamber of Commerce petitioned that increased dues should not be levied on ships which went up the Mersey without using the docks. It was agreed that improvements had recently been made, and that these should be paid for; but the anchorage and lighting dues were sufficient for this.[1] It was proposed that the Mersey, from Black Rock to Warrington and Frodsham Bridges, should be free from the Liverpool dock dues; but modified charges were to be made for conservancy, lights, buoys and telegraph, while full rates were to be charged for actual use of the docks.[2] During the next two years much correspondence went on concerning the Liverpool Dock Bill and the Mersey Conservancy Bill, with many proposals and counter-proposals, before the matter was temporarily settled by the passage of the Bills in 1842; apparently the proposals as finally passed were without serious prejudicial effects upon Manchester trade, for in 1848 the Board of the Chamber of Commerce declined to re-open the question.[3]

Within a year, however, the question had presented itself once more in a new form; and Liverpool was now divided against herself. The Dock Committee, at that time, consisted of twenty-one members, of whom eight were chosen by the dock ratepayers of £10 or over, and the remaining thirteen by the Liverpool Corporation, which also nominated the Chairman and had the right to veto any act of the Dock Committee. The question of rating the docks for parochial purposes had been discussed in Liverpool for some years, and in 1849 the parish authorities brought in a parliamentary

---

[1] *Proceedings of the Manchester Chamber of Commerce*, 20th May, 1840.
[2] *Ibid.*, 3rd June, 1840.   [3] *Ibid.*, 27th April, 1848.

bill for that purpose ; the Corporation, although it did not appear openly in the matter, agreed to pay half of the expenses incurred, and exercised its right of veto when the Dock Committee decided to oppose the bill. The proposals of the parish authorities were, however, effectively combated on their merits, and the bill had to be abandoned ; but its object continued to be pursued by less direct means. Willingness to rate the docks for parochial purposes became a test of fitness for election to the Town Council, and subsequently in the Corporation's choice of Dock Commissioners ; it therefore seemed only a matter of time before the Dock Committee itself would be converted into a " prorating " body.

To avert this danger the American Chamber of Commerce at Liverpool introduced a parliamentary bill in 1851, for the purpose of changing the constitution of the Liverpool Dock Trust, in such a way as to diminish the powers of the Town Council and to give a preponderant influence in the election of Dock Commissioners to the payers of dock rates. The Corporation naturally opposed the bill, and moved for the insertion of a clause empowering the Dock Committee to levy rates for parochial purposes ; but, with the active co-operation of the Manchester Chamber of Commerce, the promoters of the bill secured the rejection of the rating clause. To decide on the general merits of the bill itself was a more difficult task, " inasmuch as that measure only contemplated a transference of the powers to elect a majority of the Dock Commissioners out of the dock ratepayers, still leaving considerable power to the Corporation, whereas this chamber, in its memorial to the Board of Trade . . . advocated a larger principle, viz., that the dock trust at Liverpool ought to be a national trust and should be managed for national purposes only, free from all control by the municipal authorities of the town." [1]   In the end, however, the Manchester Chamber decided to support the bill, and a compromise was arrived at by which the Liverpool Corporation withdrew its opposition ; the Act as passed [2] provided that the Liverpool Dock Board should consist of twenty-four members, twelve elected by the payers of dock rates and twelve by the Liverpool Corporation.

[1] *Proceedings of the Manchester Chamber of Commerce,* 13th March, 1851.   [2] 14 & 15 Vict. c. 64.

Further friction arose in 1854, when the Liverpool Corporation sought power to borrow £3,500,000 to be expended in the construction of docks, and £1,000,000 for the construction of warehouses, on the security of the town dues ; this, from the peculiar nature of the Liverpool town dues, at once re-opened the whole question of the Dock Commission. The Manchester Chamber of Commerce sent up an indignant petition to protest :

> " That your petitioners have just heard of a Bill
> entitled ' Liverpool Improvement Bill ' which has been
> introduced into your Honourable House and, after being
> carried with unusual haste and secrecy through a second
> reading, is now before a Select Committee. That your
> petitioners are surprised to learn that this Bill contains
> a provision by which the Corporation of Liverpool seeks
> for power to mortgage that portion of its income, usually
> known as Town Dues, as security for money to be bor-
> rowed for its own use. That the said Town Dues are
> chiefly levied upon imports and exports passing *in
> transitu*, the town itself contributing to these in a very
> small degree : that they form a very grievous tax on
> the commerce of this country, which has long been a
> source of complaint not only in respect of the amount
> it produces . . . but from the most unjust manner in
> which it is levied, the freemen of certain boroughs being
> exempt. The area over which the Corporation of
> Liverpool exercises the levying of these dues is extended
> beyond that which they [the petitioners] think com-
> patible with the interests of the interior or the rights
> of the Crown, inasmuch as a local body overrides an
> estuary of the sea, and enforces payment of money dues
> over many miles of the inland course of the Mersey
> on merchandise which merely passes by and makes no
> use of the town." [1]

Similar petitions were presented in 1855 by both the Manchester Chamber of Commerce and the Manchester Commercial Association,[2] and in the end the amount which the Liverpool Corporation was authorised to borrow was cut down to £850,000.

---

[1] *Proceedings of the Manchester Chamber of Commerce*, 22nd March, 1854.
[2] Both petitions were sent on the same date, 7th February, 1855.

On the wider issue a Royal Commission had already recommended that the docks and harbours should be put in charge of a new body, to which all dues should be transferred, and that the town dues should no longer be applied in payment of interest on any debts not contracted for strictly harbour purposes ; such corporate debts should in future be a charge upon the inhabitants. In 1856 a government bill embodying these recommendations was introduced, but encountered such serious opposition that it was withdrawn. Eventually, however, a further bill for the transference of the Liverpool dock estates to an entirely new body of trustees was promoted, with the co-operation of the Manchester Chamber of Commerce, the Manchester Commercial Association, and the Great Western Railway Company.[1] The bill was referred to a Select Committee, and it was decided that in future there should be twenty-eight trustees, of whom twenty-four were to be nominated by the dock ratepayers of £10 yearly in dues (the persons elected to be payers of £25 yearly), while the remaining four trustees were to be nominated by the Commissioners of the Conservancy of the Mersey. The town dues were to go to the new trustees, who were to assume responsibility for £600,000 of the Corporation debt. The bill passed without difficulty through the Commons, and opposition in the Lords was bought off by an agreement to pay £1,500,000 to the Corporation of Liverpool as compensation for the loss of the town dues. This amicable settlement of the long dispute might be claimed not only as a victory for the organised efforts of the Manchester and Liverpool merchants but as an act of wise statesmanship for the more efficient administration of an important national waterway.

[1] *Proceedings of the Manchester Chamber of Commerce,* 29th December, 1856 ; *Proceedings of the Manchester Commercial Association,* 27th December, 1856.

CHAPTER XIV.

POSTAL SERVICES AND STEAM NAVIGATION.

To a progressive business community like Manchester, efficient postal services were almost as important as the efficient carriage of goods. The improvement of the postal services during the earlier nineteenth century was partly dependent on the contemporaneous changes in transport ; conversely, the primary aim of the Manchester merchants in encouraging the development of new means of transport was very often to secure an improvemnet of the postal services. This was especially so in the case of steam navigation ; for the steamship became important as a mail carrier long before it developed into a really serious rival of the sailing ship on the longer oceanic routes. The improvement of the postal services was not, however, exclusively dependent on the development of new means of transport ; the provincial merchants had also to work continuously for the reform of Post Office routine and organisation, which (even in those days) tended to lag far behind the business methods of commercial firms which were urged on by the spur of competition.

The antiquated organisation of the Post Office at the end of the eighteenth century may be seen reflected in the correspondence concerning the attempt of the Manchester merchants, in 1796, to obtain the more efficient transmission of any foreign mails which arrived in London on Saturday evenings. If such mails arrived in London too late for the Saturday mail coach, they were not sent off until Monday evening, and were not delivered to the Manchester business houses until Wednesday morning ; it was therefore suggested to the Postmaster-General that such mails should be dispatched from London by mail coach on Sunday evening. Among other reasons advanced by the Postmaster-General, in justification of his refusal to grant this application, it was pointed out that (a) if this request was complied with, similar concessions would be demanded by all the other northern towns; (*b*) this would probably lead to a daily post, to which there was not only official opposition, *but also the opposition of the London merchants;* (*c*) the change demanded would cause a considerable increase in expenditure : the clerks of the Inland Office would demand an increase in salary if they had to wait for the boats coming in, the expenditure on mail coaches would be increased, and an addition to the salary of the country postmasters would have to be granted. These do not seem very substantial reasons for giving the London merchants two days' start of the Manchester merchants in dealing with foreign inquiries and orders ; it is only fair to state, however, that the foreign mail failed to catch the Saturday mail coach only about once in twelve months.

Similar complaints about the delay in forwarding foreign mails from London to Manchester were still being made in 1825. A petition from the Manchester Chamber of Commerce [1] stated that letters from the Continent arriving in London after 2 p.m. were not sent on until the following day ; and that this delay was a serious injury to Manchester trade, especially if it happened on a Saturday, because in that case the foreign letters did not arrive in Manchester until Tuesday evening, " after the great market day for the sale of manufactures is over." In this respect, then, Post Office methods had not altered very markedly since 1796 ; in some other respects, however, the persistent agitation of the provincial merchants had in the post-war period resulted in substantial reforms. In 1821, for the first time, letters began to be delivered by letter-carriers, throughout Manchester and Salford, immediately after the arrival of the mail-coach from London. [2] By this arrangement the letters could be answered the same night, the post remaining open free until 10 p.m. In addition, there was a " late fee " dispatch, for which letters were received until 11 p.m. on special payment of a penny each, and until 7.45 a.m. on payment of sixpence each.

The local penny post was also made more readily available to the public at this time ; letters posted in Manchester before 5.30 p.m. were to be delivered in Manchester the same night, along with the letters from London. Further improvement in the local penny post was secured five years

[1] *Proceedings of the Manchester Chamber of Commerce,* 13th July, 1825.
[2] *Manchester Chronicle,* 6th October, 1821.

later. In 1826 the Manchester Chamber of Commerce pointed out to the Postmaster-General that, although Manchester and Salford had enjoyed the privilege of a local penny post since 1793, the boundaries within which penny letters were delivered free of charge had not been enlarged since 1795.[1] Since that time Manchester and Salford had grown enormously, and the area covered by the penny post had become quite inadequate ; at Liverpool, in similar circumstances, the Post Office authorities had enlarged the boundaries, and there seemed no reason why the same concession should not be made to Manchester. A plan marked with the wider boundaries recommended by the Chamber of Commerce was submitted to the Postmaster-General ; and before the end of the year the extended service had been put into operation.[2]

The Chamber of Commerce had less immediate success in its campaign against the double postage charged on merchants' accounts, invoices, bills of exchange, and bills of lading. This type of letter had been exempt from the ordinary postage rates until the later eighteenth century, and even until the end of the century had been exempt if included in the foreign mail. In 1801, however, this exemption had been swept away, and it had been provided that " all merchants' accounts, bills of exchange, invoices and bills of lading whatever, shall be rated, taxed, and paid for as so many several letters, or by the ounce, according to the respective rates by this Act made payable on letters and packets conveyed by the General Post." [3] This left some uncertainty as to the methods by which the letters were to be classified and the charges made ; and there can be no doubt that in many cases the action taken by the Post Office was arbitrary and inconsistent. In 1822 the Manchester Chamber of Commerce requested " to know the rules by which the Post Office is determined in charging single or double postage on foreign letters," and submitted a test case in which double postage had been charged without apparent justification.[4] Two years later the complaint was carried further in a memorial to the Chancellor of the Exchequer. The merchants objected to the system introduced in 1801, on the ground that it was impossible in many cases to ascertain how the letters ought

---

[1] *Proceedings of the Manchester Chamber of Commerce*, 2nd August 1826.
[2] *Ibid.*, 2nd September and 1st November, 1826.
[3] See *ibid.*, 25th February, 1824.
[4] *Ibid.*, 1st and 25th May, 1822.

to be charged, without opening them and thereby infringing the privacy of business communications. To avoid this, many merchants preferred to allow their letters to be overcharged, or sent their letters by private conveyance, thus diminishing the public revenue and interrupting the regularity of commercial correspondence. The remedy was (according to the memorial) a return to " the old and common-sense practice of regarding all single sheets of paper, not exceeding a certain size or weight, as single letters." The Chancellor of the Exchequer could promise no immediate relief, however, and held out only the vague hope that the grievance might be redressed in the future, " if the revenue should continue prosperous." [1]

In general, the Manchester merchants supported any suggestion for additional, quicker, or more direct mails; and in a period when the transport system of the country was being rapidly transformed such suggestions were inevitably numerous. A retrograde proposal, in 1822, to restrict the communication between Liverpool and Manchester to one mail a day called for especially energetic action. The Manchester Chamber of Commerce promptly complained that this would be unjust, since Liverpool merchants would be enabled to transmit foreign bills of exchange to London one or two days before Manchester merchants could. Moreover, the restriction would retard the circulation of commercial information, and would diminish the public revenue, since there would be a reduction in the volume of commercial correspondence and many letters would be sent by other channels. It is satisfactory to record that the memorial achieved its object, and that the proposed restriction of the mails was not made.[2] A similar grievance of commercial loss arising from postal delay was disclosed in the proposals of 1820 and 1821 that the mails between Lancashire and East Anglia should be direct and not circuitous. This grievance was especially felt in the case of letters for the continental mail from Harwich ; such letters, instead of going to Harwich direct from the north, had to travel round by London and catch a later boat. In 1820 a simple remedy was found by arranging that all the various mails from the north should be collected into one, which would leave

---

[1] *Proceedings of the Manchester Chamber of Commerce*, 25th February, 1824, and 4th Annual Report, 14th February, 1825.
[2] *Ibid.*, 22nd May and 5th June, 1822.

Birmingham at noon, picking up the mails from Manchester, Leeds and other northern industrial towns, and go direct to Harwich. It was claimed that this arrangement meant a saving of three days in transmission to the Continent ; yet apparently the Lancashire mail for Norfolk still continued to go round by London.[1]

Such efforts to secure quicker, cheaper and more efficient postal services went on all through the earlier nineteenth century, and are doubtless still necessary ; substantially the same questions often arise at different periods, in different circumstances, and in different forms. Thus the earlier movements for an extension of the local penny post, and against the uncertainties of the double postage on commercial letters, culminated before the end of the 'thirties in the movement for a uniform penny post throughout the country. In 1838 the Manchester Chamber of Commerce was very active in advocating the reduction of the postage rates ; the existing rates were declared to be not only unjust and excessive but also " injurious to the social happiness of the people," and whole-hearted support was given to the plan of reform put forward by Rowland Hill.[2] The parliamentary committee which inquired into the subject reported in favour of a uniform twopenny post, but this suggestion of compromise was by no means acceptable to merchants who had enjoyed the privilege of a local penny post for nearly half a century. More than one petition in favour of the original proposal was sent up from Manchester in 1839, and there was some co-ordination of the movement in the various manufacturing and commercial centres, apparently organised by the London Mercantile Committee on Postage.[3]

The reformers based their claim on the assertion that high postage rates led to evasion, and that the postal revenue had by no means kept pace with the growth of population and trade during the preceding generation ; whereas it seemed probable that a national penny post, with frequent collections and deliveries, would produce a considerable increase in the aggregate revenue, besides giving the country the direct benefit of cheaper communication. It has also to be remembered, in considering the provincial

[1] *Manchester Mercury*, 1st February, 1820 ; *Proceedings of the Manchester Chamber of Commerce*, 22nd October, 1821.

[2] *Ibid.*, 21st March, 1838.

[3] *Ibid.*, 11th February, 18th April, 11th July, and 22nd August, 1839.

agitation for a penny post, that much of the driving force came from the Anti-Corn-Law League, which desired cheaper rates for the purpose of distributing circulars and pamphlets. The agitation achieved its object in 1840, when a uniform penny post was established ; it is true that the promised increase in postal revenue did not accrue for many years, but in the meantime the cheaper postage rates had played no inconsiderable part in the conversion of the country to free trade in corn.

In the later 'forties, and even in the earlier 'fifties, the Manchester merchants still felt that the postal officials in Liverpool and London were unjustifiably delaying the transmission of mails to Manchester, to the great potential profit of the Liverpool and London merchants. Repeated complaints to the Liverpool Post Office about the detention of Manchester letters were apparently disregarded, and in 1849 the grievance was laid before the Postmaster-General. The specialisation between the two towns was not then so complete as it is nowadays ; Manchester and Liverpool merchants were competing to sell the same goods to America, and the advantage of a day (or even half a day) in dealing with the American mail meant that Liverpool merchants might capture the market.[1] Complaints about delays in the mails between London and Manchester turned at this time on the slowness of letter-sorting in London. Letters from the south-eastern counties and from Southampton (many of the latter containing foreign bills of exchange) arrived in London before 5 a.m., and were not sent off to Manchester until five hours later. Even by the new railways, they did not arrive in Manchester until 4.50 p.m., which was outside ordinary business hours and too late for banking transactions.[2] From a later complaint it appears that the letters were not actually delivered in Manchester until 6 p.m., by which time most of the business houses were closing. The Manchester merchants contended that it should be possible for the mail to be dispatched from London at 6 a.m., so that the letters could be delivered in Manchester before the banks closed in the afternoon. It was pointed out that the London mails were delivered in Leeds and Bradford two hours earlier than in

---

[1] *Proceedings of the Manchester Chamber of Commerce,* 3rd August, 1848 ; 1st, 9th and 12th February, 1849.
[2] *Ibid.,* 13th January, 1847.

Manchester; and that London newspapers reached Manchester four hours earlier than the London mails. For some years the Postmaster-General persisted in maintaining that earlier dispatch from London was impossible, owing to the late arrival of the French mails; but in the end it was agreed to put the Manchester mail on the 9.15 a.m. train from Euston, which arrived in Manchester at 2.40 p.m.[1] Meanwhile, another old grievance, which had caused dissatisfaction even in the eighteenth century, had been redressed in 1849, when the Postmaster-General at last authorised a Sunday dispatch of letters from London to Manchester.[2]

It will be clear that, by the middle of the century, the organisation of the inland postal system had become dependent on the railways; it must not be imagined, however, that the Post Office had given the new railways an enthusiastic welcome, or that the transfer of the mails from the roads to the railways had taken place without friction. When, in 1835, the Manchester Chamber of Commerce asked for an additional morning mail between Manchester and Liverpool, the Postmaster-General replied that he was unwilling to spend any more money on postal communications on the Liverpool and Manchester Railway.[3] This reply may have been influenced by the knowledge that many members of the Manchester Chamber of Commerce were also shareholders in the L. & M.R.; but official caution and parsimony proved equally serious obstacles to later attempts to secure (by fuller use of the railways) improved postal communications with such widely separated towns as Bristol, Hull and Southampton.[4] The London and Birmingham Railway had been sanctioned in 1833 and opened in 1838; yet throughout the earlier 'forties the Manchester merchants were still unsuccessful in their attempts to persuade the Postmaster-General to use this line for the carriage of the London-Manchester mails, which continued to go round by Newton-le-Willows on the Grand Junction Railway. Even after the Manchester and Birmingham Railway had opened up the direct through route by way of Crewe, the Postmaster-General still resisted the

---

[1] *Proceedings of the Manchester Chamber of Commerce*, 17th July, 1851; 9th December, 1852; 3rd February, 1853.
[2] *Ibid.*, 23rd October, 1849.
[3] *Ibid.*, 2nd and 9th September, and 2nd October, 1835.
[4] *Ibid.*, 8th February, 1843 (Hull); 2nd December, 1846 (Southampton); 30th December, 1847 (Bristol and South Wales).

change, on the ground of expense.[1] The solution of this problem came neither from the merchants nor from the Post Office, but from the formation of the London and North-Western Railway in 1846, which absorbed all the lines in question and thus enabled the mails to go by the most direct route.

The satisfactory acceleration of the London-Manchester mails in 1853 has already been mentioned; but even after that date the Manchester merchants still had many reforms to press upon the postal authorities. Some of the proposed improvements were outlined in the instructions given to the Secretary of the Chamber of Commerce when he was summoned to appear before the Parliamentary Committee on the Conveyance of Mails by Railway in 1854. He was to make it clear, for example, that the Post Office should not centralise all letters in London (as it then did), and that where there were means of forwarding them by more direct trains, this should be done: that the morning mail from London did not reach Manchester at a sufficiently early hour: that the foreign mails should be sorted on board ship, and should be landed at the nearest port having direct communication with their inland destination.[2] It might be thought that such reforms were so clearly desirable as to need no advocacy; but it had been the experience of the Manchester merchants, during the preceding half-century, that even the most obvious reforms were not usually carried out until the authorities had been badgered into an unwilling acquiescence.

The Manchester Chamber of Commerce first became interested in steam navigation as a potential means of quickening postal communications with India; and during the second quarter of the nineteenth century Manchester merchants actively supported the struggles of Head, Waghorn, and other pioneers to establish a regular steamship route to India, in spite of the obstructive inertia of the East India Company.[3] Captain J. H. Johnston's early attempts to establish a steamship company for trade with India, in 1822-23, received the formal approval of the Manchester Chamber,

---

[1] *Proceedings of the Manchester Chamber of Commerce*, 1st September, 1842; 28th March, 17th October and 7th November, 1844; 18th June, 1845; 9th February, 1846.

[2] *Ibid.*, 21st June, 1854.

[3] On the general topic of steam navigation to India, see H. L. Hoskins, *British Routes to India*, 1928, *passim*.

which declared that "steam navigation has already been of considerable advantage to the trading interests of the country; any extension of its use will doubtless be productive of further important benefit, especially if made subservient to the conveyance of the foreign mails." [1] Any project for obtaining steamship communication with India had, however, to encounter the passive opposition of the East India Company; and any attempt to carry letters to India by steamship seems to have been obstructed by an Act of George III's reign, which prescribed a merely nominal rate of postage for such letters. It was this latter difficulty which the Manchester Chamber of Commerce attacked in 1831, in a memorial (to the Lords of the Treasury) praying for the removal of any statutory impediment to the development of steam navigation for the transmission of letters to India.[2] Steam navigation could be established (declared the memorial) if the steam vessels were permitted to make an adequate charge for the carriage of letters; merchants would gladly submit to such postage charges, in return for the greater certainty and speed of steam navigation. No reply was vouchsafed to this memorial, however, and a renewed application in 1832 received only the non-committal answer (from the President of the Board of Trade) "that the subject was under consideration, but that it must at the same time be observed that there were many difficulties attending the case."

By this time Mr. Thomas Waghorn had begun to attract the attention of the Manchester Chamber of Commerce to his plans for a steamship service to India. In 1827 he had been touring the English towns, trying to get financial backing for a voyage by the Cape route; but Johnston's ill-fated venture with the *Enterprize* in 1826 had shown the difficulties of that route, and the provincial merchants held back. During the next three years Waghorn continued to base his schemes on the Cape route, in spite of much discouragement; but the successful voyage of the little steamer *Hugh Lindsay*, which took only about a month to steam from Bombay to Suez in the spring of 1830, converted him into a fanatical and life-long advocate of the Red Sea route. Late in 1835 the Manchester Chamber of Commerce received Waghorn's prospectus for the establishment of agencies at

---

[1] *Proceedings of the Manchester Chamber of Commerce*, 26th March, 1823.　　　　　　　　　　　　　　　[2] *Ibid.*, 8th June, 1831.

Alexandria and Suez for the forwarding of letters and parcels across Egypt, thus making the necessary land-link in the Mediterranean and Red Sea projects. The Board of the Manchester Chamber, " disclaiming any intention to prejudice or to give any opinion on the relative merits of this route, or of that by the Euphrates, which is known to be under experiment, solicited the Secretary of State for Foreign Affairs to render Mr. Waghorn such protection as he might require in prosecuting an attempt to facilitate the intercourse between this country and India. His Lordship replied that he had already done all in his power to assist Mr. Waghorn in his attempt, and that he would gladly give any further aid to the undertaking, should any unforeseen difficulties arise in its progress." [1]

By March, 1836, Waghorn was able to report that he had secured a *firman* from the Pasha of Egypt, authorising him to procure anything he required for instant despatches ; answers to letters from England could in future be received within six months. Evidently he regarded this as an important stage in his work ; for, as compensation for his labours and losses, he asked the Board of the Manchester Chamber to obtain for him a lieutenancy in the Royal Navy and a pecuniary reward from Parliament.[2] The Manchester merchants duly expressed their appreciation of " the energy of purpose, prodigality of physical exertion, and dauntless perseverance under formidable difficulties " shown by Mr. Waghorn ; but the Government and the East India Company were less enthusiastic, and Mr. Waghorn had to wait another six years before receiving his lieutenant's commission " as an official acknowledgment of exertions in establishing the overland route to India." [3] After 1836 other schemes, with more influential backing, were tending to throw Waghorn's efforts into the shade ; and the Manchester Chamber of Commerce, along with the other commercial organisations of the country, was more anxious to hasten the development of steam navigation to India than to secure a just distribution of rewards among the pioneers.

[1] *Proceedings of the Manchester Chamber of Commerce*, 11th November and 9th December, 1835 ; 15th Annual Report, 8th February, 1836.
[2] *Ibid.*, 16th March, 1836.
[3] *Asiatic Journal*, XXXVII, N.S., Pt. II, 375 ; quoted by Hoskins, *op. cit.*, p. 99, *n.* 59.

In the summer of 1836 the Board of the Manchester Chamber gave its approval to the plan of Mr. C. F. Head, chairman of a provisional committee in London, for the establishment of regular communication with India by way of the Red Sea.[1] That the Board had still a fairly open mind on the subject was shown, however, by its almost simultaneous approval of the Government's action in authorising Colonel Chesney's expedition to test the practicability of steam navigation on the Euphrates route. In May, 1837, both Waghorn and Head were appealing for the support of the Manchester merchants. Waghorn appeared in person to explain his plans, and to ask for petitions in favour of the route by Suez, Point de Galle, with Socotra as the port of call for supplies, with lines of smaller steamers for coastal transport to Bombay, Madras and Calcutta.[2] Major C. F. Head, as Chairman of the Provisional Committee of the East India Steam Navigation Company, asked the Manchester merchants to support petitions on the same subject from India and the City of London. The Manchester Chamber of Commerce accordingly petitioned for the provision of a regular system of Government steam packets, and asked that the necessary arrangements for the transmission of mails under responsible agents should be made with the Egyptian authorities.

The Government and the East India Company had by this time been stimulated to energetic action. Early in 1838 the Board of the Manchester Chamber could report with gratification that an official scheme had been agreed upon by the Board of Control and the East India Company " for establishing steam communication between the two Empires *via* the Red Sea." [3] Nevertheless, more than a year later the Indian mails transmitted by Waghorn's agency were still arriving earlier than those sent by the official channels.[4] The Board of Control's explanation of the delay was that negotiations were still proceeding with two steamship companies ; Waghorn declared that the East India Company was still raising obstacles to the comprehensive scheme approved by the Government, and that parliamentary intervention was called for.[5] In actual fact, the Government

---

[1] *Proceedings of the Manchester Chamber of Commerce*, 10th August, 1836.
 [2] *Ibid.*, 22nd May, 1837. [3] *Ibid.*, 7th February, 1838.
 [4] *Ibid.*, 21st March, 1839 : letter from Captain Barber, of the Calcutta Steam Committee. [5] *Ibid.*, 4th April, 1839.

contract for the carriage of mails between England and Egypt had already been given to the Peninsular (soon to become the Peninsular and Oriental) Steam Navigation Company ; and on this section of the shorter sea route to India the steamship service gradually improved. On the other side of the land barrier, however, the mail service between Suez and Bombay continued to be operated by the East India Company, with steamers that were inferior in both speed and accommodation. The overland journey between the Mediterranean and the Red Sea was still (in spite of Waghorn's efforts) effected precariously on camels and donkeys ; the land passage was at this time (1838-40) rendered especially uncertain by the military and diplomatic complications arising from the ambitious plans of the Pasha of Egypt, Mehemet Ali.

During the early 'forties the Manchester Chamber of Commerce was not only pressing for the further improvement of the Indian mail service, but was attempting to make the existing P. and O. service to Egypt the basis for a more general steamship service in the Levant. The export of plain cotton goods to the Levant had been greatly stimulated as a result of the Anglo-Turkish commercial treaty signed at Balta-Liman in 1838 ; and by the middle of the century the Sultan's dominions were taking more Manchester piece goods than all the European countries put together. The transport facilities for this expanding trade were at first very inadequate, and caused much delay ; while severe losses through pilfering were experienced when goods and mails were sent overland, *e.g.* through France or Austria. Expenditure on a regular British steamship service to the Levant would be more than repaid (argued the Manchester Chamber) [1] by an increase of trade, as well as by the greater speed and certainty of the mails. Countries like France, Austria and Russia had already found this out ; Russian ships were being built specially for the trade of the Black Sea and the Levant.[2] The P. and O. Company was quite willing to branch out into the Levant service if financial support was forthcoming ; but the Post Office estimated that the annual cost would amount to £8500, and the Treasury

[1] *Proceedings of the Manchester Chamber of Commerce,* 1st December, 1842 : memorial to the Lords of the Treasury.
[2] *Ibid.,* 26th April, 1843.

declined to accept this additional burden on the national finances.[1]

The Indian mail service was at this time costing £30,000 a year, and was still far from efficient, though it was better than it had been. Apparently the East India Company was still pursuing its dog-in-the-manger policy; letters arrived both in England and India a few days after the outward mail had been dispatched, and the replies had to wait some time for the next mail. The P. and O. line was experimenting with iron ships;[2] the East India Company still had faith in "wooden walls" and "hearts of oak." The P. and O. Company offered to "engraft a direct mail to the Levant upon the accelerated Indian mail at a cost of about £3000 per year, instead of £8500 as stated by the Post Office, making a gross saving of about £27,000 per annum, as compared with the present cost of the Indian mail alone."[3] Faced with this revolutionary proposal, the Directors of the East India Company remained silent, and took no steps to improve their own shipping service, with its inconvenient arrangement of the inward and outward mails. Nearly ten years later (1853) the merchants of both Manchester and Bombay were still complaining about the gross inefficiency of the mail service from Bombay to Suez, as carried on by the East India Company, and urging that the contract should be thrown open to public tender.[4] The parliamentary committee then investigating the question decided against the East India Company's continuance of the service, and thus at last the Peninsular and Oriental Company secured the contract for the carriage of the mails between Bombay and Suez at £24,700, a saving of £80,000 as compared with the expenses of the East India Company's fleet.[5]

The transference of the mails from sailing vessels to steamships had been attended with similar (though less protracted) difficulties on the other trading routes. In the post-war period the Government was already experimenting with mail steam packets for the coastal and cross-channel

[1] *Proceedings of the Manchester Chamber of Commerce*, 7th December, 1843 : Memorial to the Board of Trade.
[2] See Clapham, *op. cit.*, Vol. I, p. 440.
[3] 23rd *Annual Report of the Manchester Chamber of Commerce*, 12th February, 1844.
[4] *Ibid.*, 30th June, 1853.
[5] *Ibid.*, 10th November, 1853 ; *Proceedings of the Manchester Commercial Association*, 9th November, 1853 ; W. S. Lindsay, *History of Merchant Shipping*, 1876, Vol. IV, p. 390.

services; but the financial results were not at first satisfactory, and further progress was not rapid. In 1825 the
Manchester Chamber of Commerce strongly urged the adoption of steam vessels in the conveyance of mails from the
Continent, but ten years later the postal arrangements between Manchester and France were still causing complaints;
it was explained in 1834 that the arrangements for a daily
mail to France were still not complete, because France had
not put steam vessels on the service, as she had agreed to do
by treaty.[1]

The transference of the West Indian mails to the Royal
Mail Steam Packet Company, in 1840, did not at first
yield very satisfactory results to the provincial merchants.
Early in 1842 the Company attempted to cut down its
sailings to the West Indies from two to one each month.
This naturally led the Manchester Chamber of Commerce to
protest that serious disadvantages would result from such
a curtailment, the fear of which had already caused much
alarm among merchants dealing with those parts.[2] The
Board of Trade replied that sailings to the West Indies
would not be reduced, but that no such guarantee could be
given in favour of other places, not colonies.[3] " Other
places, not colonies " evidently included Mexico, for which
a twice-monthly mail was being demanded some months
later; but in this case the Manchester Chamber of Commerce
declined to intervene.[4] By that time the R.M.S.P. Company
had decided to effect the desired economy in working expenditure by limiting the number of ports at which West
Indian produce could be loaded. As the reduction of facilities
was accompanied by increased charges, the Manchester
Chamber of Commerce was once more moved to protest,
this time to the Secretary of State for Foreign Affairs;
but Lord Aberdeen's response was unsympathetic, and for
the time being the Manchester merchants had to swallow
their grievance.[5]

Some years later, dissatisfaction with the mail service
to North America began to be expressed. In 1847 the
Manchester Chamber of Commerce demanded direct steam

[1] *Proceedings of the Manchester Chamber of Commerce*, 13th July,
1825; 8th and 27th January, 12th March, and 6th November, 1834;
and 4th February, 1835.   [2] *Ibid.*, 3rd August, 1842.
  [3] *Ibid.*, 1st September, 1842.   [4] *Ibid.*, 15th March, 1843.
    [5] *Ibid.*, 22nd February and 20th September, 1843.

communication with New Orleans, for the more adequate accommodation of the expanding export of raw cotton from that city, which tapped the resources of the whole Mississippi basin ;[1] on this point the British Government showed ready agreement, and by February, 1848, the direct service had been established. Further friction arose, however, concerning the high British charges on American mails. The charge for letters carried between Great Britain and the United States by American ships was one shilling imposed by the American authorities for conveyance, and one shilling levied by the British Post Office (which rendered no corresponding service) ; where the letters were carried in British ships the American charge was much lower. The Manchester merchants feared that the United States would not long submit to such discrimination against her shipping ; and this fear was justified, for in 1848 a bill providing for the imposition of retaliatory charges was introduced into Congress. Promptly the Manchester Chamber of Commerce recommended to the First Lord of the Treasury that the British postal charges should be reduced to the American level, in order to secure the withdrawal of the retaliatory bill ;[2] once more the British Government hastened to comply, and before the end of the year the dispute had been brought to an amicable conclusion.

As yet no through steam communication had been established with Australia, though there was a paddle-boat service from Singapore to Australia by way of the Eastern Archipelago. In 1850 both the Manchester Chamber of Commerce and the Manchester Commercial Association gave their support to the plan of a Mr. Heyes to establish a new service of screw steamers to Australia by way of the Cape of Good Hope.[3] Two steamship companies were actually formed in 1852 to run by the Cape route—the General Screw Steamship Company for trade to Calcutta and intermediate ports, and the Australian Royal Mail Steam Packet Company ; but both alike proved signal failures on account of coaling difficulties and the competition of the Suez route. Meanwhile, the establishment of an official steamship service between Singapore and Sydney had been decided upon in 1851. The Peninsular

---

[1] *Proceedings of the Manchester Chamber of Commerce*, 13th January, 1847.
[2] *Ibid.*, 3rd February and 11th May, 1848.
[3] *Ibid.*, 11th July, 1850.

and Oriental Company secured the contract, and engaged to carry mails between Singapore and Sydney once a month each way ; but the Crimean War led to the withdrawal of this service in 1854,[1] and it was not until 1856 that an independent steamship line from Suez to Australia was established.[2]

After the middle of the century further improvements were also being demanded in the mail services with Central and South America. In 1851 the Manchester Chamber of Commerce made the reasonable suggestion that such services might be improved if postal officials were appointed to sort the letters on board ship, so that the mails could be dispatched direct from the port of arrival ; [3] but the Postmaster-General considered that such an innovation was impossible. Two years later, the Manchester Commercial Association was equally unsuccessful in attempting to secure a twice-monthly mail service with South America.[4] Independent competition in steam shipping was now, however, beginning to show itself on these routes. In 1854 the Manchester Chamber of Commerce sent to the Board of Trade a memorial, signed by seventy-three firms, in support of a projected company for the establishment of a service of twin-screw steamers to the West Indies, Mexico and the Spanish Main.[5] The application was renewed in the succeeding year,[6] and eventually a charter of incorporation was granted to the company, which was promoted by Mr. Holt of Liverpool and started with a vessel of only 535 tons. Within a very short time the company was maintaining a monthly service with steamers of increased size and power, the Holt Line had established its position, and the R.M.S.P. Company had to look to its laurels (and its contract) ; the mail contract of the R.M.S.P. was renewed in 1857, but the Company had to agree to quicken its service from sixty-three days to fifty-six days.

In the later 'fifties the victory of steam navigation was still far from complete. By that time, however, regular steamship services were being maintained on several of the

---

[1] *Cf. Proceedings of the Manchester Chamber of Commerce,* 16th February and 22nd March, 1854.

[2] Lindsay, *op. cit.,* pp. 390-6.

[3] *Proceedings of the Manchester Chamber of Commerce,* 26th June. 1851,

[4] *Proceedings of the Manchester Commercial Association,* 22nd June, 1853.

[5] *Proceedings of the Manchester Chamber of Commerce,* 28th June, 1854.

[6] *Ibid.,* 29th March, 1855.

main arterial trade routes, with the help of the mail contracts ; and on some lines the steamship was establishing
its supremacy even without the Government subsidy.   Moreover, some almost entirely new factors in long-distance communication were beginning to show themselves tentatively.
In 1856, representatives of the Atlantic Telegraph Company
explained to the Manchester merchants the wonderful po-
tentialities of the submarine cable, which was to be laid as
soon as the necessary capital had been subscribed.   The
English Government (said the Company's spokesman) had
acted with the utmost liberality.   It had already sent out
a vessel at its own expense to make further soundings.   It
had also guaranteed an interest of 4 per cent. per annum on
the entire capital required for the undertaking.   He believed
that the Government would go further and furnish vessels
to lay the cable, free of charge.   In Liverpool the enterprise
had been most warmly supported ; up to the previous night
the subscriptions in that town had amounted to £53,000,
and it was expected that they would be increased by a further
£20,000.   In Glasgow, also, great interest was manifested.
With the present system of cabling they could transmit
through a single line of wires 14,404 words every twenty-
four hours, but with the code which was being prepared
they would be able to transmit at least 30,000 words within
that time between Europe and America.   The total cost of
the undertaking would be about £250,000.[1]   In the succeeding
year the Indian and Red Sea Company was making a similar
bid for approval and support ;[2]   while Ferdinand de Lesseps
was touring the English towns to explain his plans concerning
the " proposed ship canal across the Isthmus of Suez."[3]
All these novel schemes had to undergo many tribulations
before they achieved success ; but indubitably they sounded
a modern note, and foreshadowed that contraction of
" economic distance " which has now become so marked a
feature of civilised life.

[1] *Proceedings of the Manchester Chamber of Commerce*, 20th November,
1856 (reported in the *Manchester Guardian*, 21st November, 1856).
[2] *Ibid.*, 1st October, 1857.
[3] *Ibid.*, 2nd May, 1857 ; for Birmingham, see Wright, *op. cit.*, p. 141.

CHAPTER XV.

LEGAL QUESTIONS AND JOINT-STOCK LEGISLATION.

In the work of any commercial association, a good deal of time must inevitably be taken up with tedious but necessary business concerning legal rights and liabilities. The prominence of such business in the activities of the Manchester commercial organisations of the eighteenth century has already been shown ; [1] it is hardly too much to say that the decline of the Manchester Commercial Society, after 1798, was largely due to its ill-success in coping with the complex legal questions, concerning such matters as marine insurance and under-writing, which arose as a result of the struggle against revolutionary France. Similar questions frequently arose during the early history of the Manchester Chamber of Commerce, and were more successfully handled ; though it goes without saying that even the more powerful commercial organisation of the nineteenth century did not always give its members such complete protection as they demanded.

Very often the task was to redress the grievances of individual merchants, arising from the arbitrary acts of customs officials or from the unjustifiable imposition of penalties by foreign governments. A typical case of this kind was raised in 1830 by Mr. H. Brettargh, who claimed compensation for wrongful confiscation of goods by the excise officers. In November, 1829, Mr. Brettargh sent 745 pieces of calico to be printed by Mr. Thomas Bury, of Clayton Vale. The pieces were printed and sent back to Brettargh, who paid Bury for the printing, including the excise duty. The goods were later sold to (and paid for by) Messrs. Reuss & Kling of Manchester ; but in March, 1830, when the goods were being packed for export, they were seized by the excise

---

[1] See pp. 43-50 above.

officer appointed to superintend the packing, on the ground that Bury (the printer) was a debtor to the Crown. Consequently Reuss & Kling demanded and eventually secured repayment of the purchase money from Brettargh, who had been quite innocent of any fraudulent intention. Brettargh appealed to the Government for redress, but received no answer. Eventually the Chamber of Commerce took up the case and, with legal assistance, submitted a formal memorial to the Government.[1] The Chancellor of the Exchequer replied that the seizure of the goods was legal, though Mr. Brettargh was to be commiserated with as " suffering from the odious severity of the Excise Laws, a severity represented to be necessary for the security of the revenue." The Chamber of Commerce urged in reply that the duty on printed calicoes had been levied for more than a century without the oppressive powers experienced in this case ; the change had been made " covertly, through a clause silently introduced into a general Consolidation Bill, the trade having no intimation respecting it, or any knowledge of its existence till long after the Act had passed." The dispute dragged on for about two years ; but, in the end, the Board of the Chamber was able to report that Mr. Brettargh had received full restitution for the goods seized.[2]

An almost contemporary grievance, with a less satisfactory outcome, was that of Mr. James Ferneley, who made application to the Mexican Government for the refund of duties levied in 1829 on goods which were not shipped, though they were included in the manifest of the vessel. Mr. Pakenham, the British Chargé d'Affaires, attempted to secure restitution, but failed, owing to the disturbed political condition of Mexico. On his second application, in 1833, he was told that the Government had no power to redress the grievance, because of the peremptory terms of the tariff under which it had arisen. The Manchester Chamber of Commerce laid the case before Lord Palmerston in 1837, and Mr. Pakenham was instructed to re-open the negotiations. Renewed efforts were made in 1838 ; but Mr. Ferneley does not appear to have got his money back.[3]

In the meantime, however, another Mexican dispute had

---

[1] *Proceedings of the Manchester Chamber of Commerce*, 9th February, 1831.

[2] *Ibid.*, 11th Annual Report, 13th February, 1832.

[3] *Ibid.*, 1st and 8th March, 1837 ; 26th April, 1837 ; 21st February and 4th April, 1838.

been settled in favour of the Manchester merchants concerned in it ; this was a dispute arising from the seizure by the Mexican Government of thirty-five bales of goods shipped by Messrs. Crossley & Son to Vera Cruz in 1834. The goods had been sent to Liverpool for shipment by the *Julia Arthur*, which had no specified date for sailing ; and it happened that, when final warning was given of the ship's departure, Crossley's agent had not got the necessary invoices. A letter was sent to the Mexican Customs House, explaining the omission and asking that the thirty-five bales should be kept in deposit for a few days until the invoices arrived. This was done and the goods were delivered to the consignees, although a bond of indemnification was kept. Later, however, the matter was brought before the Mexican Courts of Justice, and the goods were condemned. An appeal against this judgment failed, and Messrs. Crossley & Son therefore asked for the help of the Manchester Chamber of Commerce, which appealed to Lord Palmerston ; less than six months later, Mr. Crossley reported that a decision had now been given in favour of his firm, and the case was satisfactorily concluded.[1]

It would be tedious to multiply instances of such cases, in which the Chamber of Commerce used its influence to protect the interest and legal rights of individual merchants. The activities of the Chamber on points of legal principle, or concerning proposed legal reforms, were of more general importance ; such questions often assumed a surprising prominence in the discussions of the Manchester merchants, though the points at issue have now ceased to be of any special interest except to the legal historian. Of all the subjects which engaged the attention of the Manchester Chamber of Commerce during the middle 'thirties, one of the most keenly debated was Sir John Campbell's Bill for the Abolition of Imprisonment for Debt, which was first introduced in 1834 and was revived more than once during the next few sessions. The Manchester Chamber opposed the Bill on both special and general grounds, and persisted in its opposition year after year. A Manchester petition of April, 1835, declared that the Bill was founded on the mistaken notion that the existing laws did not give the debtor sufficient protection from a vindictive creditor. It was further

---

[1] *Proceedings of the Manchester Chamber of Commerce,* 2nd September and 7th October, 1835 ; 16th March, 1836.

contended that the holders of bonds, bills of exchange and promissory notes were given an unfair advantage, by Campbell's Bill, over the holders of simple contract debts, who would be excluded from their share in the assets of an honest but unlucky debtor, whilst they would have no protection against a dishonest debtor. This would engender a system of bill-drawing among inferior tradesmen and clerks in counting-houses, and would foster a spirit of distrust injurious to the trading community. Thus the merits of the Bill were outweighed by its defects.[1]

From a later statement it appears that the Chamber of Commerce's objection to the abolition of imprisonment for debt did not apply to arrest on mesne process. It considered that the power to arrest only affected very slightly the honest debtor, who could get quick relief from the Courts, but that it should be maintained as a remedial and preventive measure against crafty and extravagant debtors, who alone would be relieved by Sir John Campbell's Bill. Further, the provisions for punishing fraud would be nullified by the difficulty of obtaining adequate evidence on which to convict, nor would the increased powers of search, etc., be more efficient than the power of arrest, in reaching the property of the debtor. By Campbell's Bill credit would be diminished, to the serious injury of the trading community; if the Bill should pass, its operation ought to be deferred, otherwise it would have a retrospective effect of which creditors might reasonably complain.[2]

The views of the Manchester merchants were urged in the House of Commons by Mr. C. P. Thomson, (M.P. for Manchester, and also President of the Board of Trade); but in July, 1835, Mr. Thomson reported that the London movement against the Bill had collapsed, and that further opposition seemed useless.[3] Nothing daunted, the Manchester merchants appointed a deputation to give their views direct representation in London. The deputation was very coldly received by the Governor of the Bank of England, and found great difficulty in getting Members of Parliament to oppose the Bill, though many objected to parts of it.[4] In the end, however, the House of Lords shelved the Bill in September, 1835; several fresh attempts to secure its passage were made

---

[1] *Proceedings of the Manchester Chamber of Commerce*, 3rd April, 1835.
[2] *Ibid.*, 23rd May, 1835.   [3] *Ibid.*, 22nd and 29th July, 1835.
[4] *Ibid.*, 19th August, 1835.

in succeeding sessions, but the opposition persisted in challenging clause after clause, and the measure was finally abandoned.

A much more protracted struggle, extending throughout the second quarter of the nineteenth century, was waged by the Manchester merchants against excessive stamp duties on various kinds of legal documents.   This apparently minor grievance was attacked with a persistence which suggests that its real importance must have been considerable ; and it is true that the question impinged incidentally upon more than one of the main fiscal and financial controversies of the period.   Bills of exchange and promissory notes were first subjected to stamp duties in 1782 ; a general Stamp Act of 1815[1] had increased the duties, which thenceforth discriminated between short-dated and long-dated bills.   In the post-war period the average duty on all bills of less than £50 was ½ per cent. ; but this charge was felt to be prohibitive, and had in Manchester caused bills to be almost completely replaced by bank notes.   Bank notes, however, were considered to be a much more inconvenient and risky means of payment, since they were payable " to bearer " and not " to order." [2]   The Manchester Chamber of Commerce therefore moved in 1822 for the reduction of the duties, and sent up several petitions on the subject, to the Prime Minister, the Chancellor of the Exchequer, and the Houses of Parliament.   The petitioners described the serious inconvenience to business which had resulted from the virtual extinction of " a description of currency of great convenience and security " ; they suggested a greatly reduced scale of duties, and argued that, if this were adopted, not only the business community but also the revenue would benefit greatly, because of the increased use of bills of exchange.[3]

The financial crisis of 1825 emphasised still more strongly the need for bills of exchange of small amount, and the Manchester merchants again petitioned the Government for the reduction of the stamp duties ; [4] but all these petitions fell on deaf ears, and in 1827 the Board of the Chamber of Commerce had to report that " His Majesty's Ministers seemed to consider the reduction of stamp duties of small

---

[1] On the Birmingham petition against this measure, see Wright, *op. cit.*, pp. 69-70.
[2] *Proceedings of the Manchester Chamber of Commerce*, 5th March, 1823.
[3] *Ibid.*, 27th March, 1822.   [4] *Ibid.*, 10th February, 1826.

amount objectionable, conceiving (as the Board believes without foundation) that such a measure would be hurtful to the currency and would lead to improvident speculations." [1] The matter was taken up again in 1830, and yet once more in 1831 ; but the desired relief was not given until 1854, when the irregular scales of charges for long-date and short-date bills were replaced by a low and uniform percentage duty. This change, as the merchants had prophesied thirty years earlier, proved distinctly beneficial to the business community (especially in smaller commercial transactions), without inflicting any serious injury upon the revenue.

The movement aiming at the reduction of the stamp duties on fire and marine insurances seems first to have aroused the interest of the Manchester merchants in 1830, when Mr. Goulburn (as Chancellor of the Exchequer) attempted unsuccessfully to make a comprehensive reform of the duties. A memorial presented by the Manchester Chamber of Commerce to the Government in May, 1830, declared that the high rates of duty pressed very injuriously on the country, and prevented the protection of property against fire—a protection which was especially necessary in commercial communities. Notwithstanding the great increase in the number of insurance companies during the preceding twenty years, and the competition for business naturally attendant on their establishment, the amount of duty raised had not increased in proportion to the increase of insurable property. A large proportion of the capital stock of the country remained uninsured, and this imprudence could only be ascribed to the excessive duties, which in most cases of common insurances amounted to 200 per cent. on the rate of premium charged.

The duties on marine insurance were likewise excessive, being on the average not less than 20 per cent. on the full amount of the premiums paid. Such insurances could be effected abroad with equal security free of duty ; consequently merchants were tempted to place their insurance business abroad, to the manifest injury of the public revenue. Another obvious effect was to discourage the coasting trade, by imposing a burden on goods carried by sea from which those carried by land or canal were exempted. The effect on vessels engaged in foreign or colonial trade was still more

[1] *Proceedings of the Manchester Chamber of Commerce,* 6th Annual Report, 12th February, 1827.

objectionable. It was immaterial to a shipowner whether he insured his vessels in London, Amsterdam or Hamburg, and as policies executed in the last-named two cities were either wholly exempted from duties or subject to such as were merely nominal, the effect of the English duties was to transfer to the Continent a considerable amount of marine insurance business which would otherwise have been trans-acted in London.[1] No success attended these arguments either in 1830, or again in 1831, when the Manchester Chamber of Commerce, at the instigation of Lloyd's, sent another peti-tion for relief. Some reduction was made in 1833 in the duties on marine insurances for foreign voyages and time policies ; yet during the later 'thirties the Manchester merchants, still urged on by Lloyd's, made repeated applications for the further reduction of the duties, and used precisely the same arguments as they had done earlier in the decade.[2] Their petitions continued, however, to produce the same negative results ; no material reductions were secured until 1842, by which date the reduction of all kinds of duties had become much more fashionable.

The stamp duties on receipts were felt as a grievance principally by the retail traders ; yet the agitation for the repeal or reduction of the duties received most of its force from the activities of the Chambers of Commerce and similar organisations of merchants trading on a larger scale. In 1828 such towns as Birmingham, Bristol, Hull and Manchester were all sending up petitions on the subject ; and there was evidently some measure of co-operation between the various towns.[3] The Manchester petition for the repeal of the duties stated that general anxiety and alarm had been felt, especi-ally by the retail shopkeepers, who had numerous customers with small accounts. To enforce the payment of the duties in Manchester would be like the levying of a new tax, because it had rarely been the practice to give or require stamped receipts in business.[4] This same argument, that the receipt duty was vexatious though practically inoperative, was repeated in 1834, when the Manchester Chamber of

---

[1] *Proceedings of the Manchester Chamber of Commerce*, 5th May, 1830.
[2] See, for example, *ibid.*, 13th April, 1836, and 17th January, 1838.
[3] For the co-operation between Birmingham and Bristol, see Wright, *op. cit.*, pp. 101-2 ; for Hull, see *Manchester Mercury*, 18th March, 1828, and *Journals of the House of Commons*, Vol. 83, p. 155 (11th March, 1828).
[4] *Proceedings of the Manchester Chamber of Commerce*, 13th February, 1828.

Commerce again petitioned for repeal.[1] The application was partially successful, as the duty was remitted on all sums under £5 ; but a new Stamp Consolidation Bill, two years later, threatened the imposition of still more vexatious burdens, and called for renewed opposition.

In the opinion of the Manchester merchants, the pro-posed alterations in the stamp duties would increase taxation on personal and private payments ; if any alterations were made, they should be carried out so as not to tax property and commercial operations hitherto exempt, and the transference or inheritance of personal property should not be more heavily taxed than hitherto. Moreover, where an *ad valorem* duty was imposed it should cover the whole charge ; thus, there should be no probate charges on legacies after an *ad valorem* duty had been imposed, nor should there be charges on certificates of the registration of shares after their transference charge had been paid. By this Bill, also, letters of credit and the payment of transfers through banks were to be liable to an *ad valorem* duty, which was foolish, especially as the letters of credit might never be acted upon ; furthermore, why should cheques on London banks be honoured free of charge, while payment by transfer among country banks was taxed ? [2] Confronted with these and many other detailed charges of inconsistency, the Bill had finally to be abandoned ; but the Board of the Manchester Chamber resolved to maintain a careful vigilance against the introduction of similar measures in the future.[3]

The general reduction of customs and excise duties in the 'forties encouraged the provincial commercial organisa-tions to make further attacks upon the stamp duties during the prosperous years of the early 'fifties. In 1850 and 1851 the Manchester Chamber of Commerce was once more urging the abolition of the receipt duties, in co-operation with the merchants of Liverpool and Newcastle.[4] The Manchester Commercial Association was also prominent in the movement, advocating the exemption from receipt duty of all sums under £10, and recommending the adoption of a uniform 1d. receipt stamp.[5] It was, in fact, along the lines of the

---

[1] *Proceedings of the Manchester Chamber of Commerce*, 30th April, 1834.
[2] *Ibid.*, 30th March, 20th April, and 18th May, 1836.
[3] *Ibid.*, 16th Annual Report, 13th February, 1837.
[4] *Ibid.*, 30th May and 14th November, 1850 ; 16th January, 1851.
[5] *Proceedings of the Manchester Commercial Association*, 10th October, 1850, and 27th January, 1853.

latter proposal that the question was ultimately settled. The old system of stamp duties had comprised a graduated scale of charges ranging from 3*d.* on receipts for sums between £5 and £10 to 10*s.* on receipts of £1000 and upwards ; in 1853 Mr. Gladstone replaced this graduated scale by a uniform 1*d.* stamp duty on all receipts for sums exceeding £2.

The grievances of individual merchants against customs officials, and even the more general struggle against stamp duties, fade almost into insignificance compared with the legal changes which were taking place in the organisation of joint-stock companies. During the 'forties and 'fifties of the nineteenth century the foundations of modern company law were being (somewhat tentatively) laid down, and hazardous experiments were being conducted which led ultimately to the rise of the modern limited liability company. What surprises the modern mind is that the legislation which facilitated the formation of joint-stock companies had sometimes to be passed in the face of considerable opposition from groups of responsible and substantial business men. Even the Manchester Chamber of Commerce, although it agreed that the law of partnership needed clarification, was for a long time distinctly hostile to the grant of limited liability to shareholders in joint-stock companies. In 1842 the Board of the Chamber recommended the adoption of such legal reforms as were necessary to protect honest traders from ruin brought on them by fraudulent companies, and mentioned with approval " an elaborate report, from a Commissioner appointed by Government, presented to Parliament on the 14th July, 1837." [1] This was Bellenden Kerr's *Report on the Law of Partnership*,[2] which proposed the establishment of a system of registration for partnerships and joint-stock companies. Following what it considered to be the general intention of this Report, the Manchester Chamber of Commerce submitted to the Board of Trade a memorial praying that a register might be kept, containing " the place of business, the names, professions, and abodes of every individual partner : an immediate notification of every change in the partnership and, in cases of partnership to be hereafter formed, the date of their commencement and the proposed

---

[1] *Proceedings of the Manchester Chamber of Commerce,* 14th February, 1842.

[2] Printed as Appendix I of the *First Report on Joint Stock Companies,* 1844 (119), p. 245.

duration of them ; the register to be accessible to all inquirers on the payment of a small fee."

The Joint-Stock Companies Act of 1844 [1] provided some such system of company registration as had been envisaged by Bellenden Kerr, and made it both easier and cheaper for joint-stock companies to be legally established. Individual shareholders in registered companies did not, however, secure the privilege of limited liability ; and, in actual practice, the system of registration did not work satisfactorily. During the commercial depression of 1847-48 a great many of the companies registered under the Joint-Stock Companies Act of 1844 had to be wound up ; it was then made clear that the law of bankruptcy was in a most chaotic state, and that the Act of 1844 " for facilitating the winding up of the affairs of Joint-Stock Companies " [2] had made matters worse. So early as 1842 the Manchester Chamber of Commerce had been conferring with the Manchester Law Association on the reform of the bankruptcy laws ; [3] it was natural, therefore, that the Manchester merchants should display a keen interest in the Winding-up Acts of 1848 and 1849, [4] by which Parliament attempted to clear up the confusion. Both the Chamber of Commerce and the Commercial Association supported the new Winding-up Acts, in the first instance ; [5] but it soon became apparent that their confidence had been misplaced. The Acts had been intended to transfer winding-up proceedings from the Court of Bankruptcy to the Court of Chancery ; but in actual fact they seem rather to have set up a conflict of jurisdictions, which increased the legal confusion. Thus, in 1856 the Royal British Bank was wound up and declared bankrupt ; an official manager was appointed under the Court of Chancery, and official assignees under the bankruptcy laws, while an unsuccessful attempt was also made to obtain the appointment of an official receiver. [6] Such cases may explain the frequent attempts, made during the early 'fifties by bodies like the Manchester

[1] 7 & 8 Vict. c. 110.
[2] 7 & 8 Vict. c. 111.
[3] *Proceedings of the Manchester Chamber of Commerce*, 3rd August and 13th September, 1842.
[4] 11 & 12 Vict. c. 45, and 12 & 13 Vict. c. 108.
[5] *Proceedings of the Manchester Chamber of Commerce*, 24th May and 24th June, 1849 ; *Proceedings of the Manchester Commercial Association*, 5th April and 7th June, 1849.
[6] See R. R. Formoy, *Historical Foundations of Modern Company Law*, 1923, p. 94.

Chamber of Commerce and the Manchester Commercial Association, to gain information about the actual working of the bankruptcy laws and to secure their amendment.[1]

On the more general question of limited liability the Manchester merchants still refused to move with the times ; the Limited Liability Act of 1855 [2] had no more uncompromising opponents. At the Annual General Meeting of 1855, the Vice-President of the Chamber maintained that limited liability would not only ruin commercial honesty, but would call forth so much capital into business that overproduction would be caused ; and this opinion was not at variance with the evidence contributed by the Chamber of Commerce to the Royal Commission on Partnerships and Joint-Stock Companies, which was set up in 1853.[3] The Royal Commission itself considered that the advantages of limited liability had been " greatly over-rated," and that " the benefit to be acquired by the managing or limited partners will be at the expense of a more than countervailing amount of injury to traders bearing the burden of unlimited liability, who will have to enter into competition with those who enjoy the protection to be given by the proposed law." The Manchester Chamber of Commerce quoted with approval the statements of the Royal Commission, and added its own conclusion, that the principles enunciated in the Limited Liability Bills " are so subversive of that high moral responsibility which has hitherto distinguished our Partnership Laws, as to call for their [the petitioners'] strongest disapproval." [4]

Opposition to the principle of limited liability continued to be active in Manchester even after the Act had passed, and the several amending Bills of the next few sessions were scrutinised with critical suspicion. At the Annual General Meeting of 1856 Mr. John Bright told his fellow members of the Chamber of Commerce that the Limited Liability Act of the previous year had been rushed through Parliament because " the Government was very anxious to say at the end of the Session that something had been done besides voting money for the War. . . . I am one of those [he

---

[1] *Proceedings of the Manchester Chamber of Commerce*, 19th February, 1852 ; *Proceedings of the Manchester Commercial Association*, 13th February, 1850, and 25th March, 1853.

[2] 18 & 19 Vict. c. 133.

[3] *Proceedings of the Manchester Chamber of Commerce*, 10th November, 1853, and 8th February, 1855.

[4] *Ibid.*, 13th June, 1855.

continued] who believe that the expectations with regard to the effects of this legislation on this subject have been grossly exaggerated on both sides." [1]　Before his death, in 1889, Bright may well have considered that in this instance his judgment had been at fault ; by that time the smoke from the " Oldham Limiteds " was belching forth as a portent, obscuring the skies of places much further distant than Rochdale !

[1] *Proceedings of the Manchester Chamber of Commerce*, 4th February, 1856 ; *cf. ibid.*, 21st February, 6th March, 21st May, and 12th June, 1856, for further Manchester petitions against the amending Act of 1856.

CHAPTER XVI.

THE SUPPLY OF RAW COTTON.

THE Manchester merchants of the earlier nineteenth century
were primarily concerned with the export of cotton piece
goods and cotton yarns ; but the members of the Manchester
Chamber of Commerce also included many master cotton
spinners and manufacturers, to whom the plentiful supply
of raw material for their machinery was vitally important.
Manchester could hardly have visualised completely the
disastrous situation which was to arise during the early
'sixties, as a result of the American Civil War ; but the
necessity of safeguarding the cotton supply had been recognised since the earliest days of the factory system in
Lancashire. One of the main objects of the Manchester
Committee for the Protection and Encouragement of Trade
(formed in 1774) was to facilitate the importation of cotton ;
and in the same year there had been formed the Manchester
Cotton Manufacturers' Company, which financed the bulk
buying of cotton, in opposition to the specialised cotton
dealers.[1] At that date the bulk of the cotton used in Lancashire still came from the West Indies, with a dwindling
supplement from the Levant.[2] After the Napoleonic wars,
however, the situation was radically different ; North America
and Brazil were now the main sources of supply, and the proportion imported from the United States tended constantly
to increase.[3]

This growing dependence on the United States seemed
to the Manchester merchants and manufacturers fundamen-
tally unsound, and they spared no efforts to multiply the
sources of their raw material, at the same time as they were

[1] See Chap. I, pp. 3-4 above.
[2] Wadsworth and Mann, *op. cit.*, pp. 183-92, and Appendix G, pp.
520-1.
[3] Baines, *History of the Cotton Manufacture*, 1835, pp. 301-10.

striving to open up new markets for their manufactured goods. The earliest supplies of cotton had been " brought into this Kingdome by the Turkie Merchants, from Smyrna, Cyprus, Acra, and Sydon " ; [1] it was therefore natural that, in attempting to safeguard themselves against the possibility of a sudden cessation in the supply of American cotton, the Manchester merchants should look hopefully to the Levant. During the eighteenth century Levant cotton had been gradually driven out of the English markets ; nevertheless, the Lancashire manufacturers were confident that, if the Turkey trade could be freed from restrictions, Manchester might yet develop a profitable commerce with the Sultan's dominions (including Egypt), both in the import of raw cotton and in the export of manufactured goods.

After the Napoleonic wars Mehemet Ali made a systematic attempt to develop the large-scale cultivation of cotton in Egypt, and had considerable initial success. Between 1821 and 1824 the annual crop of Egyptian cotton increased from 60 bags to 140,000 bags ; and by 1823 the cotton was reported to be superior in quality to every other kind except the American Sea Island. [2] For this new supply of cotton England was the main market, importing 111,023 bags in 1825 ; on a conservative estimate, this would be equivalent to something like 23,000,000 lb., or about one-tenth of the total amount of cotton imported into England in 1825, which was a boom year. [3] The Manchester merchants lost no time in pointing out to the Board of Trade the immense potential importance of Egyptian cotton : that it could be produced in any quantity : that it was cheaper than American cotton : and that " in the event of any political change depriving us altogether of United States cotton the finer sorts of Egyptian cotton will supply the place of fine Sea Island Georgia cotton, for which heretofore no substitute could be found." [4]

This promising trade was obstructed, however, not only

[1] Wadsworth and Mann, *op. cit.*, p. 15 : quoting a London petition of 1621.

[2] Baines, *op. cit.*, p. 306.

[3] The total import was 228,005,291 lb. (Tooke and Newmarch, *op. cit.*, Vol. II, p. 155 *n*.). The average weight of bags of Egyptian cotton at this time was 210 lb. (*Proceedings of the Manchester Chamber of Commerce*, 27th April, 1833 ; *cf.* Baines, *op. cit.*, p. 307, and N. S. Buck, *Anglo-American Trade, 1800-1850*, p. 31 *n*.).

[4] *Proceedings of the Manchester Chamber of Commerce*, 9th February, 1825.

by "the capricious determination of the Pasha" but also by the vexatious regulations of the Levant Company. No English merchant was allowed to import any cotton from Egypt until he had been made free of the Company, a privilege for which substantial fees had to be paid ; and even then the merchant had still to pay 9d. on every 100 lb. of Egyptian cotton imported. In 1825 the old Levant Company was abolished ; but tariff restrictions still prevented anything like a free development of trade with the Near East, and for a long time the production of Egyptian cotton did not expand so rapidly as had been hoped.

India was a more promising field for British enterprise ; cotton was already well established there, and during the early nineteenth century there were special reasons for encouraging its cultivation as an export staple. Until almost the end of the eighteenth century fine Indian textile goods (cotton and silk) had been able to hold their own, even in England, against the finest Lancashire cotton goods ; [1] before the end of the Napoleonic wars, however, the situation had been radically altered. Indian cotton goods had now been displaced from the English market, and the Lancashire manufacturers were anxious to develop the export of cotton goods to India and the Far East. But even in the eighteenth century the Indian peasant had not had sufficient purchasing power to pay for any considerable quantity of imported manufactured goods ; and the new industrial developments in Europe had aggravated this difficulty. In order to equate the " balance of payments " it was desirable (from the Lancashire point of view) to encourage the cultivation in India of export crops ; and (again from the Lancashire point of view) there was a certain economic fitness in persuading the Indian cultivator to provide Lancashire with her raw material as well as with a market for her finished goods.

The East India Company, within the limits of its own traditional conservatism, had already done its best to improve the quality and encourage the export of Indian cotton. In the first decade of the nineteenth century bounties had been offered for improved samples of cotton, American seed had been distributed, and reports had been called for on the cotton-growing districts. The Anglo-American War of 1812-14 had given a special stimulus to the demand for Indian

[1] See Chap. IX, p. 108 above.

cotton, and even at this early date the Lancashire manu-facturing towns had realised the need for Empire-grown cotton, to supplement the American supplies.[1] Yet although American cotton was cut off from the English market for two years, only 5,200,000 lb. came during that time from British India.[2] In 1816 the East India Company allowed a drawback of the whole internal and sea duties on raw cotton exported, and in the same year the effect of the opening of the trade (consequent on the new charter of 1813) began to make itself felt. The export of raw cotton increased from 40,000,000 lb. in 1816 to 80,000,000 lb. in the following year; but thereafter the Lancashire cotton industry re-lapsed into post-war stagnation, cotton prices slumped, the superiority of American cotton reasserted itself, and the Indian supplies dwindled. Nevertheless, the Company con-tinued its efforts to bring about an improvement in native methods of cultivation, by providing selected seed and offering bounties; the Bombay administration even established a model cotton plantation.[3] But the consumption of Indian cotton in England increased only gradually; the total import of cotton from all the East Indies (including Mauritius) was only 32,755,164 lb. in 1833, as compared with 237,506,758 lb. from the United States.[4]

Indian cotton was considered suitable only for the manu-facture of the coarser cloths; it was much shorter-stapled than American cotton, and (owing to bad preparation for the market) it was extremely dirty. For these and other reasons, the use of Indian cotton was abandoned during the later 'twenties by many manufacturers who had been per-suaded to try it during the post-war years. After the change in the East India Company's constitution in 1833, European supervision of the cleaning and packing processes improved the quality of the cotton, and added considerably to its market value; but the rapid development of the crop seemed to demand that its cultivation should be taken out of the hands of the ryots, and organised under a plantation system. For this radical change of method India was not

---

[1] See petitions in *Journals of the House of Commons*, Vol. 68, 1812-13, and Vol. 69, 1813-14.
[2] J. Capper, *The Three Presidencies of India*, 1853, p. 341.
[3] *Report on the Affairs of the East India Company*, 1832, Commercial Appendix, p. 668.
[4] Baines, *op. cit.*, p. 309; the figures are not altogether reliable, owing to the varying weights of the bales or bags.

yet ripe ; the means of transport and communication were still very primitive in the interior, and there was a lack of adequate security for the investment of European capital in cotton plantations.

The interest of the Manchester merchants in Indian cotton revived rather suddenly during the ' boom ' of 1836, when there was a serious shortage of American cotton and a consequent rise in its price. In August, 1836, the Calcutta Agricultural Society reported that its attempts to obtain American cotton seed, for experimental purposes, had failed because of American jealousy. It was therefore arranged that the British consular authorities in America should procure the seed and send it to Liverpool, whence it could be shipped to India. To aid the transmission of the cotton seed to England, the Manchester Chamber voted £100 from its own funds, and the Vice-President of the Chamber (Mr. Macvicar) went in person to Liverpool to arrange for its shipment to India.[1] During 1837 and 1838 concerted efforts were also being made, by the East India Associations of Glasgow, Liverpool and London, and by the Chambers of Commerce of Bombay and Manchester, to secure an improvement in the *churka* or native machine for cleaning Indian cotton. The Manchester Chamber announced its willingness to accept subscriptions from merchants and spinners towards providing a premium for the invention of an improved machine ; and in October, 1838, the invention of an improved cotton-cleaning machine was duly announced.[2]

Shortly afterwards the Chamber's knowledge of Indian cotton-growing conditions was strengthened by an important letter from Mr. Owen Potter, who had made a first-hand investigation of the problem, principally in Guzerat(Gujarat).[3] Mr. Potter emphasised the importance of making good roads into the inland cotton-growing districts, and of lessening the burden of taxation on the cultivator. He instanced the case of Omrawuttee cotton, which cost only a penny per lb. to grow ; half the crop went to pay the Government land tax, and thus the cost per lb. was doubled, while the transmission of the cotton overland to Bombay added another penny

---

[1] *Proceedings of the Manchester Chamber of Commerce*, 3rd and 10th August, 1836, and 15th March, 1837.

[2] *Ibid.*, 8th November, 1837, 12th February and 31st October, 1838 ; *cf. ibid.*, 5th August, 1840, for the report of a deputation which had seen Indian cotton cleaned.

[3] *Ibid.*, 7th November, 1838, and 17th January, 1839.

per lb. On the other hand, in Guzerat almost all the cotton was grown within forty miles of the port from which it was shipped, and the cost of inland transport rarely exceeded two per cent. of the market value. The East India Company's methods of taxing the cotton also contributed to its defects of quality. The cotton was taxed before it was cleaned, and while the seed was still in it. If the growers were unable or unwilling to pay the tax, the cotton was buried in the ground to save the East India Company the expense of building sheds. While the cotton was buried moisture struck through it and increased the weight, but its colour deteriorated before it reached England. Pieces of brown earth often stuck to the cotton ; when the cotton was beaten to remove the earth, the pieces broke into a brown powder, which it was almost impossible to get out of the cotton afterwards. Moreover, cotton which had broken leaves mixed with it was often mingled with cotton which was free from leaves. Mr. Potter suggested that to secure the improvement of Indian cotton the East India Company should institute a system of rewards and fines ; he also recommended irrigation, which had not yet been tried, possibly because irrigated land was doubly taxed. He concluded, significantly, that until British capital and industry were utilised on the spot, little improvement would be made in the cultivation of cotton on the western side of India.

Fortified by this new information, the Manchester Chamber of Commerce presented to the Court of Directors of the East India Company [1] a memorial on cotton cultivation, and asked for the co-operation of the East India Associations of Glasgow, Liverpool and London. The memorial pointed out that Indian cotton as yet only accounted for about 5 per cent. of the total value of cotton imported, and that about 90 per cent. was drawn from foreign sources. This Indian cotton, when imported, was worth about £14,000,000 ; when it had been manufactured it was worth £40,000,000, and in the process it employed 2,000,000 people, as well as 300,000 tons of shipping. A regular and independent supply of cotton, which would be unaffected by national hostilities, would be a great boon to British manufacture, would employ British shipping, and would also

---

[1] And also to the Board of Trade (C. P. Thomson) and the Board of Control (Sir John Cam Hobhouse).

improve the condition of the Indian peasants by making taxation less burdensome to them. The continent of India was fully capable of producing every type of cotton in the desired quantities, and at a less cost than any other country in the world.[1]

The Manchester deputation which presented this memorial was very sympathetically received by the Board of Trade, the Board of Control, and the Court of Directors of the East India Company, as well as by Sir James Carnac, the newly-appointed Governor of Bombay ; the representatives of the East India Company, remembering their own unsuccessful experiments, declared that the climate and soil of India prevented much improvement in the cultivation of cotton, but promised to do all they could to help the new movement.[2] The application may possibly have had some practical effect, for in 1840 American planters were sent out to India to instruct the natives in improved methods of cotton cultivation, and prizes were offered for the best crops ; the Bengal Chamber of Commerce showed an active interest in the experiments, and cotton-growing companies began to be formed in England. Once more, however, the immediate results must have been disappointing, for the American planters returned home within a few months, and the English cotton-growing companies did not come to maturity. Even the Directors of the Manchester Chamber of Commerce did not think that the development of cotton-growing in India would be an easy or rapid process. They realised the difficulties caused by weather conditions, which necessitated excessive haste in cleaning and packing ; they knew that the *churka* gins were defective, that communications were primitive, and that the land tax was oppressive ; but the soil, they felt, was most suitable.[3] They therefore continued to send memorials to successive Governors-General of India, receiving answers which were sympathetic but (of course) non-committal.[4]

A new impetus to the cotton-growing movement was given by the financial instability of 1847, when the supply of American cotton suddenly decreased. Early in that year,

---

[1] *Proceedings of the Manchester Chamber of Commerce*, 17th December, 1838.
[2] *Ibid.*, 6th February, 1839.
[3] *Ibid.*, 13th August, 1840 (*Report on the Growth of Cotton in India*).
[4] See *e.g.* memorials to Sir Henry Hardinge (*ibid.*, 13th May, 1844), and to Lord Dalhousie (*ibid.*, 14th October, 1847).

Mr. John Bright raised the question of Indian cotton-growing in the House of Commons, and a parliamentary committee of inquiry was subsequently appointed, which once more exposed the numerous obstacles to the rapid development of Indian agriculture. The report of this parliamentary committee was discussed by the Manchester Chamber of Commerce at a special general meeting in 1850, and resolutions were passed denouncing (among other things) the " lamentable failure of the East India Company to extend the cultivation of cotton." The chairman (Mr. Thomas Bazley) said it was a disgrace that so little cotton was grown in our overseas possessions, when we were dependent upon America for nine-tenths of our supply. From India we received one-tenth of the quantity, but only one-twentieth of the quality and value. The meeting determined to present a memorial to Lord John Russell and a petition to the House of Commons, demanding the institution of a special Commission of Inquiry, in view of the fact that the charter of the East India Company was due to expire in three years.[1] Before the end of 1850 further action was taken, in co-operation with the Chambers of Commerce of Liverpool, Blackburn and Glasgow, by sending out a special agent (a Mr. Mackay) to study Indian conditions at first hand.[2] Mr. Mackay unfortunately died before his mission was ended; but before his death he had collected a great mass of information about the provinces of Guzerat and the Southern Mahratta country, tending to prove once more that the East India Company's administration had contributed to the economic backwardness of India and in particular was hampering the cultivation of cotton.[3]

Throughout the early 'fifties both the Manchester Chamber of Commerce and the Manchester Commercial Association continued persistently to goad the East India Company on the subject of cotton-growing; and the interest of the general public in the question was being stimulated by letters and articles in *The Times*, in which it was alleged that the cause of India's backwardness in developing the cultivation of cotton " lay wholly in the maladministration of the Indian Government, in its land tax, which had destroyed the security

[1] *Proceedings of the Manchester Chamber of Commerce*, 17th January, 1850.

[2] *Ibid.*, 28th October and 7th November, 1850.

[3] *Ibid.*, 10th February, 1851; 16th January and 13th May, 1852. Mackay's collected evidence was published posthumously under the title *Western India*; the mission cost about £3000.

of property and checked cultivation, and in its almost in-
credible neglect of indispensable public works." [1] It is true
that, from this time on, the special question of cotton-growing
became progressively merged into the wider " Government
of India " question, which may be said to have culminated
in the Mutiny of 1857 and Lord Derby's India Act of 1858.
It is possible, however, that the persistence of the special
agitation of the cotton towns had some influence upon
cultivation ; for in 1856 the President of the Manchester
Chamber of Commerce could report that, during the past
year, there had been an increase of 50,000 bales in the export
of cotton from India.[2]

Meanwhile, strenuous efforts were being made to foster
the cultivation of cotton in other parts of the world. So
early as 1839 the Manchester Chamber of Commerce had
received suggestions that cotton might profitably be culti-
vated at the Cape of Good Hope.[3] Nine years later the
Chamber was making detailed investigations into the suit-
ability of Natal ; evidence was given of the province's good
soil and climate, its fine harbours, the cheapness of land,
labour and food, and the excellent quality of the cotton which
grew there as a perennial. References to the formation of
a " Co-operative Land and Emigration Society," and to the
publication of an " Emigrant's Guide to Natal," suggest
that the development of the province was being taken seriously ; a more convincing sign was the purchase of 800 acres
in Natal by the Manchester firm of Galloway & Southam.[4]

By that time Australia also had entered the field as a
potential cotton-grower. In 1847 Dr. Udney tried to interest
the Manchester merchants in his project for a joint-stock
company to develop North-Eastern Australia (*i.e.* Queensland), which he thought eminently suitable for growing
cotton, or almost anything else. More attention was given
to Dr. Lang's scheme for a joint-stock company to develop
the cultivation of cotton in New South Wales, though the
Chamber of Commerce steadfastly adhered to the rule prohibiting the investment of its funds in private ventures.
In the end, Dr. Lang financed the settlement of two ship-

---

[1] See *The Times*, 15th November, 28th November, and 17th December,
1850.
[2] *Proceedings of the Manchester Chamber of Commerce*, 4th February,
1856.   [3] *Ibid.*, 21st March, 1839.
[4] *Ibid.*, 3rd and 24th February, 1848 ; 6th April, 1848 ; 5th and 12th
October, 1848 ; 12th February, 1849.

loads of emigrants at Moreton Bay (Queensland), and promoted the " Manchester and Lancashire Australian Emigration Society." The Chamber of Commerce went so far as to memorialise the Government, asking that assistance might be granted to persons emigrating to Moreton Bay for the purpose of cultivating cotton ; but Earl Grey's reply was discouraging, and the matter was not strongly followed up.[1]

West, East and North Africa were also claiming attention as possible sources of raw cotton. In 1850 the Manchester Chamber of Commerce induced Lord Palmerston to send a mission to the King of Dahomey, asking him to encourage the cultivation of cotton ; similar attempts were also being made in Liberia and Sierra Leone, as well as in Mozambique.[2] At the Paris Industrial Exhibition of 1855 there were over a hundred and fifty exhibitors of Algerian cotton, and 9000 acres were reported to be under cultivation. In that same year the Manchester Commercial Association investigated proposals for the establishment of an " Anglo-French Cotton Spinning Company," which proposed to stimulate cotton-growing in Algeria ;[3] but later reports were pessimistic, and by 1860 there had been a considerable falling away in the quantity and quality of Algerian cotton. Egypt, also, was now once more claiming special attention as a cotton-growing country. In 1851 the Pasha of Egypt asked the Manchester Chamber of Commerce to send out an expert adviser, principally to superintend the classification of cotton. A young man named Swinglehurst was recommended, and went out to Alexandria at a salary of £200 a year ; but he does not seem to have got on well with the Egyptian authorities, and after two years the arrangement broke down. The production of Egyptian cotton, which in 1852 was more than double what it had been in the previous year, relapsed sadly after (perhaps even before ?) the termination of Mr. Swinglehurst's contract ; though by the later 'fifties some progress towards recovery had been made, stimulated by a sharp rise in the price of American cotton in 1856.[4]

[1] *Proceedings of the Manchester Chamber of Commerce*, 22nd July and 26th August, 1847 ; 3rd August, 1848 ; 19th July, 1849 ; 10th January, 1850.
[2] *Ibid.*, 10th January, 7th February, and 14th March, 1850 ; and numerous references thereafter.
[3] *Proceedings of the Manchester Commercial Association*, 27th June, 1855.
[4] *Proceedings of the Manchester Chamber of Commerce*, 4th September and 23rd October, 1851 ; 4th February, 1856 ; 9th February, 1857. Statistics in J. A. Mann, *The Cotton Trade of Great Britain*, 1860, pp. 82-3.

This renewed threat that the Lancashire manufacturers might, sooner or later, have reason to rue their continued dependence on American cotton, caused the question to be attacked with even greater zeal than before, though not with much practical success. Suggestions for the development of cotton-growing began to pour in from most unlikely places, and from all quarters of the globe. According to Mr. Clegg's *Report on a Journey to the East, and on the Cultivation of Cotton* (1856), districts suitable for cotton-growing had been found in Algiers, Morocco, Malta, Egypt, Palestine, Sicily, Italy and Spain. Other correspondents reported that excellent cotton was growing wild in the hinterland of Buenos Ayres and Monte Video. Samples of cotton grown in Monte Video were valued by the Secretary of the Manchester Chamber as worth 7*d.* to 9*d.* per lb., and were reported to be of very strong staple.[1] Other samples of cotton were arriving in Manchester from as far afield as Peru and Tahiti, and the volume of correspondence on the subject was becoming somewhat burdensome. The time seemed ripe for the formation of a special organisation, and the President of the Manchester Chamber of Commerce found ready support when, in February, 1857, he suggested the formation of a Cotton League for promoting and encouraging the growth of cotton in every part of the world.[2] Two months later the Cotton Supply Association was formed in Manchester, and thenceforth all letters and samples of cotton addressed either to the Chamber of Commerce or to the Commercial Association were handed over to the new organisation.[3]

The articles of faith of the Cotton Supply Association were set forth in resolutions passed at a public meeting, held in the Manchester Town Hall on the 19th June, 1857. The meeting believed that " the colonial and other dependencies of Great Britain afford ample resources for the cultivation and development of the cotton plant, and that it is the duty as well as to the interest of the British nation to aid in the promotion of those efforts by means of which its growth may be extended not only in the British dominions, but in all accessible countries." The methods which the Association proposed to adopt were explained in an early

[1] *Proceedings of the Manchester Chamber of Commerce,* 7th October, 1852 ; 24th February, 1853 ; 27th October, 1856.
[2] *Ibid.,* Annual General Meeting, 9th February, 1857.
[3] See *e.g., ibid.,* 5th December, 1857.

issue of its own fortnightly paper, the *Cotton Supply Reporter* : " By bringing the necessary influence to bear upon our own and other Governments for the removal of restrictive duties or legislative obstructions to cotton-growth or exportation in the British dominions or elsewhere ; by obtaining and diffusing all available information as to countries capable of growing cotton, with a view to stimulating and directing private enterprise in its production ; by circulating printed instructions as to the best methods of cotton farming and the preparation of cotton for the market ; by grants of cotton seed, cotton gins, and machinery of the most approved kinds of construction, as inducements to private persons or associations to enter upon cotton culture ; by sending out competent teachers or agents . . . , by awarding honorary and other prizes to successful cultivators . . . ," etc.   During the next few years the Association showed great energy in attempting to carry out this arduous programme ; and its existence was abundantly justified during the early 'sixties, when the American Civil War caused the failure of cotton supplies fron the southern States.   No doubt the Cotton Supply Association was amateurish in its methods and over-ambitious in its scope ; but the Empire Cotton Growing Corporation and British Cotton Growing Association of a more scientific age need not be ashamed of their ancestor.[1]

[1] See W. O. Henderson, " The Cotton Supply Association, 1857-72," in the *Empire Cotton Growing Review*, Vol. IX, No. 2, 1932 ; *cf.* I. Watts, *The Cotton Supply Association : Its Origin and Progress* (Manchester, 1871).

CHAPTER XVII.

CONCLUSION.

It would be an endless task to analyse all the multifarious problems which such organisations as the Manchester Chamber of Commerce attempted to solve during the first half of the nineteenth century. Some questions, especially those concerning industrial relations, the Manchester merchants seem to have regarded as outside the scope of their deliberations. Almost the only references in the early records of the Chamber of Commerce to the growth of trade unions or employers' associations were two colourless declarations of industrial pacificism made just before the repeal of the Combination Laws in 1824 : " Combinations, whether of masters or workmen, produce a hostile feeling towards each other which is directly opposed to the best interests of society. . . . The Chamber of Commerce specially recommends that punishment for violence or intimidation, either by masters or workmen, should be as severe as possible." [1] In the following year the Chamber of Commerce defined its attitude towards factory legislation in terms which, having regard to the economic and social atmosphere of the time, may be regarded as comparatively enlightened. It was acknowledged that the introduction of machinery had given employers a stronger incentive " to work their people to excess," and that " the Factory System also renders the labourer less able to regulate his hours of work according to his inclination and his physical powers." It was therefore admitted that legislative interference with industrial working conditions might be regarded as reasonable ; but the Chamber of Commerce thought (with some measure of justification) that such interference should be general, and not restricted to the cotton industry, as it had been down to

[1] *Proceedings of the Manchester Chamber of Commerce,* 15th March and 26th May, 1824.

that time.[1]   Such an attitude may appear to the modern mind unduly hesitant and cautious ; but it was certainly less obstructive than that of many similar organisations in that generation.   The Birmingham Chamber of Commerce, for instance, thought that legislative restrictions might be necessary in the cotton industry, but would (if applied to the Birmingham trades) be " erroneous in principle, vexatious and embarrassing to the manufacturer, inquisitorial in their nature, oppressive to the labouring class, and in their tendency injuriously affecting the public interests." [2]

Apart from these more or less formal definitions of attitude, the early records of the Manchester Chamber of Commerce contain practically no references to narrowly industrial problems.   Many members of the Chamber were also manufacturers, and some of them (*e.g.* John Bright) took a prominent part in the industrial controversies of the time ; but they did so as manufacturers, not as members of the Chamber of Commerce.   The same method of explanation may be applied to the Chamber's neglect of social questions.   It is true that the early records of the Chamber contain much valuable information about the condition of the working-classes of Manchester ; [3] but the Chamber, as a general rule, collected such information only when requested to do so by the Board of Trade.   Members of the Chamber were prominent, however, among the founders of the Manchester Statistical Society in 1833 ; and one of the original objects of the Statistical Society was to investigate the economic and social problems of the district.[4]   A search through the early records of the Society shows that many of its social investigations were undertaken by members who were also prominent in the Chamber of Commerce, such as Samuel and W. R. Greg, P. Ewart, John Douglas, Thomas Boothman (the Secretary of the Chamber of Commerce), and Richard Birley.   The Chamber's apparent apathy to-

[1] *Proceedings of the Manchester Chamber of Commerce*, 30th March, 1825 ; *cf.* Helm, *op. cit.*, p. 81.

[2] Wright, *op. cit.*, pp. 70-2, 76.

[3] See, for example, the Chamber's important report to the Board of Trade in 1833, from which some extracts are given in Appendix A, pp. 237-42 below.

[4] See the article by Theodore Gregory on " The Early History of the Manchester Statistical Society," in the Society's *Transactions*, 1925-26, pp. 1-32.   For a more extended study of the activities of the Society, see T. S. Ashton, *Economic and Social Investigations in Manchester, 1833-1933* (1934).

wards social problems is thus seen to be due not to moral callousness but to a deliberate specialisation of function. In studying the early records of the Chamber of Commerce this limitation of purpose has constantly to be remembered ; it accounts for many curious omissions, and helps to explain why some problems were viewed from an apparently obtuse angle.

A further difficulty arises from any attempt to fit the deliberations of the Manchester merchants into the general framework of economic history. The streams of local controversy often flow across the main watersheds of national history in a most disconcerting fashion ; some of the commercial questions raised during (or even before) the French wars were still being discussed in the eighteen-fifties, after more than thirty years of peace. There may be some justification for assuming that a new rhythm entered into English economic life round about the middle of the nineteenth century ; [1] but any attempt to fix upon a particular year, as marking the end of one phase of economic life and the beginning of another, breaks down completely in national and local history alike. Historians to whom the Free Trade Movement appeared to be the dominant issue in the economic life of the earlier nineteenth century have commonly regarded the repeal of the Corn Laws, in 1846, as marking the culmination of economic liberalism, and as an important turning-point in national economic history. Yet the Manchester Chamber of Commerce was still busily advocating the reduction or abolition of customs duties in the 'fifties ; and Gladstone himself (who knew as much as anybody about the tariff changes of the 'forties) [2] considered that the movement in favour of free trade " reached its zenith " in 1860, with the negotiation of the Cobden-Chevalier Commercial Treaty between England and France.

A similar consideration of the main issues with which the Manchester Chamber of Commerce concerned itself during that generation would show that most of the problems entered upon a new phase at some point between 1850 and 1860. In Indian affairs, the dividing line between periods

[1] See Redford, *Economic History of England, 1760-1860,* 1931, Chap. XV.
[2] As Vice-President of the Board of Trade, he had been largely responsible for the detailed revision of the customs schedule, under Peel's supervision.

would be determined either by the Mutiny of 1857 or by Lord Derby's India Act of 1858, which finally settled the protracted struggle against the East India Company. The influx of Californian gold into England, after 1849, gave a new turn to the currency and banking controversy which had raged all through the preceding half-century ; but the limits within which the controversy was henceforth to be carried on could be discerned more clearly after the financial crisis of 1857 than during the first years of gilded prosperity. In joint-stock organisation the initial triumph of the limited liability principle in 1855 might be considered an important turning-point, though the Companies Act of 1862 was a much more decisive measure. By 1850 the steam railway had already transformed the inland transport system of the country ; but in Manchester's local transport problem more than one reason might be given for regarding the year 1856 as a significant date. In that year the Manchester Chamber of Commerce and the Aire and Calder Navigation Company, after bickering with each other for more than half a century, at last found themselves fighting alongside each other in a struggle against the monopolistic schemes of the railway companies ; at the same time, the Manchester Chamber of Commerce had one of the great railway companies as its ally in negotiations which were to settle the protracted disputes concerning the administration of the Liverpool docks and the navigation of the Mersey.

In the general movement towards commercial organisation, a new phase was entered upon in 1860, with the foundation of the Association of Chambers of Commerce, which was eventually to become regarded as " a kind of parliament of trade." Throughout the preceding decade the consolidation of British commercial organisation and commercial law had been energetically championed by Leone Levi, a brilliant young Italian Jew from Ancona (but a devout Presbyterian) who was later to become an economic statistician of considerable prominence.[1] Levi first attracted public notice with his pamphlet on *Chambers and Tribunals of Commerce, and Proposed General Chamber of Commerce in Liverpool*, which was published in 1849.[2] In this pamphlet, Levi had (among

[1] See biographical notices in *Dictionary of National Biography, Dictionary of Political Economy*, etc.

[2] Cf. *Proceedings of the Manchester Commercial Association*, 24th November and 27th December, 1849. The Liverpool Chamber of Commerce was founded in 1849, with Levi as its first Secretary.

weightier matters) urged the formation of an advisory body to the Board of Trade, composed of one member elected annually from every Chamber of Commerce throughout the United Kingdom ; and this scheme for " a deputation to form a standing committee to the Board of Trade, to aid the Government in preparing commercial measures," was recommended by him to various commercial organisations during the next few years.

The Manchester merchants did not display any great enthusiasm towards the idea ; but some of the smaller and newer Chambers of Commerce were more fully alive to the benefits of co-operation, for the purpose of increasing their influence with the Government. In 1855 the newly reconstituted Birmingham Chamber of Commerce received from the Bristol Chamber a suggestion that the provincial commercial organisations should co-operate in the appointment of a salaried agent to look after their parliamentary interests in London, and to build up what would nowadays be called a bureau of commercial intelligence.[1] The proposal was subsequently approved (after a joint conference) by the Chambers of Commerce of Birmingham, Bristol, Hull, Belfast, Bradford, Stoke-upon-Trent and Worcester ; and early in 1856 the associated bodies of merchants appointed Levi as their London agent.[2] Three years later, the movement towards the national consolidation of the commercial organisations took a further step forward when arrangements were made for an Annual Congress of Delegates from the various Chambers of Commerce " to discuss questions bearing immediately on subjects within their peculiar province." From this stage there was a quite natural transition to the establishment in 1860 of a permanent Association of Chambers of Commerce, with (of course) a London agent.[3]

The year 1860 thus witnessed a notable development in the national consolidation of the commercial interests. It may be remarked, however, that the Manchester merchants had so far held themselves aloof from the new movement, and had not joined the national Association. There is, indeed, a special reason for considering 1858 a more significant date than 1860 in the history of commercial organisation in Manchester. This reason has to do with the curious relationship between the Manchester Chamber of Commerce and the

---

[1] Wright, *op. cit.*, pp. 125-6.   [2] *Ibid.*, p. 134.
[3] *Ibid.*, pp. 162-3.

Manchester Commercial Association. Although the Chamber of Commerce was strongly in favour of Free Trade and the repeal of the Corn Laws, yet in the 'thirties and 'forties there had been a considerable dissentient party within the Chamber.[1] In 1845, at the very height of the campaign, the conflict of opinion had become so great that the malcontent members seceded to form a rival body, the Manchester Commercial Association.[2] Yet, although the rebellion originated as a protest against free-trade fanaticism, the Commercial Association soon became as enthusiastic as the Chamber of Commerce in support of free trade. Why the two organisations should have kept up their separate existence for so long is a great mystery ; for it is not possible, by reading through their *Proceedings*, to find any important question on which they represented opposite points of view. In the end, their reunion came about partly through the fortuitous circumstance that Thomas Boothman, the Secretary of the Chamber of Commerce, retired in 1857 after twenty-seven years' service. The *Manchester Guardian* made Boothman's retirement the occasion for a leading article on the rival commercial organisations, and described the situation very caustically :—

> " Two separate knots of grave and elderly gentlemen, ensconced, one in Cross Street and the other in King Street, anxiously discussing the same questions, commonly arriving at the same inevitable conclusions, and dispatching a couple of deputations, and a brace of secretaries, at double charges, to occupy a jaded minister on two precious mornings—and all for what ? Why, to din into his ears the self-same story ! And, then, the great man blunders as to the identity of the body before him.
>
> " ' Let me see, don't you represent the—the—Chamber of Commerce ? '
>
> " ' No, my lord, the Commercial Association.'
>
> " ' Oh, yes ! The gentlemen from the Chamber were here yesterday. Do they speak for the home trade, and you for the foreign ? '

[1] *Proceedings of the Manchester Chamber of Commerce*, 9th and 11th February, 1839, and many later references.
[2] *Ibid.*, 28th March, 4th, 11th and 23rd April, and 2nd May, 1844 ; 10th and 21st February, 3rd and 6th March, 1845 ; *Proceedings of the Manchester Commercial Association*, 14th April and 1st May, 1845.

"'By no means; each society is composed of men from all the branches of industry among us.'

"'I presume, then, that yours is a protectionist, and the other a free-trade chamber?'

"'Indeed, my lord, we are as good free traders as they!'

"'But, at any rate, you are here on different errands? . . . Well, I declare, you ask for the same thing almost in identical words! Here is division of labour of a novel sort—more work without more fruit! You are, certainly, strange people in Manchester.'"[1]

The satirical shaft struck home; on the very next day, the subject of amalgamation was discussed by the Chamber of Commerce, and negotiations with the Commercial Association were decided upon. At the next annual general meeting of the Chamber, the President referred to "the very public and pointed manner in which the Press had indicated the necessity for such an amalgamation," and announced that provisional terms of reunion had been arranged. By the 19th February, 1858, the fusion had been safely effected, and the funds of the Commercial Association were transferred to the Chamber of Commerce.[2]

The President of the Chamber of Commerce, in welcoming the prospect of united action in the future, emphasised the historical importance of the reunion, and issued a challenge to local economic historians: "In 1820 the present Chamber was formed, and from that time the proceedings of this Chamber have been regularly and explicitly recorded, so that from their books and those of the earlier Society a history might be written of the Trade and Commerce of Manchester." Local historians have not shown any great readiness to accept the challenge; and, in the meantime, the records of another seventy-five years have accumulated in the archives of the Chamber.

[1] *Manchester Guardian*, 25th November, 1857.
[2] *Proceedings of the Manchester Chamber of Commerce*, 26th November and 16th December, 1857; 1st February, 1858. *Cf. Proceedings of the Manchester Commercial Association*, 27th November and 17th December, 1857; 19th February, 1858.

APPENDIX A.

THE POPULATION, COMMERCE AND INDUSTRY
OF MANCHESTER, *c.* 1820–32.

QUESTIONS proposed by The Board of Trade per Letter, 3rd September, 1832, and Answers returned thereto.[1]

QUESTION 1. *A statement of the principal branches of Commerce and Industry carried on in the town of Manchester.*

The branches of Industry which may be said to engage the almost exclusive attention of this town and its immediate neighbourhood, are the spinning and manufacture of Cotton Wool. The Silk Trade has, since the change in the laws which regulated that trade, made considerable progress, and is gradually increasing. The spinning of flax has also been lately introduced.

A very large population is employed in the making of machinery, in the printing and dyeing of goods, and in every variety of process which the finishing of manufactures for the market requires; those however we consider as employed in manufacture. Other branches of industry exist in Manchester, but not to an extent which calls for special mention.

The Commerce of the town therefore consists in a very great degree in the sale and exportation of Cotton Yarns and Cotton and Silk goods; but in the prosecution of its commercial operations, Manchester draws largely from the woollen markets of Yorkshire, and, in fact, from every district where manufactures exist.

QUESTION 3. *Some approximation to the number of Factories at work and of persons employed in each, distinguishing men, women and children.*

In answering this question the Board supposed, that allusion is made solely to such establishments as are engaged in the spinning or manufacture of cotton wool and silk. The enumeration of these is subjoined, but no mention is made of those buildings in which other branches, such as the making of machinery, the printing or dyeing of goods, etc., etc., are carried on.

As respects the number of persons employed therein, this Board regrets, that it has not been able to procure the information, altho' it cannot account for the difficulty which exists in procuring it. If the Board of Trade require this information for

[1] *Proceedings of the Manchester Chamber of Commerce*, 27th April, 1833.

237

any special purpose, a renewed attempt shall be made to procure an exact statement ; if not, it may be correctly assumed, that the whole population of this town is either employed in manufacturing pursuits or dependent upon their prosperity.

COTTON MILLS AT WORK IN MANCHESTER.

	1820	1821	1822	1823	1824	1825	1826	1827	1828	1829	1830	1831	1832
Manchester	44	45	46	49	55	60	63	65	63	63	67	67	68
Salford .	4	5	5	5	8	8	10	10	11	10	10	7	7
Chorlton .	12	11	12	12	12	12	12	13	13	13	13	12	12
Ardwick .	2	2	2	2	2	3	2	3	3	3	3	3	3
Hulme .	2	2	2	2	2	2	2	2	2	2	2	2	2
Newton .	—	—	—	—	—	1	1	1	1	1	1	1	1
Pendleton .	2	2	2	2	2	2	2	2	2	2	2	2	2
Beswick .	—	—	—	—	—	—	—	—	1	1	1	1	1
	66	67	69	72	81	88	92	96	96	95	99	95	96

SILK MILLS.

	1820	1821	1822	1823	1824	1825	1826	1827	1828	1829	1830	1831	1832
Manchester	2	3	4	4	4	5	9	9	9	10	11	11	12
Salford .	1	1	1	1	1	—	—	1	1	1	1	1	2
Newton .	—	—	—	—	1	1	1	2	2	2	2	2	2
	3	4	5	5	6	6	10	12	12	13	14	14	16

WOOLLEN OR WORSTED MILLS.

	1820	1821	1822	1823	1824	1825	1826	1827	1828	1829	1830	1831	1832
Manchester	1	1	1	1	1	1	1	1	1	1	1	2	2
Salford .	1	1	1	1	1	1	1	1	1	1	1	1	2
Ardwick .	1	1	1	1	1	1	1	1	1	1	1	1	1
	3	3	3	3	3	3	3	3	3	3	3	4	5

FLAX MILLS.

		1827	1828	1829	1830	1831	1832
Manchester Salford		— I	I I	I I	I I	— 2	— 2
		I	2	2	2	2	2

QUESTION 4. *The rates of wages paid to each class.*

It is difficult to quote the rates of wages earned in the mills in Manchester, they are governed by a great variety of circumstances, amongst which the nature of the work performed, the state of the machinery, and the talents and steady conduct of the operative himself have great influence. The following may be quoted as the average clear weekly earnings of the average of workers.

SPINNERS:

Men (*i.e.*, mule minders). — 20/- to 25/- — All are paid by the quantity produced. These may be considered the average clear weekly earnings of that class of spinners, who in point of talent and steadiness form the great bulk of that body. Many however will make a clear weekly average of from 28/- to 32/-.

Women. 10/- to 15/-

STRETCHERS:

Men. 25/- to 26/- — Not numerous.

PIECERS:

Boys and Girls, Young Men and Women. 4/7 to 7/- — The great majority will average 6/-. The wages of this class increase with the age of the operatives until they attain about 18 years, when they become spinners.

SCAVENGERS:

The smallest class of children of both sexes employed. 1/6 to 2/8 — These are employed in cleaning machinery. Some of this class earn 4/- but they are few. Scavengers become piecers when they attain sufficient age and size.

CARD ROOM:

Men. 14/6 to 17/-

Young Women, 15 years and upwards. 9/- to 9/6

Under 15. 6/- to 7/-

THROSTLE SPINNERS.

5/- to 9/6 — These are almost wholly girls of 14 years and upwards. The great majority earn 8/6 per week.

REELERS :
This work can be and is frequently performed at home. } 7/- to 9/-

All females. The wages of this class vary exceedingly. The work is not difficult and can be performed by very young persons ; the consequence is, that there are more workers than can be supplied with employment. The rates quoted suppose full work.

WEAVERS BY POWER :
Men. 13/- to 16/10

Some men earn higher wages than these.

Women. 8/- to 12/-
DRESSERS :
Men. 28/- to 30/-
WINDERS AND WARPERS. 8/- to 11/-
MECHANICS. 24/- to 26/-

These are employed in making and repairing machinery. Many receive more, few less than the rates quoted.

We have added the rates of wages of other artisans and persons employed in the town ; the sums affixed are estimated as paid to such persons as form the average of each class in point of ability and steadiness of conduct, and supposing 12 hours labour per day.

WEAVING BY HAND :
Nankeens—
Fancy : Men. 9/- to 15/-
Common : Men, women and children. } 6/- to 8/-

It ought to be remarked, that Hand-loom Weaving has ceased, except in a few of its branches or under peculiar circumstances, to be the work of adults. When the father of a family has pursued this occupation until his family has attained the age of puberty, he will go on, because he and his family may, when all employed, earn a fair means of support. When this is not the case, an adult cannot compete with a machine.

Checks :
Fancy. 7/- to 7/6
Common. 6/- to 7/-

Cambrics :
All ages. 6/- to 6/6
Quiltings :
Men and Women. 9/- to 12/-
CALICO PRINTERS.
FUSTIAN CUTTERS. 10/- to 12/-

This class are receiving something better Wages than these at present : this is the average for some time past, and there is no doubt but that their wages will recede. There are ordinarily more workers than employment.

MACHINE-MAKERS.	26/- to 30/-	Proportionate talent ensures higher wages.
IRON FOUNDERS.	28/- to 30/-	Men of superior ability can earn more.
DYERS AND DRESSERS :		
Men.	15/- to 20/-	
Young men, 15 to 18 years.	12/- to 14/-	
Boys.	5/- to 10/-	
TAILORS.	18/-	This the average for the whole year.
PORTERS. Men.	14/- to 15/-	
PACKERS. Men.	20/-	
SHOEMAKERS.		
Men.	15/- to 16/-	These are the wages which may be earned rather than what are generally earned. It is an idle, combining and dissipated class.
WHITESMITHS.	22/- to 24/-	
SAWYERS.	24/- to 28/-	
CARPENTERS.	24/-	
STONE-MASONS.	18/- to 22/-	Allowing for loss of time in winter months.
BRICKLAYERS.	17/- to 20/-	Allowing for loss of time in winter months. (A combination has lately procured an advance of 6d. per day.)
BRICKLAYERS' LABOURERS.	12/-	
PAINTERS.	18/-	
SLATER'S CHARGE	3/8 per day,	but are not employed more than half-time.
PLASTERERS.	19/- to 21/-	
SPADEMEN.	10/- to 15/-	

QUESTION 6. *A statement of the rate of rents, and of the prices of several principal articles of consumption in each year from 1820 inclusive.*

The rates of rents in Manchester vary exceedingly according to locality. We have endeavoured to procure the rates of rents which are not governed by any extraordinary circumstances, which might either raise or depress the rental.

Rate on Outlay.   Will realize

Cottage property under £15—7½ to 8½ P. Cent.   5 to 6 P. Cent.

The collection of the rents extremely precarious, and the damage done by tenants very great.

Rental.

Houses—from £15 to £40—7 P. Ct.   5½ P. Cent.
         £40 to £100—6 P. Ct.   5 P. Cent.
         above £100—5½ P. Ct.   4 to 5 P. Cent.

Warehouses. Locality has more effect upon the rents of Warehouse property than even upon houses, and as changes are constantly taking place in the gradual removal of the most active scenes of business from one street or district to another, so in proportion do the rates of rent fluctuate. At the present moment, houses in the best streets are being converted into Stores. The average rate of rent may be quoted at from 6 to 7 P. Cent. upon outlay.

Rents when not strongly influenced by locality have fallen in Manchester since 1820, about 10 P. Ct. upon the rental, arising from a continued cheaper cost of building.

PRICES OF SEVERAL PRINCIPAL ARTICLES OF CONSUMPTION IN MANCHESTER, IN EACH YEAR FROM 1821 TO 1831.

	Beef.		Pork.	Bacon.	Bread Flour.	Oat Meal.	Malt.	Cheese.	Potatoes.
	Best.	Coarse.							
A.D.	pr. lb.	pr. lb.	pr. lb.	pr. lb.	pr. 12 lb.	pr. 10 lb.	pr. 9 lb.	pr. lb.	pr. 252 lb.
1821	5d.	3d.	4¾d.	5¾d.	2/2	1/4	2/2	6½d.	5/8
1822	5d.	3½d.	4½d.	5½d.	2/3-2/10	1/3	2/-	7½d.	4/6
1823	5d.	3¼d.	5¾d.	7¾d.	2/-	1/4	2/1	7-7½d.	5/-
1824	5¾d.	3½d.	6d.	8d.	2/6	1/6-1/7	2/3	8-8½d.	8/-
1825	6¼d.	4¾d.	6½d.	7¾d.	2/7	1/5	2/6	9d.	6/-
1826	6¼d.	4¾d.	6½d.	7½d.	2/5	1/7-1/8	2/1	7½d.	9/9
1827	6d.	4d.	7d.	8d.	2/5	1/8-1/9	2/4	7½d.	4/9
1828	6½d.	4d.	6¼d.	7½d.	2/7	1/7	2/2	8d.	5/8
1829	6d.	3¾d.	6¼d.	7½d.	2/9	1/5	2/2	6½d.	6/6
1830	5½d.	3d.	5d.	6½d.	2/7	1/6	2/1	7½d.	6/-
1831	6d.	3½d.	5½d.	7d.	2/6	1/6	2/4	8d.	6/3
1832			5½d.	7d.	2/4	1/3	2/2-2/3	7½d.	4/3

The Prices attached to Beef are the contract prices at our Royal Infirmary for large quantities. The price paid by the poor will lie between the two prices quoted. The Prices of Potatoes are the contract prices at the workhouse; the poor pay much more, as they generally purchase in quantities of 20 lb. and under; the difference will perhaps amount to 30 P. Cent.

All the other prices here quoted have been procured from retail shopkeepers. It is proper to remark, that the poor find the quality of Bread Flour called "Best Seconds" the most useful, although it is not the lowest in price.

DECLARED VALUE OF BRITISH AND IRISH COTTON MANUFACTURES AND TWIST AND YARN, EXPORTED TO THE UNDER-MENTIONED COUNTRIES IN THE YEAR 1853.[1]

Countries to which Exported.	Cotton Manufactures entered by the Yard.	Hosiery, Lace, and Small-wares.	Cotton Twist and Yarn.	Total.
	£	£	£	£
Russia—Northern Ports .	34,333	8,592	137,324	180,249
Ports within the Black Sea	9,462	102	4,186	13,750
Sweden . . .	7,166	2,176	45,295	54,637
Norway . . .	27,303	1,728	25,399	54,430
Denmark (including Iceland) . . .	34,989	2,027	64,142	101,158
Prussia	537	200	26,508	27,245
Mecklenburg-Schwerin .	—	—	60	60
Hanover . . .	612	13	146,795	147,420
Oldenburg and Kniphausen	—	—	—	—
Hanseatic Towns . .	785,395	202,268	2,076,717	3,064,380
Heligoland . . .	—	2	—	2
Holland . . .	473,700	81,435	1,692,043	2,247,178
Belgium . . .	62,170	57,390	179,676	299,236
Channel Islands . .	46,565	1,253	474	48,292
France . . .	65,552	46,574	43,584	155,710
Portugal Proper . .	611,195	10,858	42,310	664,363
Azores . . .	47,609	803	1,140	49,552
Madeira . . .	16,945	721	18	17,684
Spain—Continental and Balearic Islands . .	73,283	6,897	5,953	86,133
Canary Islands . .	61,839	3,035	401	65,275
Gibraltar . . .	374,289	21,926	7,455	403,670
Italy,etc.—Sardinian Territories . .	242,213	17,795	46,775	306,783
Duchy of Tuscany .	236,676	26,695	104,742	368,113
Papal Territories .	80,423	613	78,740	159,776
Naples and Sicily .	148,621	13,272	199,630	361,523
Austrian Territories .	200,304	6,052	135,113	341,469
Malta and Gozo . .	108,445	2,099	30,447	140,991
Ionian Islands . .	67,026	623	18,411	86,060
Kingdom of Greece .	95,590	307	12,161	108,048

[1] Appendix to Thirty-Fourth Annual Report of the Manchester Chamber of Commerce, 8th February, 1855.

Countries to which Exported.	Cotton Manufactures entered by the Yard.	Hosiery, Lace, and Small-wares.	Cotton Twist and Yarn.	Total.
	£	£	£	£
Turkish Dominions, exclusive of Wallachia, Moldavia, Syria, and Egypt.	1,510,622	13,529	158,368	1,682,519
Wallachia and Moldavia	77,460	538	75,332	153,330
Syria and Palestine	242,639	651	33,430	276,720
Egypt—Ports on Mediterranean	318,143	7,601	27,795	353,539
Tunis	—	—	—	—
Algeria	—	—	—	—
Morocco, etc.	63,532	218	60	63,810
Western Coast of Africa	384,719	1,167	617	386,503
British Possessions in South Africa	207,785	12,714	541	221,040
Eastern Coast of Africa	1,580	—	—	1,580
African Ports on the Red Sea	—	—	—	—
Cape Verde Islands	2,737	—	—	2,737
Ascension and St. Helena	979	486	—	1,465
Mauritius	124,257	5,732	3	129,992
Aden	535	—	—	535
Persia	—	—	—	—
Continental India, with the contiguous Islands, viz., British Territories	4,447,413	64,392	1,168,264	5,680,069
The Birman Empire	—	—	—	—
Islands of Indian Sea : Java	412,194	5,727	30,344	448,265
Philippine Islands	333,160	8,855	2,140	344,155
China	1,028,074	329	101,396	1,129,799
Hong Kong	177,921	3,624	97,089	278,634
Japanese Islands	—	—	—	—
British Settlements in Australia	806,715	225,588	8,218	1,040,521
South Sea Islands	18,704	176	—	18,880
British North America	665,635	60,161	23,456	749,252
British West Indian Islands and British Guiana	370,016	24,828	182	395,026
Honduras (British Settlements)	52,400	3,114	1,351	56,865
Foreign West Indian Islands :—				
Cuba	341,294	43,092	8	384,464
Porto Rico	4,773	144	–	4,917
Guadeloupe	—	—	—	—
Martinique	—	—	—	—
Curaçoa	11,316	662	—	11,978
St. Croix	—	—	—	—
St. Thomas	275,046	16,379	4,283	295,708
French Guiana	—	—	—	—
Dutch Guiana	1,010	21	—	1,031
Hayti	73,441	2,953	80	76,474
United States of America	3,524,629	648,601	9,671	4,182,901
California	82,979	6,914	670	90,563
Mexico	473,216	47,720	11,719	532,655

Countries to which Exported.	Cotton Manufactures entered by the Yard.	Hosiery, Lace, and Small-wares.	Cotton Twist and Yarn.	Total.
	£	£	£	£
Central America	116,787	6,801	7,741	131,129
New Grenada	289,994	12,489	248	293,731
Venezuela	152,456	6,385	82	158,923
Ecuador	18,922	622	25	19,569
Brazil	1,727,537	60,009	820	1,788,366
Oriental Republic of the Uruguay	253,072	10,988	382	264,442
Buenos Ayres, or Argentine Republic	238,431	17,164	213	255,808
Chili	543,413	45,599	4073	593,085
Bolivia	—	—	—	—
Peru	623,054	33,780	1481	658,315
Falkland Islands	108	100	2	210
Greenland and Davis Straits	—	—	—	—
Total	23,901,940	1,915,309	6,895,653	32,712,902

Estimated Consumption of Cotton Manufactures in Great
  Britain and Ireland £21,224,494
Amount of British Cotton Manufactures supplied for the
  whole World 53,937,396

According to the above table, the Cotton industry of Great
Britain and Ireland yielded in the year 1853 about 54 millions
sterling, and which may be regarded as half the Cotton industry
of the world ; but foreign countries, besides taking half the
raw Cotton sent to market, receive large supplies of Cotton Yarns
from Great Britain, and in Asia and Africa Cotton is still largely
spun by hand ; hence the world's Cotton industry may be valued
at 120 millions sterling, and which would therefore afford to every
man, woman, and child on the face of the earth 2s. 9¾d. worth of
Cotton Manufactures, or about 14 yards each, per annum, of excellent Calico.

THOMAS BAZLEY.

(It is, however, necessary to remark, that in studying this
table, certain large entrepôts exhibit an amount of consumption
which must not be taken as the consumption of the place indicated
—for example, the Hanseatic Towns, Gibraltar, Hong Kong, and
St. Thomas are to be considered as representing the districts
which draw their supplies from each mart respectively.)

INDEX.

ABERDEEN, Lord, 102 n., 103, 106, 201.

Africa, 25, 37, 106, 225-7, 244-5.

Agriculture and agricultural labourers, 79, 94, 133-9, 153, 158, 221-5, 228. *See also* Corn Laws.

Alexandria, 197, 226.

Algeria, 226-7, 244.

Althorp, Lord, 140-1, 148-9.

America: *see* United States, North America, South America, Brazil, West Indies, etc.

Amiens, Peace of, 56, 59-65, 87, 128-9.

Amsterdam, 21, 211.

Argentine Republic, 101, 105, 245. *See also* Buenos Ayres.

Arkwright, Richard, 5.

Armitage, Elkanah, 154.

Ashton, T. S., 7 n., 10 n., 13 n., 230 n.

Attwood, Thomas, 158.

Australia, 165, 202-3, 225-6, 244.

Austria, 21, 59, 81, 86-7, 91, 95-6, 199.

BALTIC Trade, 31, 33, 44, 91-2, 169, 175: Sound Dues, 91-2.

Banking and currency, 17, 21-3, 50-3, 58, 75-7, 81-4, 122-5, 158-68, 193, 209-12, 232.

Bank of England, 17, 50, 76-7, 81-3, 158-68, 208.

Bankruptcy and bankruptcy laws, 76, 81, 160, 164, 166-7, 214-5.

Banks: Jones's, 53; United States Bank of Pennsylvania, 83; Jones Loyd & Co., Heywood Bros. & Co., Daintry, Ryle & Co., 159; Western Bank of Scotland, City of Glasgow Bank, 166; Royal British Bank, 214.

Baring, Alexander, 69, 176-7.

Bazley, Thomas, 107 n., 224, 245.

Belfast, 105, 140, 148, 233.

Belgium, 92, 94, 243.

Bengal, 124, 145, 223.

Biddle, Nicholas, 83.

Bills of exchange, 21, 23, 26, 37, 40-1, 48-50, 82-3, 123-5, 162, 166-7, 190-3, 208-10.

Birley, H. H., 178.

Birley, Richard, 71, 230.

Birmingham, 6-13, 27, 34, 38, 47-8, 54-60, 99, 101 n., 115-7, 127, 131-7, 158, 164-8, 173, 192, 194, 204 n., 209 n., 211, 230, 233.

Blackburn, 111, 224.

Bleaching and crofting, 6-7, 14.

Bohemia, 86, 96.

Bologna, 38, 49.

Bombay, 119, 124, 196-200, 220-3.

Boothman, Thomas, 230, 234.

Boulton, Matthew, 9, 12.

Bounties, 8, 127, 219-20.

Bowden, W., 3 n.-5 n., 8 n., 9 n., 14 n., 18 n., 127 n.

Bowring, Dr. John, 96.

Bradford, 170, 173, 193, 233.

Brandenburg, 86, 130.

Brandt, C. F., 16, 18, 53-7, 64-5.

Brazil, 19, 81, 97, 99, 101-6, 146, 217, 245.

Bremen, 32-3.

Bright, John, 154, 215-6, 224, 230.

Bristol, 116, 194, 211, 233.

Brunswick, 26, 95.

Buck, N. S., 83 n., 97 n., 98 n., 218 n.

Buenos Ayres, 97, 100, 102-5, 227, 245. *See also* Argentine.

CADIZ, 55, 98.

Calcutta, 119, 124, 198, 202, 221.

Calenderers and finishers, 6, 14.

Calico and calico-printing, 6, 14, 17, 25, 67, 98, 112, 140-3, 205-6, 237, 240, 245.

California, 165, 232, 244.

Cambrics, 95, 240.

Canada, 97, 156, 244.

Canals, 169-79, 181-2, 232: Aire and Calder Navigation, 170-7, 181, 232; Calder and Hebble Navigation, 169 ; Duke of Bridgewater's Canal, 177, 181 ; Leeds and Liverpool Canal, 177 ; Rochdale Canal, 174-5, 181.

Cannan, E., 73 n.

Canning, George, 88, 92-3.

Canton, 115, 117, 119-21, 124.

Cape of Good Hope, 202, 225.

Central America, 97-8, 103-5, 203, 244-5.

Checkmaking, 25, 240.

Chile, 100, 101, 103, 245.

China, 19, 70, 111-25, 244-5.

Clapham, J. H., 93 n., 98 n., 133 n., 200 n.

Coasting trade, 35, 112, 173, 198, 200, 210.

Cobden, Richard, 151-5, 231.

Coffee and coffee duties, 144-51.

Colombia, 97, 100, 103.

Colonial trade, 8, 25, 98-9, 144-9, 156, 210 : colonial preferences, 144-9, 156.

Commercial organisations : Commercial Committees, 2-16, 20, 23, 27, 43, 52-6, 63-70, 113, 127-8, 217 ; Commercial Societies, 2, 6, 15 ff., 45 ff., 63-4, 67-8, 72, 86, 109, 127-30, 170-5, 205 ; " United Commercial Societies of England," 58-62, 127-8 ; Chambers of Commerce, 2, 6, 13, 16, 19, 47, 54-8, 63 ff., 232-5.

Commercial treaties and reciprocity, 8, 11-15, 21, 24, 40, 55, 85 ff., 102, 104, 120-2, 126-9, 146, 199, 201, 231.

Companies and company laws, 3, 4, 72, 160-1, 173, 178, 195, 198, 202-3, 213-6, 217, 223-6, 232.

Confiscation of property, 24, 26, 37-41, 44-5, 50, 55, 57, 59, 61, 104, 119, 205.

Convoys, 15-6, 24 ff., 46, 56, 69.

Corn Laws and Anti-Corn-Law Movement, 72, 132 ff., 150-7, 193, 231, 234.

Corsica, 37, 39, 41.

Cotton, raw, 1-5, 65, 75-83, 93, 97, 99, 124, 139-41, 144-9, 151, 177, 202, 217-28, 245 ; Cotton Supply Association, 227-8.

Credit, 4, 14, 20-3, 49, 76-7, 81-4, 101, 123-5, 158-68, 180, 212. See also Banking and currency, Bills of exchange.

Customs duties, 8, 11, 43-4, 65, 85 ff., 109, 110, 113, 121-2, 126 ff., 139-57, 205-7, 219-20, 231.

DANIELS, G. W., 4 n., 74 n.

Debts, collection and repudiation of, 23, 45, 48-50, 55, 58-9, 61, 69, 207-9 ; imprisonment for debt, 207-9.

Denmark, 91-2, 243.

Derby, Lord, 125, 225, 232.

Dinwiddie, William, 64-5.

Disraeli, Benjamin, 150.

Douglas, John and William, 64-5, 230.

Drinkwater, John and Thomas, 64.

Drinkwater, Peter, 10, 20.

Dyeing, 6, 7, 14, 17, 75, 98, 143, 237, 241.

Dyer, J. C., 155.

EAST INDIA COMPANY, 14, 29, 30, 108-25, 149, 195-200, 219-25, 232 ; financial operations, 122-5.

East Indies, 108-9, 112-6, 144, 198, 220, 244. See also India.

Ecuador, 105-6, 245.

Egypt, 90, 148, 196-9, 218-9, 226-7, 244.

Embargoes, 25 ff., 45-7, 58, 69, 97.

Emigration, 225-6 ; of artisans, 5, 7, 67, 131.

Employers' organisations, 1-14, 20, 23, 66-8, 126-7, 229.

Employment and unemployment, 75-6, 81, 83, 98, 108-9, 129, 130, 139, 164, 222, 229, 237-41. See also Social Distress.

Ewart, Peter, 178, 230.

Exchanges, foreign, 23, 50, 58, 103, 119, 123-5.

Exchequer Bills, 76-7, 82, 161.

Excise duties, 7, 8, 11, 110, 140-1, 149, 205-6.

Exeter, 6, 18, 27, 48, 54, 57-60.

Exports, 1, 7, 8, 11, 16, 20-3, 25 ff., 61, 63, 67, 75, 78, 81, 85 ff., 97 ff., 106 ff., 237, 243-5.

FACTORIES and factory system, 1, 20, 72-3, 76, 78-80, 98, 108, 131, 229, 237-9.

Fairs, 25-36, 86, 95.

Falmouth, 28-9, 34, 46.

Finance, 158-68. See also Banking and Currency, Taxation and Taxes, Bills of Exchange, Exchequer Bills, Exchanges, etc.

France and the French, 3, 11-12, 14 ff., 39, 46, 48-9, 55-61, 68, 81, 86, 89, 93-4, 101, 104-5, 126-9, 194, 199, 201, 226, 231, 243.

Frankfort-on-Main, 26, 33, 86, 95-6.
Free Trade Movement, 8, 11-12, 37, 69-72, 85 ff., 108 ff., 126 ff., 139-57, 193, 231, 234-5.
Fustian manufacture, 6-9, 12-14, 20, 25, 75, 240.

GARNETT, William, 178.
Germany, 21, 25-6, 32-5, 42, 61, 81, 86, 94-6, 110, 129, 130, 155, 175 ; Zollverein, 95-6, 155. See also Prussia.
Gibraltar, 39, 41-2, 90, 243, 245.
Gladstone, W. E., 150, 213, 231.
Glasgow, 7, 76, 90, 92, 95, 104-6, 111, 116, 118 n., 123, 131, 134-5, 140, 145, 148, 166, 204, 221-4.
Goddard, Samuel, 164.
Gold and the gold standard, 158-68, 232.
Grain trade, 91, 134, 136. See also Agriculture, Corn Laws.
Greg, Samuel, 65, 230.
Gregory, T. E., 162 n., 166 n.
Grenville, Lord, 40, 87, 128.
Gujarat, 221-4.

HALIFAX, 6, 27, 30, 38, 54-60, 170-3.
Hamburg, 21, 31-4, 42, 95, 211.
Hammond, J. L. and B., 66 n., 79 n.
Hanse Towns, 32, 91, 245.
Harwich, 191-2.
Head, Major C. F., 195, 198.
Heckscher, E. F., 15 n., 44 n., 85 n., 158 n.
Helm, Elijah, 68 n., 230 n.
Hill, Rowland, 192.
Holland, 21, 25, 32, 48, 61, 92-3, 110, 115-6, 126, 243. See also Netherlands.
Hoskins, H. L., 195 n., 197 n.
Housing, 79, 241-2.
Huddersfield, 131, 169-73.
Hull, 31-5, 44, 92, 95, 169-75, 194, 211, 233.
Huskisson, William, 136-7.

IMPORTS, 1-5, 41, 65, 85, 88, 94, 108-11, 115-6, 128-9, 134, 136-7, 139-57, 217 ff. : Import duties, see Customs, Tariff.
India, 19, 25, 30, 65, 70, 108-25, 129, 144-5, 148-50, 195-200, 204, 219-25, 231-2, 244. See also East India Company.
Insurance : marine, 26, 32, 42-8, 69, 145, 170-4, 205, 210-11 ; fire, 210 ; "averages," 45-7 ; Lloyd's, 69, 211.

Ireland and the Irish, 6, 8, 9, 80, 105, 126-9, 141-3, 156, 183, 243, 245 ; "Irish Propositions," 6-11 ; Irish Catholics in Spain, 41 ; Irish in England, 79-80 ; Irish Union Duties, 141-3 ; Irish potato famine, 156.
Iron and steel industries, 7-13, 54-5, 80, 177, 241.
Italy, 21, 25-44, 48-50, 55, 57-8, 61, 81, 86-9, 169, 227, 243.

JERVIS, Sir John, 39, 41-2.
Johnston, Capt. J. H., 195-6.

KAY, Dr. J. P., 79.
Kerr, Bellenden, 213-4.

LABOUR legislation, 65-6, 131, 229-30.
Lansdowne, Lord, 8, 100.
Leeds, 6, 16, 19, 27-30, 38, 47, 54, 57-60, 92, 111 n., 117, 123, 131, 142, 170-3, 176-7, 192-3.
Legal cases and questions, 45 ff., 205 ff.
Leghorn, 28, 37-40, 46, 48-9, 55-6.
Leipzig, 26, 33, 86, 95-6.
Lesseps, Ferdinand de, 204.
Levi, Leone, 232-3.
Lindsay, W. S., 200 n., 203 n.
Linen industry, 2, 5-7, 72-3, 78, 93-4, 143, 149, 237, 239.
Lisbon, 41-4.
Liverpool, 19, 28-9, 34, 38, 54-9, 73 n., 76, 81-3, 92, 98, 102-6, 115-6, 120, 123, 125, 131, 142-6, 150, 177-8, 182-6, 190-4, 203-4, 207, 212, 221-4, 232.
London merchants, 11-13, 27-31, 37-8, 41, 43, 48, 54-6, 59, 65, 69, 90, 92, 104, 109-10, 128, 130, 144-5, 189, 192-3, 221-2.

MACHINERY, 1, 4, 5, 67, 73, 75, 78, 80-1, 93-4, 108, 128, 130-3, 221, 228-9, 237-41 ; exportation of, 67, 131-3.
M'Connel, James, 65.
Mann, J. A., 122 n., 226 n.
Mann, J. de L., 2 n., 3 n., 4 n., 25 n., 217 n., 218 n.,
Manufacturers, General Chamber of, 9-13, 56, 85-6, 126-7.
Marsland, Samuel and Peter, 64-5.
Mediterranean trade, 18, 22-4, 28-9, 31, 33-45, 55, 60-1, 81, 87-90, 169, 218-9. See also Italy, Naples, Spain.
Mehemet Ali, 199, 218-9.

Mercantile System, 85, 98-9, 127.
Merchant employers, 1, 2, 55.
Mersey navigation and conservancy, 177, 181-7, 232.
Metal industries, 7, 8, 115, 117, 127. *See also* Iron and Steel.
Mexico, 81, 97, 100, 103-5, 201, 203, 206-7, 244.
Milan, 38, 49.
Milnes, Richard, 170-4.
Monte Video, 101-2, 105, 227.
Muslin manufacture, 14, 95, 108-9, 112-3, 141 ; muslinets, 130.

Nanking, 120-1.
Napier, Lord, 118-9.
Naples, 23, 28, 32, 39-42, 87-8, 243.
Napoleon I., 26, 37-8, 44, 60, 65, 68-9, 86, 158.
Navigation Laws, 3, 4.
Navy and naval operations, 27-32, 35-45, 69, 97, 120-1, 197 : press-gangs, 35 ; St. Vincent and Camperdown, 42 ; Battle of the Nile, 43. *See also* Ships and shipping, Convoys, Embargoes.
Netherlands, 48, 92-3, 175. *See also* Holland, Belgium.
Newcastle-upon-Tyne, 165, 212.
Norman, James, 51, 59, 60, 63-4, 129.
North America, 25, 201-2, 217, 244. *See also* Canada.
Norwich, 54, 57, 59, 60, 173.
Nottingham, 13, 34, 140, 148, 173.
Nuremberg, 26, 95.

Oldknow, Samuel, 10, 64-5.
Opium trade, 119-20, 124.

Palmerston, Lord, 90, 95-6, 104-6, 119-20, 206-7, 226.
Papacy and Papal States, 32, 87, 243.
Peel, Lawrence, 14, 53, 64.
Peel, Robert (1750-1830), 5, 8, 14, 20, 64-5, 134.
Peel, Sir Robert (1788-1850), 103, 140, 146-7, 152, 156-8, 231 n.
Peking, 119, 122.
Peru, 100-3, 227, 245.
Philips, George and Francis, 64.
Philips, S., 69 n.
Pitt, William (1759-1806), 7, 8, 13, 43, 48-50, 57, 126-8.
Poland, 21, 61, 86, 95-6.
Population, growth of, 72-3, 78, 116, 158, 192.
Portsmouth, 46-7.
Portugal, 32, 42, 44, 61, 89, 98-101, 129, 243.

Postal Services, 188-204 ; penny posts, 189-93.
Potter, Benjamin, Thomas and James, 53, 64, 154.
Potter, Owen, 221-2.
Pottery industry, 9-13, 127, 142.
Prentice, Archibald, 134 n., 135, 153 n.
Prices, 1, 3, 74-8, 81-3, 102, 115-6, 123-4, 129-37, 143, 153, 164-5, 174, 220-1, 242, 245.
Prussia, 26, 32, 61, 86, 95-6, 243.

Railways, 169, 177 ff., 193-5, 232 : Liverpool and Manchester Railway, 178, 194 ; Manchester, Staffordshire and Cheshire Railway, South Union Railway, Midland Railway, North Union Railway, 179 ; Grand Junction Railway, 182, 194 ; Great Western Railway, 187 ; London and Birmingham Railway, Manchester and Birmingham Railway, 194 ; London and North-Western Railway, 195.
Reinhard, Charles, 26 n., 95.
Richardson, Thomas, 16, 57, 64.
Roberts, Richard, 82.
Rochdale, 57, 170-5, 216.
Rose, George, 20, 21 n.
Russell, Lord John, 125 n., 150, 224.
Russia, 21, 59, 61, 86, 91, 95-6, 126, 199, 243.

Salerno, 25-6, 28, 30-1, 34.
Salterhebble, 169-72.
Salt, T. Clutton, 165, 167-8.
Satterthwaite, Thomas, 64.
Scotland, 9, 95, 166, 183. *See also* Glasgow.
Seddon, Joseph, 64, 67-8.
Sharp, Thomas, 178.
Sheffield, 13.
Ships and shipping, 4, 14, 20-3, 25 ff., 45 ff., 69, 85, 91-2, 98, 105, 110, 114-9, 122, 139-40, 144-5, 169, 172-7, 182-8, 195-204, 222. *See also* Convoys, Embargoes, Navy.
Sicily, 88-9, 227, 243. *See also* Naples.
Silk industry, 5, 11, 65, 72, 76, 88, 91, 109-10, 119, 124, 129, 143, 149, 219, 237-8.
Silver, 105, 119, 122-3.
Silvester, J., 6, 52-4, 63-4, 67.
Singapore, 202-3.
Slavery and slave trade, 106, 144-7.
Smith, Adam, 1, 85.

Smith, J. B., 154-5.
Smuggling, 6, 96, 109-10, 114, 124.
Soap duty, 143, 151.
Social distress and unrest, 74-83, 161-5, 230-1.
South America, 60, 78, 81, 96-106, 203, 207.
Southampton, 193-4.
Sowerby, 169-74.
Spain, 18, 21, 26-7, 30, 32, 39-41, 44, 50, 55, 57, 61, 86, 89, 90, 98-100, 103, 127-9, 227, 243.
Speculation, financial, 4, 21, 76-7, 80-3, 98, 125, 163-6, 180, 210.
Spencer, Lord, 41-2, 54, 60.
Spinning and spinners, 1, 5, 20, 66-7, 72-3, 76, 80, 108-9, 129-33, 217, 221, 237, 239.
Spithead, 28-9, 39.
Spooner, R., 167.
Staffordshire, 9, 13, 127.
Stamp duties, 209-13.
Steamships, 169, 182, 188, 195-204. See also Ships and shipping.
Stockport, 159.
Stoke-upon-Trent, 233.
Suez, 196-204 ; Suez Canal, 204.
Sugar and sugar duties, 144-51.
Switzerland, 31-2, 34, 81.
Sydney, 202-3.

Tariff protectionism and prohibitions, 11-12, 15 ff., 44, 61, 65, 69, 85 ff., 97 ff., 108-13, 126 ff., 139-57, 219. See also Customs duties, Free Trade Movement.
Taxation and taxes, 6-11, 37, 43-4, 57, 85 ff., 108-9, 127, 129, 133, 136-7, 139-57, 209 ff., 221-2.
Taylor, John Edward, 154.
Tea trade and duties, 115-9, 124, 149-51.
Telegraph, 184, 204.
Telford, Thomas, 176-7.
Thomson, C. Poulett, 82, 208, 222 n.
Tientsin, 121-2.
Timber trade and duties, 91, 151.
Tooke, Thomas, 69, 76 n., 151, 165 n., 218 n.
Touchet, James, 64.
Trade, fluctuation of, 69, 74 ff., 98, 101, 125, 138, 148, 150-3, 158-68, 180, 209, 214, 218, 220-3, 232. See also Speculation.
Trade unionism, 5, 66-7, 229, 241.
Transport and communications, 169 ff., 188 ff., 221-2, 232. See also Canals, Railways, Ships, Telegraph, Postal Services.

Turkey and the Levant, 37, 41-2, 87, 90-1, 95-6, 199, 200, 217-8, 227, 244 ; Levant Company, 36, 90, 218-9.
Turnbull, Mr. (of Turnbull, Forbes & Co., London), 27-31, 36, 37 n., 41, 43, 50, 54-62, 128.
Tuscany, 26, 37-8, 243.

United States of America, 43, 75-83, 86, 92, 97-100, 105, 115-6, 148, 193, 201-4, 217-28, 244.
Uruguay, 101-3, 245.
Usury Laws, 160-2.

Wadsworth, A. P., 2 n., 3 n., 4 n., 25 n., 217 n., 218 n.
Wages, 1, 8, 75, 78-81, 108-9, 127, 134-5, 139, 163, 174, 239-41.
Waghorn, Lieutenant Thomas, 195-8.
Wakefield, 172-7.
Walker, George, 4.
Walker, Thomas, 10, 14.
Wars : American War of Independence, 4, 6, 126 ; French Revolutionary Wars, 6, 13 ff., 45 ff., 61, 86-7, 169, 170, 205, 231 ; Napoleonic Wars, 65, 68-9, 74, 86, 95-8, 158 ; Anglo-American War of 1812, 219-20 ; Anglo-Chinese Opium Wars, 119, 121 ; Crimean War, 150-1, 167, 203, 215 ; Indian Mutiny, 225, 232 ; American Civil War, 217, 228.
Warrington, 179, 182-4.
Watt, James, 12-13.
Watts, Isaac, 107 n., 228 n.
Weaving and weavers, 65-6, 76, 78, 80, 108-9, 113, 129-33, 237, 240.
Wedgwood, Josiah, 9, 13.
Wellington, Duke of, 117, 137-8.
West Indies, 3, 4, 18, 19, 25, 29, 36, 62, 92, 97, 144-8, 201, 203, 217, 244.
Wolverhampton, 168.
Wood, Charles, 64.
Wood, G. W., 69 n., 158.
Woollen and worsted industries, 2, 21, 73 n., 78, 93-4, 109, 111, 149, 237-8.
Wright, G. H., 6 n., 11 n., 13 n., 55 n., 99 n., 101 n., 114 n., 116 n., 117 n., 133 n., 134 n., 137 n., 168 n., 204 n., 209 n., 211 n., 230 n., 233 n.

Yates, Richard, 68.
Yorkshire, 34-5, 78, 111, 169 ff., 181, 237. See also Woollen and worsted industries.